Making Writing Matter

Making Writing Matter

—➤•◀—

Composition in the Engaged University

Ann M. Feldman

STATE UNIVERSITY OF NEW YORK PRESS

Published by
State University of New York Press, Albany

For information, contact State University of New York Press, Albany, NY
www.sunypress.edu

Production by Kelli Williams-LeRoux
Marketing by Michael Campochiaro

Library of Congress Cataloging-in-Publication Data

Feldman, Ann Merle.
  Making writing matter : composition in the engaged university / Ann M. Feldman.
    p. cm.
  Includes bibliographical references and index.
  ISBN 978-0-7914-7381-8 (alk. paper)   1. English language—Rhetoric—Study and
teaching (Higher)   2. Report writing—Study and teaching (Higher)   I. Title.

PE1404.F38 2008
808'.0420711—dc22

                                                                    2007035092

10 9 8 7 6 5 4 3 2 1

For my parents,
Florence Feldman and Morton Feldman (of blessed memory) and
For my husband and partner, Robert Jay Meyerhoff

Contents

Part Two: Designing Instruction to Make Writing Matter

Acknowledgments

I am indebted to many scholars, students, colleagues and friends, whose unwavering support made it possible to write this book. I received a Great Cities fellowship that gave me a place to work and colleagues who inspired and challenged me. I thank David Perry, Lauri Alpern, Marilyn Ruiz, Lauri Schaffner, Irma Olmedo, Sharon Haar, Nacho Gonzalez, and Chang Lee. An internship in the office of Academic Affairs with Uday Sukhatme, Toby Tate, Anne Cruz, Chris Messenger, Clark Hulse, Carol Snow, Debra Hale, and Lon Kaufman furthered my understanding of the urban university. My colleagues in the English department provided all manner of support. Among the many, I thank Jerry Graff, Walter Benn Michaels, Ralph Cintron, Dierdre McCloskey, Judy Gardiner, Jessica Williams, Cathy Birkenstein-Graff, Tonia Nikopoulos, Ginny Tunnicliff, Mark Canuel, Virginia Wexman, John Huntington, Tom Bestul, Todd DeStigter, David Schaafsma, Patty Harkin, Sharon Holland, Jennifer Ashton, and Kyoko Inoue.

The Corporation for National and Community Service funded the three-year pilot project I write about in the second half of the book. Many friends and colleagues from near and far contributed to this project: Barbara Holland, Diane Chin, Tom Moss, Jeffrey Howard, Kathy Engleken, and Linda Landis Andrews. Candice Rai and Megan Marie, who collaborated with me on chapter 5, have been staunch allies throughout. Many years before, I worked with Tobi Jacobi and Cordelia Maloney on what I know now was the beginning of this project. Our many community partners continue to teach me about reciprocity; I thank The Resurrection Project, Gads Hill Center, Latinos United, Changing Worlds, the Center for Neighborhood Technology, Metro Chicago Information Center, the Illinois Institute for Entrepreneurial Education, World Relief Corporation, the Chicago Metropolitan Agency for Planning, Center on Halsted, Openlands Project, Chicagoland Bicycle Federation, Stroger Hospital of Cook County, and several others.

The First-Year Writing Program is a formidable force at UIC largely because of our staff, graduate students, lecturers, and, most of all, our students. It has been a joy to work with these folks and many more over the years: Tom Moss, Nancy Downs, Ellen McManus (now at Dominican University), Nikki Cox,

Mimi Rosenbush, Ryan Brooks, Chad Heltzel, Pete Franks, Nicole Russo, Kristen Schaffenberger, Glenda Jones, Kirk Robinson, and Brian Bergen-Aurand, Caroline Gottschalk-Druschke, Tim Henningsen, Stephanie Reich, Bridget Sullivan, Rebecca Haggerty, Nadya Pittendrigh, Matt Pavesich, and Tracey Layng-Awasthi. All the students who took part in the Chicago Civic Leadership Certificate Program over the past three years deserve my heartfelt thanks for all their efforts and good humor.

I thank David Takacs and his students Julia Brown, Antoinette Mantz, and Nick Hack for sharing thoughts about their writing and their community-based work, which I include in chapter 1. I acknowledge Pete Franks for sharing his *faux* film review, which appears in chapter 2. And I thank artist R. J. Kitaj and the Marlborough Gallery for allowing me to use *The Billionaire in Vincent's Chair* in chapter 2 and on the cover. I thank Beatríce Salas for allowing me to share her work and her ideas in this book. And, I thank Candice Rai for allowing me to include her "Wilson Yard" writing assignment in chapter 2. I am indebted to Chancellor Sylvia Manning, who allowed me to include in chapter 3 her version of "The Raven" presented at the reception honoring Stanley Fish's retirement as dean. The graphics in chapter 4 that illustrate the curricula for English 160 and 161 were designed by Megan Marie. Chapter 6 includes work by graduate students who have, over the years, contributed to English 555, our teacher training seminar. These students include, among others: Kristen Schaffenberger, Chad Heltzel, James Arnett, Nicole Russo, Mary Hibbler, and Jennifer Bryant. Mr. Stephen Mifsud generously allowed me to reprint his photo, *Old Bread Factory in Vaasa*, in chapter 6.

I thank State University of New York Press's anonymous reviewers for their careful readings of this manuscript and for challenging my thinking on a number of topics. I thank my editors at SUNY Press as well for their support and enthusiasm.

I must also thank my yoga teachers who provided spirit, fortitude (without struggle), and, of course, the breath one cannot do without: Ana Forrest, Jonathan Bowra, Steve Emmerman, Talya Ring, Bridget Boland, and Umani.

My family, too, sustained me throughout this project. Bob Meyerhoff responded with superb vision to too many drafts. Our combined brood—Amy and Philip Matsuhashi and Jonah and Aaron Meyerhoff offered heartfelt support and plenty of comic relief.

Introduction

Making Writing Matter

In this book, I argue that scholarship at metropolitan, engaged universities is changing and these changes offer an opportunity to redesign first-year writing in ways that make students better writers. First, you may ask, what precisely is an "engaged university," and what new opportunities does it provide for scholarship? Second, how can first-year writing programs benefit from the emergence of engaged scholarship? I offer brief answers to these questions in this introduction, and I elaborate on them throughout the book. Most simply, this book should be taken as a proposal for a new sort of relationship between faculty members, students, and the community based on a mutual interest in writing.

When I speak of making students better writers, I invoke a much broader definition than is usually attached to academic writing. A better writer is a situated writer, who is motivated by the particular context in which a piece of writing is imagined, designed, executed, and delivered. Writing, in this book, is taken to be a performance that emerges out of a consequential situation. When faculty members see writing as a situated performance, they can consider how writing, conceived of as a rhetorical activity, makes a difference in their research, whether traditional scholarship or engaged research conducted in partnership with others. When students see writing as a situated performance, they see themselves as agents called to action; writing becomes something other than a means to demonstrate to the teacher that the student has learned something. Students, along with faculty, will see how writing matters by developing new knowledge that contributes to material change. My goal is that writing be seen as a core intellectual activity of undergraduate education in the engaged university. First-year writing classes should provide university students with a set of footprints, the first of many, marking a path that makes writing matter wherever they go and whatever they do.

What Is Engaged Scholarship?

Though I argue that scholarship at engaged universities is changing, I admit that the term engagement is itself problematic. Engagement is frequently used to replace the more traditional term service, which has come to signify a sort of noblesse oblige. Service, in this sense, means an attempt to do good works for the communities surrounding the university in a way that identified the served as deficient in some way. Sometimes, engagement still means a traditional form of outreach or public service in which the university provides information and services to its community. Or, it might mean an effort to provide remedial education to neighborhood students, or to establish recreational opportunities for surrounding communities. Frequently, the university considers engagement to mean the development of service-learning programs in which undergraduates add a community-based experience to university classes. Each of these efforts might be referred to as engagement, making it hard to know what the term means. At the very least, the term signals a university's intent to be more socially useful than it has been in the past, creating a closer link between academic work and the community. Engagement, as the term is used today, aims for a more reciprocal relationship than had been possible before, a new way for the university and its surrounding communities to improve the social fabric. Even so, efforts to define that new relationship are often confused and fraught with contradiction. Thus, I'm resigned to use the term while defining it carefully for my purposes.

Engagement, as I use the term here, is more ambitious: it means that a university makes a commitment as part of its core intellectual agenda to a relationship with its context that depends on the mutual creation of knowledge. Engaged scholarship represents a reconception of traditional faculty members' work, one in which faculty members consider how their scholarship impacts public contexts. Faculty members find themselves establishing reciprocal and collaborative relationships with partners who may not be university faculty, and the research itself proceeds with new criteria and different goals. These changes will have an impact on the way that faculty see relationships both in and outside of the university; they will expand the faculty members' options for writing; and they will change the faculty members' view of what constitutes the production of knowledge. The institution, too, will have to reconsider and broaden the way it evaluates faculty research for promotion and tenure.

Imagine, for instance, a historian who now applies traditional, disciplinary scholarship on landmark buildings to a new community-based project. This scholar has decided to work with a local community group to study the role of historic buildings in plans for community development. Understanding how particular buildings have functioned historically in this community may suggest new ways to shape current proposals for economic or cultural development. Engaged research in this case means that the knowledge created in collaboration with others will result in community-based consequences as well as traditional scholarly publication. The historian now finds him or herself embedded in a community outside the university, which leads to new opportunities for writing and communication. The historian might contribute to a newsletter, co-author proposals and reports with community partners, or offer workshops for other communities interested in how historical knowledge of landmark buildings can contribute to emerging agendas for community development. These activities broaden traditional notions of scholarly work, scholarly writing, and the production of knowledge.

Admittedly, this view of how scholarship should change may be more proposal than fact; it may bear only slight resemblance to life as we know it in many departments and on many campuses. Not all faculty members are interested in the possibilities of engaged scholarship, nor need they be. Further, this book is not as much about faculty as it is about students. Yet change is in the air and universities are considering what this change might mean; this potential for change holds promise for the ways that universities view writing programs.

Faculty scholarship that used to be conducted as purely discipline-based research is now increasingly reconceived as a principled, reciprocal interaction with a variety of stakeholders in communities surrounding the university. Such an approach to scholarship aims to close the gap between scholarship and advocacy, which, of course, opens the door to an entirely new set of complications. Conducting research in an engaged university requires faculty members to carefully consider how they see themselves embedded in their particular situations and how they collaborate with others to define research partnerships. Such considerations always concern the language and discourse used to represent the realities and relationships under study.

Making Writing Matter for First-Year Students

This emerging, institution-wide change in faculty scholarship provides a promising new direction for redesigning writing classes. When faculty members find that research in these new, more public situations changes their habitual approaches to writing, new sorts of conversation with students become possible. Faculty who work in reciprocal partnerships with colleagues outside the university to study literacy, public transportation, economic development, architecture, gentrification, public art, asthma in low-income communities, or the impact of poverty on high school graduation rates naturally become concerned with how to write or speak effectively in new situations and thus in new genres. Expanding research interests such as these do not in any way exclude the humanities, as one might think; rather they provide a new agenda for rich cross-disciplinary conversations.

The possibility of a renewed focus on language use as an important feature of engaged research opens doors for reconceptualizing student writing. For one thing, it allows freshman writing classes to draw on the intellectual resources of a broad range of faculty research rather than only on the scholarly questions raised by English departments. As engaged research gathers momentum on college campuses, we can design student writing projects that emphasize how specific situations—real or simulated—shape the use of language in those settings. The increasing interest in engaged research, I argue, offers an important opportunity for faculty to connect to students about writing as an intellectual activity rather than either a remedial one or a hurdle students must get over.

It's true that many university faculty do not think about first-year writing as an intellectual activity. "Just teach students the basics," they say, "so that their papers show me they've learned my course material." Or, faculty plead, "Please, teach my students to put together a decent sentence." For many faculty members student writing serves as no more than a conduit that delivers the learned material to the teacher. Even with the steady scholarship produced by the writing in the disciplines movement that emphasizes how situation and genre contribute to disciplinary scholarship, faculty still largely see their own writing activities as unconnected to their students' writing. The thrust of my proposal asks faculty to rethink their writing activity as they rethink traditional approaches to the production of knowledge.

What will it take to design instruction that positions students as rhetors, sophisticated shapers of language and discourse, who craft sentences and shape genres to make a material difference in a situation? Most important, entering students should understand that what is being asked of them grows out of an institutional mission for engagement and that this mission raises the bar for learning to write. Students should understand that they are being asked to write as part of a broader intellectual and political agenda that involves faculty members, students, and community partners. Perhaps, in some cases, this far-reaching goal will ask for more than can reasonably be achieved given the current economic dilemmas encountered by most first-year writing programs. Even so, I sketch my proposal to imagine what is possible.

As part of this university-wide agenda, first-year writing classes will teach students to imagine themselves as participants embedded in specific situations that give rise to writing. This means paying special attention to two features of writing that are usually ignored in the self-contained writing class. To understand writing as a situated performance, students must learn about the important roles played by written and spoken discourse in public settings, the historical uses of language for social action, the imagination necessary to see how social contexts might change, and how patterns of circulation and delivery impact writing projects. The unfortunate assumption that the teacher, as the imagined audience, can stand-in as the sole recipient of student writing eliminates rich possibilities for inquiring into the conversations, histories, laws, experiences, traditions, and assumptions that surround any particular situation that may give rise to writing.

Perhaps most important, students must understand that because engaged research often creates new situations for writing, genre takes on heightened importance in student writing. Genre cannot be seen as a container that packages content for delivery to a solitary instructor. However, even with the exciting work on genre theory by Charles Bazerman, Carolyn Miller, Anis Bawarshi, Aviva Freedman, David Russell, Tom Deans and others, conventional writing instruction often means selecting new or alternative genres for students to analyze or experiment with. This is not enough. Students need to understand genre as a way to enact social motives. Genre analysis provides a tool for thinking about the relationship between institutions' habitual ways of knowing and the use of writing to accommodate and to revise patterns of knowledge production (Bawarshi 2003; Miller 1984, 1994). In imagining the shape a particular piece of writing takes, students must do no less than ask themselves how their writing will reshape their world. Genre, then, when linked to a specific situation, provides a portal for identifying and employing all of the other writing practices important to that project.

Writing for Civic Engagement

I am not alone in suggesting that writing plays an important role in connecting civic engagement to undergraduate education. Although it would take another book to review these efforts adequately, I offer a sampling of projects that have incorporated writing instruction into community-based learning. Most recently, David Coogan argued that the role of rhetorical education should enable "student-citizens to write for social change," which, for him, means investigating the "historical and material conditions that have made some arguments more viable than others" (2006, 667–668). In *Tactics of Hope: The Public Turn in English Composition*, Paula Mathieu (2005) breaks new ground in examining the pitfalls and possibilities for university-community partnerships. Mathieu documents, in stunningly direct narrative, her own experiences with street newspapers and her misadventures with service learning. Her notion of tactics offers a powerful corrective to arguments for engagement (such as mine) and encourages "accepting the contingent and vexed nature of our actions" (xv). In the mid-1990s, Linda Flower and a group of colleagues launched a community literacy project that identified a particular sort of inquiry as the driving force behind university-community collaborations (Flower 1997). Flower's practice of inquiry, rivaling, creates an intersection between divergent situations for making meaning among students on campus and among urban youth off-campus. The analysis of varied perspectives and conflicting evidence by students, researchers, and community members acknowledges the agency of a wide variety of stakeholders (Flower, Long, & Higgins 2000). Ellen Cushman has, for years, grappled with the challenges of engagement between unwieldy institutions, individuals, and groups who frequently end up on the unsavory side of server-served equations (1996, 2002).

Much of the early work on service learning in composition and rhetoric appeared in a landmark volume titled *Writing the Community: Concepts and Model for Service-learning in Composition* that was part of an ambitious, discipline-specific series edited by service learning scholar Edward Zlotkowski (Adler-Kassner, et al. 1997). Nearly a decade later, we will be able to chart the trajectory of service learning or civic engagement approaches through an agenda-setting, bibliographic survey funded by the National Council of Teachers of English (Bacon, et al. 2005). This survey, based on over 370 sources, lauds the broad learning outcomes available through service learning, but notes that we still do not know whether service learning improves student writing (however, see Feldman, et al. 2006). The group who conducted this survey, all service-learning practitioners, noted a shift toward "local publics," and inquiries about how rhetoric can inform participation in the social sphere (Bacon, et al. 2005, 3). The project I introduce below and develop more fully in the second half of this book responds to this public turn in composition and rhetoric.

At the University of Illinois at Chicago (UIC), we have developed a civic engagement program for undergraduates that aims to embed students in consequential writing situations that entail scholarly lessons. This program, the Chicago Civic Leadership Certificate Program (CCLCP), expands on principles already in place in the conventional first-year writing classes. The examples below illustrate how our students began to see themselves as participants in particular situations that gave rise to writing projects. As part of a community-based first-year writing course, Tiffany France designed and produced a fact sheet for Gads Hill, a community organization modeled after the Jane Addams Hull House. In her first-year writing course, Tiffany studied rhetoric, visual design, and argument; at the community organization, she worked with Janet Beals, the director of development and a newly hired grant writer to learn how to craft a fact sheet for the organization. At a fundraiser, Janet Beals used the fact sheet to introduce Gads Hill to Club Couture, a group of women who design couture fashion and donate their proceeds. Club Couture responded to the presentation by donating the entire $3,500 from their recent fund-raiser to Gads Hill for their community-based programs.

Universities' agendas for engaged scholarship aim to strengthen communities; so when Janet Beals e-mailed us to tell us about her recent funding success with Club Couture we were very excited. But we also realized that this sort of immediate consequence to a piece of writing makes it look as though we view writing as entirely practical and utilitarian—a well-written piece can bring in the money. In fact, our point is to make writing more intellectual and scholarly, to help students understand more fully how writing works in rhetorical situations such as the one Gads Hill found itself in. Tiffany learned from this project how to draw on a rich set of resources to represent Gad's Hill's activities, strengths, and needs. The fund-raising coup was an unexpected bonus.

In CCLCP's second required writing course on academic inquiry, Jee Eun Nam studied health care for undocumented immigrants and wrote a position paper that not only fulfilled the course's requirements for a research paper, but also provided useful material for Latinos United, the not-for-profit she had been working with, who used the research to support its expanding agenda. The next year, in an urban planning class, several students worked with a faculty member in urban planning, composition instructors, and a nonprofit agency, Center for Neighborhood Technology (CNT), to conduct research on the impact of transportation costs on housing affordability. Students conducted site inspections of transportation availability and cost in particular neighborhoods with varied housing costs. They applied and tested an algorithm developed by CNT called the "affordability index," developed a presentation, and wrote a paper based on their findings. Their research was included in a larger report CNT produced for the funders of their project which will guide several cities' development efforts. Here, too, students were able to work jointly with a community-based agency and university faculty to produce knowledge that once disseminated and used by potential home buyers, would have a tangible impact on the lives of Chicago residents. These writing projects and ones like them produced around the country emphasize the ways in which participation in civic contexts can make writing matter.

How I Came to Write This Book

I feel uniquely qualified to pursue this project, having been at the University of Illinois at Chicago (UIC) over the past twenty-five years, a period in which it has struggled to redefine itself as an engaged institution. During my years at UIC, I directed our Writing Center, published composition textbooks, taught graduate courses in composition and language theory, and as Director of First-Year Writing taught new graduate students how to design first-year writing courses. Along the way, I was fortunate to have two fellowships at UIC's Great Cities Institute that allowed time to contemplate how I could connect the work of first-year writing with the university's broader notions of engagement. And most recently, a group of colleagues and I received a grant from the Corporation for National and Community Service to launch the service-learning project discussed above.

Throughout my time at UIC, the university has struggled to define its institutional identity. UIC is one of a few college campuses built from scratch and intended to be a presence in the "inner city" (Muthesius 2000, 200). This fact continues to raise questions about UIC's relationship with Chicago. Its brutalist architecture, starkly modern and concrete, was designed by Walter Netsch. This wholly new campus, built in 1965, was in part a response to urban renewal intended to provide higher education to the mixed-race, low-income population that surrounded it. However, this hoped-for legacy is tainted by the memory of a vigorously fought battle by local residents for their homes and neighborhood. From another perspective, the campus that rose on the grounds of that local battle reflected the hubris of the *uber* architect who operated in a space beyond local neighborhoods. According to an editorial published in *Architectural Forum*, UIC embodied the "design of the ideal while the refuse of the real accumulates around us" (Oscar Newman 1966, quoted in Muthesius 2000, 196.) This complicated beginning influences everything that UIC is and does.

In the early 1980s, after merging with the University of Illinois Medical School, which resulted in the Carnegie Research I designation, the university continued to build its profile as a research university, putting aside its founding mission to serve the surrounding city. Eventually, a group of administrators and faculty members responded to the lingering concern for the "urban mission" that UIC had ignored and now imagined a way to resuscitate its legacy as part of a land-grant college system. Rethinking how the university could develop a more symbiotic relationship with its metropolitan surroundings led to the development of the Great Cities Institute (GCI) and to designate itself, in the new parlance, an engaged university. Included under the GCI's umbrella are: two urban policy research centers, community partnerships with two adjacent neighborhoods, a year-long, campus-wide faculty scholar program, a campus-wide seed grant program, research programs conducted by institute fellows, and a professional education initiative. In short, then, the university developed a new infrastructure to house its Great Cities Initiative, but more important than that, it had launched an institutional agenda that could offer faculty members an opportunity to reframe their research as engaged scholarship.

I became involved at GCI from its earliest days by applying for and receiving seed grants and faculty fellowships. GCI turned out to be an incubator for the ideas I propose in this book. I participated in campus-wide discussions about the meaning of engaged scholarship and I interacted with a wide range of faculty who were struggling to define what it meant to conduct research collaboratively with partners based in the city at not-for-profits or government offices. This brief historical review explains in part why my project focuses so intently on "the urban." Understanding universities as producers of knowledge depends on understanding the historical, economical, and political roles universities have played in cities (Perry 2004; Perry and Wiewel 2005, 3; see also Weber, Theodore, and Hoch 2005). This book offers a tightly focused discussion of how engagement plays out in metropolitan, or urban, settings. Similar issues are also at work in rural settings and the fact that this case study focuses on urban settings should not suggest that its ideas are not applicable to a wide variety of institutional settings including rural areas.

The Great Cities Institute provided a home outside the English department that broadened my perspective and informed my continual redesign of the first-year writing program. Further, the institute's continual efforts to encourage and support faculty in what they call "engaged research" has radically changed the way the university values such research as well as the way the city interacts with the university. While many faculty members continue to conduct traditional, discipline-centered work, the growing group of Great Cities faculty scholars has carved out a respected place for engaged scholarship. Thus, this institutional trajectory toward engaged scholarship made it possible for me to contemplate how first-year writing classes might be redesigned to take up engaged scholarship as well.

The Organization of This Book

Part 1: The Place of Writing in the University

Chapter 1. "Engaged Scholarship at the University" explores how embeddedness and participation contribute to producing the agile student writer we desire. Historian Thomas Bender proposes that universities and cities each contribute differing forms of knowledge: the university produces discipline-based scholarly knowledge while the city produces descriptive, pragmatic knowledge. Engaged scholarship offers the possibility of moving beyond such binaries and repatterning knowledge production based on the intersection of these different cultural trajectories. This chapter first offers a definition of engaged scholarship for faculty members and then illustrates how student writing can meet them on the ground of engagement.

Chapter 2. "Writing as Participation" begins with two historical scenarios in which a text that might be taken as a diary turns out to function differently in its particular social context. An examination of genre, specifically the art of portraiture, illustrates how a contemporary painter used genre as a discursive opportunity rather than as a limiting form. The chapter then turns to student writing and the instructional tensions between writing about what others have written and writing experienced as participation in lived space.

Chapter 3. "Telling Tales Out of School" offers a narrative interlude that challenges our preconceptions about genre. With its diary-like entries in narrative form, the chapter looks like a diary but it is not. The chapter's *faux* diary entries afford the reader a view of the underbelly, so to speak, of the author's lived experience while writing this book. The purpose of the chapter, however, is not to reflect on the author's circumstances; rather, it aims to extend her argument that rethinking first-year writing requires hard-won institutional change.

Part II: Designing Instruction to Make Writing Matter

Chapter 4. "Rethinking Reflection in Community-Based Writing" does two things. It describes the development of the Chicago Civic Leadership Certificate Program (CCLCP), an undergraduate program that integrates writing instruction with community-based learning. To explain the importance of genre in the CCLCP curriculum, the chapter also tells the story of Vivian Gornick's memoir, *Fierce Attachments*, and her reception by a group of angry reporters who contested the factuality of her memoir. The Gornick tale illustrates the complex relationship between genre and experience, which suggests the importance of performative and consequential features of writing for classroom writing. The cautionary tale about Gornick's memoir informed the curriculum design for CCLCP and, in particular the decision not to include literacy narratives or reflective essays as key writing assignments. Instead, the curriculum focused on the ways that analyzing particular writing situations gave rise to careful consideration of the participatory nature of writing.

Chapter 5. "Assessing Writing and Learning in Community-Based Courses" calls attention to how CCLCP writing projects are rhetorically crafted for particular situations. We point out that assessment in this context is particularly difficult because designing, conducting, and reporting on assessment is, itself, a rhetorically motivated writing activity. This chapter illustrates the development of an assessment matrix that articulates what we wanted students to learn. Next, the chapter reports on two pilot projects. The first uses a survey to ask students whether specific aspects of writing became easier over the semester. The second relies on discourse analysis to learn how students characterize leadership. (This chapter was co-authored with Candice Rai and Megan Marie.)

Chapter 6. "Teaching the Teachers" describes a seminar that prepares new graduate teaching assistants to design courses that engage students in the approach to writing recommended in this book. Preparing graduate students to plan and teach such writing classes requires that they recognize how their own embeddedness in literary studies shapes their expectations for the first-year writing class. This chapter also responds to the recent debates about whether writing courses should be required during the first year of university studies. Included here are examples of writing projects designed by graduate students that emphasize students' participation in a social scene. The chapter concludes with a graduate student's poetic manifesto for first-year writing.

Part One

The Place of Writing in the University

Chapter 1

⟰⟰⬥⟰⟰

Engaged Scholarship
at the University

The complex relationship between the university and the city provides the context for this chapter, which explores not only the changing nature of scholarship in the metropolitan research university, but also how its changing intellectual climate should, in turn, change our conception of writing instruction for students who attend college in the city. Historian Thomas Bender argues for "a university *of*, not simply *in*, the city" (1998, 18). Each entity, the university and the city, has a particular intellectual or cultural trajectory. Their needs are different but each provides a measure of balance. Bender describes the preferred modality of each:

> The university is best at producing abstract, highly focused, rigorous and internally consistent forms of knowledge, while the city is more likely to produce descriptive, concrete, but also less tightly focused and more immediately useful knowledge, whether this is generated by businessmen, journalists, or professional practitioners. The academy risks scholasticism, but the culture of the city is vulnerable to the charge of superficiality and crude pragmatism. (19)

Even as Bender sets up this series of binaries, he cautions against solidifying this set of differences into monolithic, self-contained institutional entities. Outside of universities, Bender finds examples of exciting opportunities to reconnect research and advocacy, such as Lower Manhattan's Silicon Alley, an "incredibly dense interdisciplinary world of writers, artists, and computer freaks, making multimedia CD's and other interactive media creations, some commercial products, [and] some art ..." Rather than promoting a hardening of the two camps, Bender wishes to see a transmutation in which engagement suggests a repatterning of knowledge production, intellectual activity, and advocacy for change. The university *of* the city heightens its emphasis on localized knowledge without foregoing its historically purposeful approach to scholarship (21).

I begin this chapter with Stanley Fish's argument against engaged scholarship. Stanley Fish raised issues of writing instruction and civic engagement in both national, professional venues as well as in local contexts while he was Dean of the College of Liberal Arts and Sciences at the University of Illinois at Chicago (UIC). Since UIC, has, itself, for the past decade and a half, encouraged an increasingly dialogic relationship with the city, this debate creates a fitting opening for the chapter. Fish—a vigorous opponent of both service-learning and engaged research—argues for disciplinary scholarship as a self-contained, coherent practice that depends on a particular body of knowledge. I, however, argue that disciplinary scholarship is changing as institutions reconsider knowledge-making practices. Fish's focus on the scholar's embeddedness in a particular set of practices rather than on the discipline's content provides an unintentional opportunity to use his argument against him. Fish's notion of embeddedness, I demonstrate, provides a strong argument *for* engaged research. When both faculty members and students focus on engagement, we enhance our relationship to the city while also enhancing undergraduate education and, in particular, writing instruction.

After a brief discussion of what engaged scholarship and research is not, in the section, "How Discourse Drives Engagement," I argue that this sort of participatory, reciprocal research depends on an awareness of research as a discursive practice; that is, on how language and rhetoric are used to shape emerging knowledge. In the section, "The New Learner Writes," I make the transition to student learning. Certainly students should learn to engage in public debate and to produce written arguments that take positions on important issues, but the more subtle and hard-won pedagogical prize will be a student who takes part in the sort of transdisciplinary, discourse-focused scholarship conducted by faculty members. In this section, I liken the contemporary student's foray into new spaces and new genres to Keith W. Hoskin's "new learners" of the latter half of the eighteenth century for whom writing and its new uses supersedes the traditional of oral exams. Student writing also defines the next section, "Educating Citizens to Write." Here, I offer a critique of the reflection essay, a prominent service-learning classroom activity typically employed to capture the learning generated by community-based service activities. This critique, continued in chapter 4, illustrates how the embedded nature of the students' activity contributes to both scholarly understanding of the issues under exploration as well as to a sophisticated awareness of how writing supports learning. The final section, "When Students 'Walk' the City," suggests that the repatterning of knowledge-making practices suggested above by Thomas Bender can be achieved by conceptualizing the university as a spatial entity.

Changing the Kind of Thing We Do Around Here

Traditionally, faculty members at research universities do two things: they teach students and they conduct research. In the popular press as well as in his scholarly work, Stanley Fish has insisted that university faculty should do these two things within the context of disciplines and not as political action. Further, he insists, our teaching should focus on bringing students into the practices of a particular discipline—in his example, literary criticism. This is "the kind of thing we do around here" (Fish 1995, 16). In the discussion that follows, I will enlist Stanley Fish, almost certainly against his will, to support my agenda for redesigning first-year writing classes. I argue that one needn't choose to be "inside" or "outside" a discipline. Rather, the notion of disciplinarity and our core ideas about making knowledge need to change. Most readers of Fish understand his argument validating discipline-centered work as one focused on the key questions asked by the discipline. I focus instead on his interest in embeddedness, which places a writer inside a situation and which defines the choices that might be made by that writer.

This feature of scholarly activity, embeddedness, which Fish claims for disciplinarity, I claim for the engaged university and for first-year writing instruction (see also Butin 2005). Engagement, which focuses on making knowledge in partnership with others, depends on a scholar's embeddedness in a particular context as well as in a particular discipline. When a first-year writing student or a faculty member writes from an embedded position, that writer makes rhetorical decisions drawn from the complexities of a particular context. The student writer must see him or herself in a "lived situation" that calls for writing. This is what Fish claims for scholars of literature and I extend this claim to first-year students who study writing at an engaged institution.

Fish describes the work of the disciplinary specialist as one who is defined by, "traditions, histories, techniques, vocabularies, and methods of inquiry" (Olson 2002, 9). Specific academic practices are built on these features and help participants say what is distinctive about literary studies and what it is not.[1] Fish's discussion of literary scholarship depends on a sense of what it means to be a professional in this particular area. He relies on the notion of "immanent understanding" from legal philosophy to characterize an insider's grasp of the profession's practices: what questions might be asked; what answers might be given; what routines are habits of mind or hallmarks of the specific profession (Fish 1995, 20–21). The work of a literary critic is distinct not because of any particular content—the study of eighteenth-century British literature and drama, for instance—but because that participant grasps, "a coherent set of purposes . . . that inform an insider's perception," that allows him or her to listen with a critic's ears (1995, 21).

As an example, Fish takes us through a reading of the first three words of John Milton's *Lycidas*. Just three words, "Yet once more," sustain Fish as he illustrates the rich interpretive context that a traditional literary critic draws on to say what the poem means. His purpose, however, is not to argue for the truth of his analysis; rather he wants us to see the practices he engages in to articulate the words' meaning. Fish asks: does 'yet' mean despite, or, does it refer to a sense of exasperation—must we do this again—as in 'yet once *more?*' (1995, 4). These alternative analyses—and he presents many rich and varied examples of others—depend on a set of discipline-based questions—routines, if you will. He explains:

> To choose between these readings . . . is to choose between the alternative imaginings of the situation from which the words issue, where "situation" is an inadequate shorthand for such matters as the identity of the speaker—what kind of person is he? where has he been? where is he going?; the nature of his project—what is he trying to do?; the occasion of its performance—what has moved him to do it? (1995, 4)

The answers to these questions cannot come from the text. If they come from anywhere, Fish argues, they come from the critic's embeddedness in disciplinary practices, practices that are immediately obvious to anyone who engages in them but equally mysterious to anyone outside that group of professionals (1995, 6). The distinctiveness of these practices helps to characterize the discipline as what it is and more importantly for Fish, what it is not.

Political work, such as efforts to redress inequality or support diversity are outside the scope of literary work and, Fish claims, will dissolve the distinctiveness of disciplinary ventures. If we want to influence legislators, we should hire a lobbyist; and, if we want to change the world, that's all right, just don't call it literary criticism. He offers a quip attributed to Samuel Goldwyn who said about his films, "If I wanted to send a message, I'd use Western Union" (Fish 1995, 2). Or, in *The Chronicle of Higher Education*, Fish proposes that if you, a scholar of literature, attempt to interpret a poem to advance a political cause, "you will be pretending to practice literary criticism, and you will be exploiting for partisan purposes the discipline in whose name you supposedly act" (Fish 2002a). Thus, Fish separates disciplinary activity and political activity into two mutually exclusive spheres. Political activity, which he lumps together with engagement, outreach, and service learning has no place in the context of literary work and further, no place in English departments.

Fish offers his tightly conceived definition of disciplinarity, based on distinctiveness, as an argument against the idea of the engaged university. On the other hand, the Kellogg Commission says that disciplines and their distinctiveness are precisely the problem with universities. This commission, created by the National Association of State Universities and Land-Grant Colleges (NASULGC) and funded by a $1.2 million grant from the Kellogg Foundation, assembled a group of twenty-four presidents and chancellors of public universities who, through a series of reports, proposed a new understanding of engagement for public, land-grant universities and colleges.[2] The Kellogg Commission's 1999 report responded in part to the fact that universities are seen by the public as unresponsive and out of touch with societal needs for access to knowledge. The public, they say, perceives academic governance as a "near-inscrutable entity governed by its own mysterious sense of itself" (1999, 20). They go on to say, "although society has 'problems,' our institutions have 'disciplines'" (20). Disciplines, like silos, are self-contained entities, concerned only with narrowly focused research agendas. Thus, the commission reasons, they have lost sight of the institution's mission to solve contemporary social problems. The solution, according to Kellogg, must be found in interdisciplinarity because no single discipline has the answer to society's problems.

To summarize: Fish argues that disciplines *should* be like silos, distinctive and self-contained. The Kellogg Commission says no, disciplines-as-silos are precisely the problem. The Commission offers interdisciplinarity as the way that universities can help solve contemporary dilemmas. Fish, however, anticipating such a response, cautions that interdisicplinarity is, in fact, a logical impossibility. How can disciplines with their unique ways of knowing, their deeply embedded practices, collaborate to solve a social problem? Such a Utopian synthesis would collapse under the weight of its own grandeur and the component disciplines that labored in particular fields would disappear (Fish 1995, 73). It is important to note here that Fish aimed this critique of interdisciplinarity directly at the then-burgeoning field of cultural studies which hoped, quite apart from ongoing discussions of the engaged university, to (*a*) transform literary studies into a more social relevant and consequential endeavor; and (*b*) combat disciplinary fragmentation by "taking the entire social 'text' as its object of study" (Olson 2002, 19).

Now, you may reasonably ask, what do these arguments about disciplinarity and interdisciplinarity have to do with first-year writing programs or with the engaged university? Both disciplinarity, as defined by Fish, and interdisciplinarity as wished for by the Kellogg Commission, *appear* to depend on the movability of borders. This focus on borders points us to content: what content is appropriately studied in a particular discipline and what content is outside the purview of that discipline? Fish seems focused on content when he separates political work from literary criticism. Yet, the discipline of composition and rhetoric, with its responsibility for both teaching and research, does not depend on the distinctiveness of content to define itself. Rather, it draws on a deeper feature of disciplinarity, embeddedness, discussed by Fish but hardly mentioned in recent discussions of his work. In Fish's argument, embeddedness refers to a scholar's participation in the particular practices of his or her discipline, however, in this book embeddedness characterizes a participant's deep involvement in specialized communities of practice populated by community and faculty participants working together to find solutions and responding to pressing concerns.

While the idea of distinctiveness allows Fish to make the case for preserving a particular kind of literary studies, it is his idea of embeddedness that drives successful writing instruction. Think back, if you will, to Fish's reading of "yet once more," the first three words of *Lycidas,* and his description of what the literary critic must do: the critic, who, let us not forget, is also a writer, must "choose between the alternative imaginings of the situation from which the words issue." The critic must become part of the context in which the text was written and imagine the rhetorical and textual issues that apply. This embedded work, cast by Fish as literary-specific, discipline-centered work, is, in fact, what all writers do and provides the key message we want to send students who learn to write in the context of an engaged university.

Thus, a key feature of Fish's "distinctiveness" argument, embeddedness, helps us to understand the potential that writing instruction offers for students in writing or service-learning classes. Embeddedness places the writer inside a writing situation so that the language he or she uses constructs that situation. Whether interpreting a poem or writing a needs statement for a local not-for-profit, the writer must construct an imagining of the situation: of its key features, of the ways it has been represented historically, of the need that the writing responds to, and of one's writerly position in that situation. It's not the subject matter one is being asked to write about, but as Fish argued above, it's grasping, "a coherent set of purposes . . . that inform an insider's perception," and listening with a critic's [or writer's] ears (Fish 1995, 21; my addition). Notice how embeddedness subverts the usual distinction between literary studies, in which students are seen not only as consumers of text, and writing instruction, but also in which students become producers of text. Writing practices, when embedded in specific situations, allow students to be both consumers and producers of discourse.

I believe it is his deep appreciation of this feature of disciplinarity—embeddedness—that prompted Stanley Fish to proclaim in the *Chronicle of Higher Education* that "Every dean should forthwith insist that all composition courses teach grammar and rhetoric and nothing else . . . Content should be avoided like the plague it is, except for the deep and inexhaustible content that will reveal itself once the dynamics of language are regarded not as secondary, mechanical aids to thought, but as thought itself" (Fish 2002b). This diatribe, repeated again and again in horror on composition listservs, was taken by many to be a cold and self-serving dismissal of composition and rhetoric's years' long development as a discipline. For now, let's ignore Fish's administrative approach—change by decree. By excluding content and by isolating grammar and rhetoric to be taught with "nothing else," Fish appears to be brandishing the "grammar hammer," a putative tool that, wielded with heft and accuracy, can pound students' errant sentences into correct forms. Fish's argument is more complicated than most assume.

When Fish refers to content in the first-year writing classroom, he is point-ing, I believe, to the sorts of readings used by cultural studies theorists in first-year writing classes. These readings carry out the aims of cultural studies, and as Fish sees it, point students toward a particular brand of critical self-consciousness and, to his dismay, toward particular political positions. Cultural studies writing as-signments, usually academic essays, ask students to analyze the social landscape they have just read about or observed. Students write about how racism takes its toll, how gender defines our lives, or how shopping malls reshape our desires. Cast as radical pedagogy, this sort of teaching actually traps students into writ-ing for teachers about their newly won critical consciousness. It is, as Fish points out, a form of reflection that does not stem from an imagining of any situation other than the classroom.

There is, according to Fish, another sort of content, which is "the deep and inexhaustible content that will reveal itself once the dynamics of language, or writing practices, are regarded not as secondary, mechanical aids to thought, but as thought itself." This other content, "deep and inexhaustible," emerges from the function of words within syntactic structures. Those syntactic structures, crafted through a rhetorical desire for meaning, can only emerge from a writer's deeply participatory presence in a particular situation. When, as you'll see later in this chapter, students produce a brochure to warn parents about lead poison-ing, they, too, are performing in language as part of a larger project.[3] Unlike the school-based argumentative essay or research report in which students manipu-late content for the teacher, the brochure requires something different. Teaching first-year writing classes that build on the sort of deep participation desired by Fish cannot be accomplished by individual teachers or in the context of partic-ular disciplines. Such a change requires that we imagine a geo-rhetorical space that extends across disciplines and, more important, beyond the university's intellectual and physical space.

Important Work, But Not University Partnership

Before elaborating on engaged scholarship, I wish to respond to two alternative definitions for engagement that are receiving significant attention. First, I dis-cuss the role of the public intellectual who speaks out on public issues but who, I argue, does not contribute to the sort of institutional change necessary to re-shape our knowledge-making practices. Another popular model for engage-ment is public work, which involves both activist agendas and efforts to improve public dialogue. The work of activists who pursue agendas for social justice as well as the work of organizations that support public dialogue on crit-ically important issues contribute to improving our lives. My purpose in this book, however, takes on that unwieldy entity called the university and asks how it, as an institution, can reshape its teaching and learning activities in ways that engage all stakeholders in reciprocal and collaborative practices.

While the public intellectual has always played an important role in academia, this high-profile faculty member does more to divide the university from the city than to connect the two. Even so, the public remains interested in this public figure, hoping that his or her contribution will improve the social fabric. This interest in the public intellectual is not new; in some ways it recycles a long-standing debate about the university's terms of engagement with its public. Richard Posner cautions against an academic pedestal for the public intellectual, a role which he says is in decline. Posner offers a market-driven analysis focused narrowly on academics who direct their intellectual activity through the media at a public audience to comment on political matters or to function as a social critic (2003, 23–24). Posner's economic analysis suggests that the potential supply of public intellectuals might be greater than the demand for them. Many bright young assistant professors can design careers that produce outward-directed scholarship, but most will not achieve success. The costs to the scholar for this activity, Posner argues, are considerable. First, the ability and intellectual maturity to perform successfully in public are not talents held by all. Second, a young scholar who jumps the track of his specialty risks the derision of his colleagues who see this move as a bid for notoriety that precludes scholarship. Third, publications with a trade press bypass the traditional methods of ensuring quality through academic peer review placing the young scholar in a precarious position for internal academic reveiw (Posner 2003, 81). Finally, only a small number of performing academics who have an interest in being a public intellectual ever reach the superstar status that Posner says marks their success (2003, 402).

The public intellectual's activities serve to distinguish this individual from other faculty members and from other communities both within and outside of the university. Superstars like Cornel West, Stanley Fish, Norman Mailer, or Susan Sontag who, it is agreed, produce important and consequential scholarship, will not contribute to a broad, institution-wide reshaping of faculty activities or of a renewed mission for the engaged university. The terms of their engagement as public intellectuals is not reciprocal; their task is to comment on, explore, or translate current issues. The direction of their work is typically one way, a form of broadcast from the university outward toward the masses. And, the public intellectual's comments highlight the individual, not the institution. Thus, public intellectuals perform a valuable function, but they do not contribute to a re-imagining of the university as an engaged institution.

Several universities have defined engagement as public work, which sometimes depends on activist traditions and sometimes on improving public discourse. In this section, I offer a definition of public work and an example of a very impressive organization, The Public Square, that supports public dialogue, but that operates outside of a university's infrastructure and as such can't contribute to the institutional changes necessary to undergraduate education needed to design opportunities for students to write in embedded contexts. Some argue that the idea of public work should regain its former dignity and further, it should characterize the work of the engaged university. Public work, according to H. C. Boyte and N. N. Kari, means "patterns of work that have public dimensions (that is, work with public purposes, work by a public, work in public settings) as well as the 'works' or products themselves"(1996, 202). Boyte and Kari look back to colonial times for a model of public work that could connect the everyday activities of work, home, and family with participation in the public sphere. The early settlers knew that they would only prosper if they worked together to keep homes, churches, pastures, and roads functioning. Working for the common good, or as it was known then, "the commonwealth," soon extended to a concern for solving social problems.

Chicago's Public Square offers an example of a contemporary form of public work. Its 2003–2004 agenda, for instance, focused on democracy and citizenship and aimed to "foster[s] debate, dialogue, and exchange of ideas about cultural, social and political issues with an emphasis on social justice" (The Public Square). I attended a symposium sponsored by this not-for-profit organization at which three speakers, known for their contributions as teachers, activists, and writers, engaged the audience in a discussion of what constitutes activism. Their conversation also shed light on the nature of public work. I sat on a folded chair watching the speakers prepare for the event. Juvenile Defense Attorney, Bernardine Dohrn, director of Northwestern University's School of Law's Center for Children and Family Justice, sat in the middle of the three speakers on a long black sofa; she jotted down notes and questions on a yellow pad. To her left sat Barbara Ransby, the executive director of The Public Square, a social activist, and faculty member at the University of Illinois at Chicago. On the right sat the invited speaker, Grace Lee Boggs, a social activist, now eighty-eight years old, who would talk about her memoir, *Living for Change* (1998), which examined her evolving Asian-American identity in the context of her work with the Black Power movement.

This thriving enterprise, The Public Square, was established by Lisa Yun Lee and a group of former graduate students from Duke University to create a space for important public conversations. The board of directors includes several faculty members from the University of Illinois at Chicago who have been aggressive supporters of this fledgling experiment in promoting public discourse. At the Grace Boggs event, Barbara Ransby explained that, after decades of experience in direct organizing for social justice, she has shifted her priorities toward the critical goal of getting people to talk to one another. She admitted that she doesn't have a blueprint for The Public Square, but she was eager to talk about what she learned from her biographical and historical research on Ella

Baker's participation in the Black Freedom movement (Ransby 2003).[4] More than studying the "big marches or the eloquent speeches," Ransby argued, "we need to look at human relationships and networks of relationships that were sustained around a certain set of values and a commitment to struggle." Ransby learned from her study of Baker's life that "how we talk to people, how we disagree, how we come to a different understanding is more important than getting to that "correct position." What Ransby found in the work of Ella Baker and what the audience at the Grace Boggs event found in the three speakers was a sense of embeddedness in particular historical contexts that drove each person's speaking and writing activity. The Public Square, through its events and coffee shop conversations, has gifted Chicago with an opportunity for ordinary citizens to participate in improving public life. The question before us, however, concerns how *the university* can re-imagine a form of engaged scholarship that contributes to improving public life.

How Discourse Drives Engagement

An increasing number of universities have, through mission, through historical legacy, and through administrative infrastructure, redefined themselves as engaged universities. This sort of institution is committed, Barbara Holland explains, to "direct interaction with external constituencies and communities through mutually beneficial exchange, exploration, and application of knowledge, expertise and information."[5] Such a university mission not only changes the relationship of the university to its surrounding metropolis or region, but it also changes student learning. The often invisible link, I claim, between engagement and student learning becomes visible through our use of language and in particular, written discourse.

Engaged scholarship begins with a sense of embeddedness, not in the self-contained, disciplinary sense, but in specialized communities of practice that exist across departments and across institutional boundaries. I expand on the notion of communities of practice in chapter 2, but for the present, I'll define them as groups of people who come together strategically to solve particular problems rather than groups that come together as members of historically established institutional structures like academic departments. However, to grow and take root, engaged scholarship also depends on an institutional mission that values reciprocal partnerships and the mutually beneficial production of knowledge. In *Knowledge Without Boundaries: What America's Research Universities Can Do for the Economy, the Workplace, and the Community*, Mary L. Walshok challenges universities to respond more effectively to the "knowledge needs of a postindustrial society" (1995, xvii). In order to remain viable, research universities need to continually revise their response to these knowledge needs, which means not only finding new ways to access, sort, synthesize, and exchange information, but also to develop discourse communities that transform mere information into powerful new understandings through the use of language (1995, 19). This complex view of knowledge-making must, however, be supported by institutional structures that provide a conceptualization of knowledge based on multiple sources of information and reciprocity among academic faculty and off-campus constituents (13, 26).

The urban research university's push for engagement aims to redefine the, admittedly, oversimplified town-gown relationship in which the university on the hill is seen as spreading wisdom to the town below. This new direction offers a radical departure from the possibilities initiated by the Morrill Act of 1862 and the decades-long efforts and outreach and extension by which universities provided support to communities in need. New understandings of engagement function as an antidote to the "server-served" relationship (Keith 2005; Feldman 2003). Engaged scholarship also provides an antidote for the research-based practice of raiding communities for data and for savaging thriving communities to build college campuses (Maurrasse 2001; Muthesius 2000; Wiewel and Broski 1999; Perry and Wiewel 2005).

In this new context, faculty research is defined not solely by historical disciplinary standards, but by its ability to incorporate a wide range of stakeholders who bring to the table both vernacular and academic ways of knowing. The new dialogues that result from collaborative projects that cross university boundaries produce radically different kinds of knowledge. Michael Gibbons working with an international team of sociologists (Gibbons, et al. 1994) characterized this institutional shift as a radical, epistemic change that is transdisciplinary, demand-driven, entrepreneurial, and collaborative. For example, UIC Professor Olivia Gude initiated the Chicago Public Art Group which partners with "city agencies, private firms, and other organizations to produce community-oriented, site-integrated public artworks in which artists work with architects, designers, and engineers" (Gude 2000, 2). This group illustrates how transdisciplinary, reciprocal partnerships work. To proceed, the organization identifies a site-specific idea for developing a "place" and engages all stakeholders in a dialogue. The group moves ahead collaboratively to carry out research, to explore the site, to develop a budget, to actually create the space, to evaluate its use, and to celebrate its presence (cited in Feldman, et al. 2006).

We are very familiar with the traditional model of discipline-based knowledge production in which research problems are conceptualized and studied through the academic interests of a specific group. This mode of knowledge production, called Mode 1 by Gibbons' group, emerged from a view of hard science in which activities and practices take place within an agreed upon paradigm. An emerging model for knowledge production, called Mode 2 by Gibbons and his group, emphasizes its "broader, transdisciplinary, social and economic contexts" (Gibbons, et al. 1994, 1). In this materializing paradigm, knowledge is produced in a "context of application" that will likely extend outside the institution's walls to take part in a network of knowledge sources and interested parties (1994, 3). Rather than being guided by the conventions of a particular discipline, problem solving is organized and carried out in response to a particular application. Such research typically crosses disciplinary boundaries, encourages new methods of knowledge production, and involves stakeholders as participants in research rather than as the subjects of research. Changes in research practices are having a ripple effect through the rest of the academy, creating tension around time-honored processes for evaluation research for promotion and tenure. The shift to Mode 2 research has certainly been driven by the rise in globalization and computing technology, but perhaps more important is an ongoing and multisided conversation about who can produce knowledge and about what constitutes expertise (Brukardt, et al. 2004, 11). Whereas the quality of traditional research has been determined by peer review, the quality of a Mode 2 project suggests additional considerations such as: "Will the solution . . . be competitive in the market? Will it be socially responsible?" (Gibbons, et al. 1994, 8). This expanded view of making knowledge has been a driving force for engaged universities as they imagine what might be gained by research embedded in transdisciplinary contexts.

Thus far I have argued for engaged research as transdisciplinary, participatory, and reciprocal. However, above all, engaged research is discursive; as the academic faculty member proceeds in collaboration with others, he or she constructs a representation of a situation through language. Indeed, such writings, or discursive representations, can be thought of, as "situated rhetorical performances" (Petraglia 2003, 163) that advocate for specific realities. Visionary thinker, Ernest Boyer, argued that universities should be seen as "staging grounds for action." In his last talks, however, he elaborated his notion of engaged scholarship by underscoring the importance of language for taking action. He explained, "the scholarship of engagement also means creating a special climate in which the academic and civil cultures communicate more continuously and more creatively with each other, helping to enlarge what anthropologist Clifford Geertz describes as the universe of human discourse and enriching the quality of life for all of us" (cited in Glassick 1999; See also Boyer 1990).

Most important, Boyer notes that it is the discourse, itself, that allows the making of knowledge to occur among the many stakeholders who work under the aegis of the engaged university. In this context for making knowledge, the rhetorical function of language is the critical commodity. Yet we must also acknowledge that the university does not own the production of knowledge. The university is only "one of many" knowledge centers and the relationships we establish with others must be "more fluid, more interactive, and more activist" (Walshok 1999, 85). The engaged university is defined by its communicative potential and scholars, students, and community partners should see thick discourse at the center of their work. This increased attention to discourse, often characterized as "the rhetorical turn," is an established feature of scholarly work in the humanities, yet its lessons are quickly subsumed by the overwhelming belief that writing mirrors reality. Discipline-based scholars increasingly notice the ways that language constructs reality (Nelson, Megill, and McCloskey 1987). More important, this turn or return to rhetoric, has "rejected the conventional split between inquiry and advocacy," pushing us to consider how guidelines for thick discourse can also become guidelines for action (Simons 1990, 4). Where advocacy was once seen as the province of the public and making knowledge was seen exclusively as the province of the university, the rhetorical turn brings the two together through writing. Writing, or discourse, can now be seen as critical and consequential rather than as, "writing it up," or the final step in a research project. We will learn more about the possibilities of thick discourse not from ancient rhetoricians' emphasis on invention, arrangement, and style, but from seeing rhetoric as an epistemic activity that concerns the ways that discourse makes meaning. Deirdre McCloskey called this perspective "Big Rhetoric" and has used this notion to argue for a more robust presence of rhetoric in the academy (1997). Even with calls for a greater emphasis on the role of rhetoric in the making of knowledge, language and rhetoric often function invisibly, obscured by the more tangible features of a university's work—labs and classrooms, tests and tenure.

Composition scholar Charles Bazerman's study of Thomas Edison illustrates the transformative value of discourse for institutions (1999). Contemporary universities have departments of electrical engineering, where research is conducted and knowledge, presumably, socially responsible knowledge, is produced. We would not have departments of electrical engineering without electricity. However, rather than focus on the particular scientific inventions, the "generators, meters, switches, and lamps," Bazerman focuses on the way that Edison's entrance to the scene constituted a discursive moment (1999, 333). He further argues that the success of a technological innovation must do more than accomplish a material change; it hinges on understanding the ways that symbols are circulated through language (335–336). Bazerman argues that incandescent lighting achieved value because of the "development of symbols that . . . give presence, meaning and value to a technological object or process within a discursive system" (335). As we rethink the role of the engaged university, our task is to consider how discourse lends value to research and knowledge, especially when the making of socially useful knowledge results from reciprocal activity with partners in government, communities, and businesses. We are not simply producing "generators, meters, switches, and lamps." Together, the university and its partners produce a value system that surrounds these objects and that marks them as socially useful in some way. Bazerman's research on Edison reminds us that language, or discourse, seen as a system of practices, creates symbolic value in specific contexts.

Contemporary urban theorist Robert A. Beauregard provides a provocative example of how an epistemic view of rhetoric and an ethic of reciprocity and advocacy can drive the production of knowledge (1995). Beauregard explores the rhetorical practices employed to represent the city in a three-part series in the *New York Times* early in 1991 that subscribed to a tale of urban decay and objectified the city and its residents. He makes clear his perspective by announcing that

> the city, of course, cannot tell us of its problems or its prospects, its
> successes or its failures. The city is not a speaking subject. Rather, it is
> the object of our discourse. We speak for the city; it is spoken about.
> (1991, 60)

The *New York Times* series presents an argument that shapes our view of urban cities as sites of decay that defy amelioration. The rhetorical strategies employed in the series of articles created a situation so dire and so emotionally fraught that the proposed solutions seem to dissipate into "resignation and despair" (67). The image of the city is then equated with wholesale civilization so that the decline of the city means the decline of civilization (65). The experts—sociologists, politicians, political scientists, and public policy types—produce a discourse that marginalizes and locates the poor "in a social space that few of us occupy" (67). The discussion is so devastating that it leaves the reader immobilized. The articles further suggest that solutions will lead us into economic recession and the resulting failure might either be familiar or novel, but, in any case, we will fail to solve the problem (88). Beauregard's analysis of the articles deftly illustrates how poverty is defined in a social space quite apart from the readers and as such solutions seem impossible (67).

Rather than objectifying the problems of poverty though a rhetorically driven narrative of despair, Beauregard, as both faculty member at the University of Pittsburgh and community resident, constructs quite a different response, which he calls "collective action." He tells the story of working with a group of community residents to mobilize against a vigilante nightclub that contributed not only to noise, but that also contributed to drug sales and other illegal activity. The residents, who had already begun organizing a neighborhood watch, worked through the city's licensing bureau to have the club shut down. Beauregard details the work of this group and how they achieved a positive result through collective action. Interestingly, we do not know of Beauregard's participation in this collective action until the last section of the chapter.

In the article's coda, Beauregard announces his participation in the community activity. He titles this section, "Reflections," to signal his reader that once he has completed his academic analysis, he can become a participant of the collective action. He justifies his presentation in a footnote by citing Clifford Geertz's argument for "presence" as a way to legitimate narratives (1995, 78). Beauregard's discursive move, while cast as an apology—a reflective comment rather than an assertion, moves him toward engaged scholarship. The act of working with his community to shut down the club is activism and certainly could have been conducted outside of the university. However, the act of publishing a report of this effort and creating an analysis that illustrates how discourse works in two very different settings constitutes a scholarly contribution based on collaborative work. The reciprocal partnerships that made Beauregard's community participation possible also contributed to an alternate vision for a situation characterized by the *New York Times* in a discourse of urban decay.

As I argued earlier in response to Stanley Fish's definition of disciplinarity, the crucial feature of Beauregard's scholarship is his embeddedness in a community of practice. We can also characterize the context for Beauregard's work as a geo-rhetorical space. Postmodern geographer, Edward W. Soja, offers a way to understand the nature of this geo-rhetorical space through his notion of "thirdspace." Thirdspace is a site that honors the dynamic way that "lived space" connects discourse with location. Thirdspace, according to Soja, functions as a counterspace that can foreground a writer's lived experiences through the all-encompassing "relations of dominance, subordination, and resistance" that define each and every writing situation (1996, 68). Although Soja offers distinct definitions for first, second, and third spaces, his intent is to explore the complexity among these ways of thinking about social space. Drawing on the work of H. Lefebvre's *The Production of Space* (1991), Soja proposes a "dialectically linked triad" that features thirdspace as a tool that can be used to reconstitute social spaces.

Firstspace. Firstspace, or perceived space, houses a spatial practice in which space is perceived, measured, and described. Information about space is presented as the process of human activity (1996, 66) For instance, geographers who map technology use in urban neighborhoods are functioning in firstspace.

Secondspace. Secondspace, or conceived space, offers representations of space where writers, artists, ethnographers, cultural theorists, urban planners, and other artist-scientists construct visionary interpretations, produce knowledge, and dominate through their design. While firstspace privileges "objectivity and materiality," (75) aimed at a formal science that can represent information, secondspace privileges "abstract mental concepts" through which, for instance, the good intentions of artists and architects will improve material reality (79).

Firstspace and secondspace are intertwined and define our ontology, that is, our ways of being. Soja argues that the ontological basis of first and second space has been privileged by a view of history that relies on time and narrativity to "make" the historical subject (173). Time defines how life was lived, how societies developed, and how human beings enter the future having accumulated a collective past. In sharp contrast, space was treated as "something fixed, lifeless, immobile, a mere background or stage for the human drama" (169). Space, in this intellectual tradition, is seen as a container—the physical surrounding, environment, or context for being-in-the world (71). Thirdspace offers a way to counteract the illusion of reality presented by the overwhelming influence of time and historicity on the way we understand our participation in social contexts.

Thirdspace. Soja proposes thirdspace as a tool for an ontological rebalancing. Thirdspace, or lived space, forwards a political agenda "that gives special attention and particular contemporary relevance to the spaces of representation, to *lived space as a strategic location* from which to encompass, understand and potentially transform all spaces simultaneously" (68; Soja's emphasis). Soja, who writes, in part, to broaden the disciplinary space allowed to geographers, offers a productive way, as well, to broaden the space allotted to first-year writing classes.

When engagement is defined as service, locations for service are seen as the perceived, natural spaces of *firstspace* and the sometimes the Utopian spaces of *secondspace.* When we value the lived experience of all participants—in and outside the university—who endeavor to make useful knowledge, we can connect discourse with location in *thirdspace.* Likewise, when this restructuring moves into first-year writing classes, the reified genres that constitute its *firstspace* and the interpretive analysis that consititute its *secondspace* will be transformed by the possibilities of *thirdspace,* where writing becomes a way to advocate for the options available in a lived space.

In the terms of Edward W. Soja's *thirdspace,* Beauregard has created a geo-rhetorical, lived space in which to enact change; this is different than studying poverty through a narrative that objectifies the poor as a marginalized "other." Beauregard's participation in the lived experience of the same marginalized poor that were objectified in the *Times* analysis provides a more dynamic notion of scholarship than allowed by self-contained disciplinary work. Of course, some might reasonably point out that Beauregard's position as a tenured faculty member affords him privileges that his community-based colleagues don't have. And, this example might be strengthened by an illustration of some written or spoken documents produced collaboratively by the community-based group. Even with these concerns, the example illustrates the difference that embeddedness can make in the use of language and discourse to construct what we know about poverty. This illustration, as important as it is, can help me make a further point that, I think, may be difficult to grasp. Beauregard, I'm sure, doesn't think of himself as a teacher of first-year writing. Yet, as an engaged scholar, he has demonstrated how discourse analysis drove his critique of the *New York Times* piece. Further, and even more to the point, Beauregard, has much to say to undergraduate writing students about how his participation in the events he writes about demonstrates the ways that discourse drives engagement.

The New Learner Writes

The purpose of this section is to imagine what engaged scholarship means for student writing and learning. As university faculty across campuses engage more fully in partner-centered, reciprocal, and transdisciplinary research, rich opportunities for students open up. If the writing in the disciplines movement taught students the genres and the ways of knowing of particular disciplines, then engaged scholarship will provide a cross-disciplinary and even cross-institution approach to learning. Engaged scholarship is not the product of individual scholars working alone; it is not service; and it is not public work. As Barbara Holland says, it is a mode of teaching and research: "The scholarship of engagement and the idea of community partnerships are not about service. They are about extraordinary forms of teaching and research and what happens when they come together" (quoted in Brukardt et al. 2004, 2).

Following the work of Keith W. Hoskin, I call students who learn, along with faculty members, in the context of an engaged university "new learners." My argument for a post-disciplinary approach to scholarship will benefit from a brief historical note on the relationship between disciplines and learning. Keith W. Hoskin, in "Education and the Genesis of Disciplinarity," reminds us that the Latin *disciplina* is a "collapsed form of the *discipulina*, which means to get 'learning' (the *disci-* part) into 'the child' (the *puer* here represented in the *pu-* syllable in—*pulina*)" (1993, 297). The notion of discipline has always had these two functions: first, producing and disseminating knowledge and second, a concern for learning. Hoskin argues that the idea of disciplinarity began, surprisingly perhaps, through its educational function. Disciplinarity was born in the latter half of the eighteenth century through examinations, the numerical grading of those examinations, and interestingly, through the escalation of writing by and about students (Hoskin 1993, 272).

It was not oral examinations, which had been conducted since medieval times, but the insistence on written examinations and the concomitant surveillance and assessment of them that provided a foundation for the development of disciplines. A new "economy of knowledge" emerged in the German university, first, from the ranking of written work, which could now measure the inner value of the external performance. This focus on evaluation provided the starting place for a "credential society," which could identify what Keith W. Hoskin calls the "new learners," as proficient in some way. Second, and of particular interest for thinking about engaged scholarship, Hoskin argues that these new learners discovered that there was another side to the coin. Not only were students subjected to "disciplinary power" as they were evaluated on their exams, but also conversely, they, "discovered a new knowledge-power for themselves: a mirror power. . . . [that] imposed a systematically new way of constructing knowledge upon these new learners. In these new contexts for learning, students questioned, thought, and literally wrote in a new register. As a result, they produced qualitatively new forms of knowledge" (1993, 274). It is hard to imagine what it felt like to be a learner in the late eighteenth century but Hoskin suggests that this time held a good deal of excitement. Writing, for these new learners, held a sense of discovery and a sense of participation that was lost as disciplines became formed, or as some say, naturalized.

During the latter half of the eighteenth century, when, Hoskin claims, our current notion of disciplinarity was being formed, these writers, or new learners, produced what might be called "engaged scholarship." As time went on, genres of writing and ways of learning would become reified into standardized texts and tests. But at this moment, these writers wrote in response to novel situations, taking into account the immediate rhetorical exigencies. This context for writing gave rise to both disciplines and to identities. We have the scientist with his equipment and the sociologist with his survey. But we also now have the student, whose identity in the context of university life, enacts a lively engagement with the work of writing and who, only later, becomes primarily the taker of graded examinations and the recipient of knowledge from pure disciplines. Understanding disciplines as Hoskin proposes, in this historical trajectory, helps us to imagine universities and disciplines as part of a particular time and a particular place.

Who are the new learners? What do they look like in the contemporary, metropolitan engaged university? An event at Princeton University in the late 1990s raises this question and the broader one of what constitutes engagement. When, in 1998, Princeton University hired controversial ethicist Peter Singer, their decision set off a campus debate that reverberated across the country. Student groups launched protests against what they understood as Singer's support of euthanasia for severely disabled infants. Further, students accused Princeton of turning its back on its commitment to its community by ignoring the needs of the disabled. Princeton's President, Harold Shapiro, countered that the university's role is to ask the most difficult and penetrating questions we face about human life, framing these questions with rigor and integrity.[6] But this principled debate did not occur. The standoff escalated, prompting an editorial writer for the *Philadelphia Inquirer* to ask, "What's the point of a university? . . . Is it only to cram a society's settled opinions into the minds of young adults, to prepare them to ease smoothly into the workplace once they've snagged a diploma? Or is it also to spur those minds to become more agile and powerful, capable of challenging and improving upon the received wisdom, able to stretch the boundaries of theory and research?" (*Philadelphia Inquirer* 1999). While this event clearly raises questions about how a university can aspire to be *of* a community, I want to focus here on student learning. What might be the shape of the "agile minds" the editor argued for?

As the ripples widened, Judith Rodin, then president of the University of Pennsylvania and director of a commission aimed at improving public dialogue, stepped into the fray.[7] Rodin argued that universities can participate, even lead, in this national quest to improve public discourse; they should be exemplars of a new kind of thoughtful civic engagement and robust public discourse" (Rodin 2003, 233). Rodin suggested strongly that students learn to participate in debates about important issues like the one that surrounded the Singer hire. Certainly an ability to participate in deliberative discourse, in public debate and argument, is an important academic skill and one that needs honing. Learning how to argue and debate in a public forum has always been a valued academic skill. Rodin suggests that service learning, too, should become a valued part of the academic landscape. What Rodin misses, as I illustrate below, is the importance of discourse use in service-learning contexts.

Rodin offered the work of a Penn geologist, chair of his department, who provided field-based experiences for his students as part of a service-learning course in environmental toxins. This faculty member asked students to work with families in low-income communities to assess the presence of lead in their homes and yards. I want to call to your attention an activity that Rodin mentioned only briefly: students designed brochures to be disseminated to neighborhood families (2003, 234). These student-written brochures, aimed at a community-based audience, I argue, contribute significantly to the agile minds (and agile bodies) we desire for our undergraduate students. Agile writers depend on a sense of active participation in solving important problems. The Penn geologist who asked his students to go beyond their research in environmental toxins to produce brochures understood the participatory and reciprocal nature of knowledge production.

It is important to realize that the geologist understood his students needed to learn how language functions in the production of knowledge. Designing and writing a brochure depends on a sophisticated understanding of how language works to shape reality. Students, who are adept only at school-based writing, face several challenges in this field-based context. On the one hand, the comfortable, well-practiced, classroom-based modes of argumentation and narrative are of little help. On the other hand, students' familiar template for the brochure—flashy visuals and minimal text packaged in a triple-fold format—makes it seem deceptively easy.

Writing the brochure requires, more than anything else, a sense of participation in a consequential situation. This is a new and complex experience for most students. Students must synthesize their general scientific knowledge and their community-based research with the particular needs of the community members who will read their brochures. Formal aspects of writing such as paragraph coherence, syntax, style, and punctuation are now connected to a consequential aim.

Students will need to consult with community organizations and field-test the document with its potential audience, but they also will need to consult with a teacher who provides disciplinary as well as rhetorical expertise. When Penn students design written and graphic materials for use in an ongoing public situation, they write as participants, performing rhetorically to produce language and genre out of, as Stanley Fish would say, "a coherent set of purposes."

Educating Citizens to Write

In this section, I take a close look at a service-learning course at the University of California at Monterey Bay in which students undertake a complex writing project. I compare the Monterey Bay students' writing with a certain kind of writing used commonly in service-learning courses called "reflection." I learned about the service-learning class I describe below from *Educating Citizens: Preparing America's Undergraduates for Lives of Moral and Civic Responsibility* (Colby, et al. 2003; see also Fish 2003), which, in the context of arguing that universities should teach moral responsibility—a premise I disagree with—also promotes a pedagogy called "structured reflection." (See chapter 4 for a lengthy discussion of the reflection essay.) It is important to note that not all service-learning programs focus on moral development. Most, in fact, understand service learning as a way not only to prepare students for participation in contemporary society, but also as a pedagogy that connects disciplinary knowledge to applications outside the classroom.

Educating Citizens offers a manifesto for the engaged university, arguing that all types of colleges and universities can promote a mission of moral education through civic engagement. Structured reflection is the method for preparing undergraduates for lives of moral and civic responsibility. As I read *Educating Citizens* and followed its descriptions of service-learning activities, in which structured reflection was central, I noticed several classroom projects that seemed to be doing something closer to what I was after; students were using writing to shape reality rather than report to the teacher on what was learned. Let's take a close look at one of them.

Two faculty members at California State University, Monterey Bay, teamed up to teach a service-learning course for upper-level earth science majors that filled their undergraduate requirement for California history and democratic participation. Gerald Shenk, a historian, and David Takacs, in earth systems science and environmental policy, wanted students to "see history as a tool they can use to understand and shape the world they live in" (Colby et al. 2003, 160). For their major project, and for 75 percent of their grade, students were required to produce a written document call the "HIPP," or, "Historically Informed Political Project." To complete this project, students identified an ongoing California issue that had both environmental and social implications. They articulated their own perspective on the issue; they conducted historical and constitutional research on the issue; they did ten hours of community work related to that issue; and they developed a set of policy recommendations.

Educating Citizens describes, in detail, an introductory portion of the course in which students engaged in high-energy conversations about what counts as political action. Students grappled "with defining politics in ways that reflect their personal values" and they asked each other challenging questions (2003, 163). The authors of *Educating Citizens* focused on what they call the "cycles of action and reflection" that occurred throughout the course. Students continually discussed the relationship between "their definition of politics, their personal values, and . . . political action" (2003, 163). Further, students learned "to articulate, revise, and refine the values and other assumptions that inform their beliefs about their responsibilities as citizens" (2003, 163). The result of these discussions, the authors posit, "is that they will internalize habits of mind that involve careful reflection, followed by action, which is followed by a return to reflection on the action and possible changes in values and other assumptions as a result of the cycle of action and reflection" (2003, 163).

As I read the description of this project in *Educating Citizens*, something seemed wrong. The authors of *Educating Citizens* claimed, that these discussions, what they called "an internalized cycle of reflection and action" contribute to learning. I wasn't buying it. The discussions of values and moral capacities described in *Educating Citizens* seemed to float in a sea of abstract ideas. I sensed a disconnect between students' discussions, albeit important ones, and the Historically Informed Political Project (HIPP) that students would produce that semester. I wondered what sort of "action" students could take on the basis of their discussions about values. The sort of learning that would take place in an upper-level earth science class should prepare students to take action based on the discipline-specific knowledge they gained in the course. I couldn't imagine how these class discussions about values could contribute to the sentence-by-sentence craftsmanship required to produce a complex, major paper project that, among other things, developed policy recommendations. So, I called David Takacs and told him I wanted to learn more about the writing students did in his course; he kindly sent me a copy of the syllabus and three student papers. The syllabus, a thirteen-page document, states that an important goal for the course is that students become "effective participants in the civic lives of your communities after college." Students will both observe "systematic relationships in the world," and learn to make sense of those systematic relationships through the study of history and environmental policy. As suggested in *Educating Citizens*, students also would discuss what it means to take political action and how their own attitudes and experiences inform their beliefs.

The most striking feature of this syllabus, however, which is not even hinted at in *Educating Citizens*, is its emphasis on writing. This syllabus is, in fact, a handbook for how to conduct a detailed, investigative writing project. The HIPP integrates discipline-specific knowledge with ongoing social, environmental, and political issues; it requires students to use writing to take a stand on these issues. Takacs and Shenk divide the class work into eleven short writing projects which build toward the final project. Each week, students produce some writing toward the project and receive written feedback before the next week. An early writing assignment teaches students how to take field notes. Students annotate a reading from Patricia N. Limerick's book, *Something in the Soil: Field-Testing the New Western History* (2000), take field notes at a location pertinent to California's social and environmental history, and synthesize their observations with Limerick's work. In subsequent weekly writing assignments, students define the term politics and the sort of political action they might take; then they further define their political project. Next, they write a proposal outlining the historical research that underlies their project. As the class unfolds, students work on developing annotated bibliographies that evaluate the usefulness of particular sources; they study the constitution and state, federal, and local laws that apply to the issue they are studying, and they continue to turn in drafts of specific segments of their project. The syllabus offers explicit rhetorical advice for the paper's introduction that asks students to consider their audience. Along with progress reports and continued drafts of the project, students were also expected to develop and write up policy recommendations that could drive the recommended political change.

In an interview, David Takacs stressed how important the students' fieldwork was to their academic and professional development. By studying California history in the classroom as well as in community-based settings, students came to see how historical themes—such as the history of migrant labor—emerge in contemporary situations. Students also came to see how social and environmental policies developed, and they learned how to evaluate and critique these changing policies. In addition, students learned to participate in public discourse—to get over the fear of speaking up in a town meeting or participating in a public forum on a controversial topic. Julia Brown, a student in Takacs' class, worked with LandWatch, an organization that promotes responsible land policy and legislation through grassroots activism. For a case study that could illustrate patterns of land use and urbanization, she focused on Spreckels, a company town built to support the sugar beet industry in the early twentieth century. She opened her paper as follows:

> I keep an AAA map of Salinas in my glove compartment because I have a habit of getting lost. My map is well worn and very much appreciated. It tells me that Salinas is a densely populated island, surrounded by

what the map shows as blank space. But what's that little grouping to the south? That's Spreckels; you don't need your map there. It's only twelve square blocks, and no one thinks of it except to say, "Isn't that sugar or something?"

Julia told me that this project differed substantially from other history papers she had written. She said she felt much more "a part of the paper" and that she didn't have to remove herself. She learned as much from data gathered through her field-based experience as from textbooks. In particular she was struck by the way the project helped her to synthesize across a wide variety of sources. "Books," she said, "don't have to be about the same topic I'm writing about in order to speak to the same issue." This comment, stated very simply, gets at a crucial feature of writing from sources. Here, the writer, immersed as a participant in ongoing land use issues, now sees written source material for how it contributes to her developing project even if it was written about another site or a different situation.

Nick Hack, who investigated the contributions of various immigrant groups to California's agricultural history, felt that the "traditional model" for writing papers is "detached" and "distant." From his research on immigrant contributions, Nick chose to develop a policy statement on the controversial bill signed by California Governor Gray Davis allowing undocumented workers to use their Mexican National ID cards to obtain driving licenses. This bill played a crucial part in the recall election won by Arnold Schwarzenegger, who repealed the bill soon after taking office. As a result of his experience, Nick said that he was more likely to contribute letters to the editor, participate in forums sponsored by his school, and write to his congressman and senator about issues he felt important.

Antoinette Mantz, who studied the rise of corporate agribusiness, worked with the Community Alliance with Family Farmers (CAFF) on their "Buy Fresh Buy Local" campaign. As part of her community-service activity, she developed a survey for shoppers and wrote a report evaluating the media campaign's success. Writing a short report on her survey results made her realize that the information she had gathered for the organization's annual report would be read by current and potential funders and could have significant consequences. These students told me that they saw their writing as doing something important in a public context. Julia Brown, Nick Hack, and Antoinette Mantz did not produce structured reflections in their final paper for this history class. If they had, they would have missed an important opportunity to meld disciplinary knowledge with their field-based experiences.

Asking the question posed by *Educating Citizens* about whether or not these three students developed moral capacities presses the wrong agenda. What interests me most in these students is not whether they saw their work as political, but how much these students saw themselves as embedded, that is, as participants in situations for which writing and speaking are crucial rhetorical activities. Two of the three students were majors in Earth Systems Science and Policy and for this major their professional interests will require them to interact with local communities. Students in this course became not only situated rhetors, performing as writers in a discipline-based major, but also as participants in a larger public discourse. Even though these students' projects were, to a large extent, conventional classroom papers, they wrote from embedded positions. They emerged from their course with a sense of themselves as professionals who had learned a lot about participating in complex rhetorical settings and about how to employ a particular set of skills to navigate in these settings. Instead of finding moral growth, I found agile writers and competent rhetors who see writing as a way to make knowledge and to create change.

When Students "Walk" the City

In this chapter, I argue that the engaged scholar approaches research by seeing one's self as a participant and writing from that position. This perspective offers us a valuable lesson that is difficult but not impossible to reenact in the first-year writing classroom. Contemplating the redesign of first-year writing requires the kind of repatterning suggested by Thomas Bender at the beginning of this chapter. We must provide opportunities for students to move back and forth between the university's scholasticism and the city's pragmatism (Bender 1998, 19).

Scholars of composition and rhetoric have struggled to achieve the field's current disciplinary status yet some say that we achieved this status in spite of first-year writing classes. Hoping to repair their entering students' poor writing skills, Harvard initiated, in the late 1800s, a writing requirement, which, some say began the entrenchment of composition. This nineteenth-century American starting point is preceded, of course, by the much longer history of instruction in classical rhetoric. Even so, after decades of momentum built through instruction, through publication, and through professional organizations, composition evolved into an academic entity during the early 1960s when disciplinarity was both sought after and contended with. In the middle to late decades of the twentieth century, much research was driven by "paradigm hope," the idea that composition would become a science (North 1996). Composition now claims for itself—with some continuing discomfort—a disciplinary status evidenced by graduate programs, highly specific job descriptions, bibliographies, book series, conferences, and federally funded research centers. David Bartholomae, who himself regularly teaches first-year writing classes, expresses surprise at the irony that a composition specialist may not ever teach writing to undergraduates. The composition and rhetoric career path, Bartholomae argues, "has everything to do with status and identity in English and little to do with the organization, management, and evaluation of student writing, except perhaps as an administrative problem" (Bartholomae 1996, 23).

Maureen Day Goggin has developed an elaborate critique of first-year writing programs, characterizing them as stuck in a "well-worn groove" (Goggin and Beatty 2000, 30). Once imagined as a short-term solution to students' ill-preparedness, as was the case at Harvard, freshman writing courses never seemed to solve the problem; they became entrenched in a classic, self-perpetuating economic scenario that goes as follows: if instruction is kept simple, with a focus on skill development, then anyone can teach the course. With an unending supply of anyones, large numbers of courses can be launched at a very low cost. At the same time, administrators and faculty members complain that the course does not teach students how to write. Goggin quotes Donald McQuade from a piece I have regularly asked my new graduate teaching assistants to read. McQuade quips, "composition studies remains one of the few academic disciplines in which outsiders insist on naming and authorizing its activities, without accepting the intellectual responsibility—and intellectual consequences—of doing so" (McQuade 1992, 484). (See chapter 6 for further discussion of this issue.) We need to rethink this institutional pattern.

Universities that pursue an academic agenda based on reciprocal research practices with community partners will provide support for first-year writing programs that wish to announce such a direction. Composition and Rhetoric faculty members should reassert the power that the teaching and learning of writing can have on a university located in the middle of a city with an articulated mission to be *of* the city and not merely *in* it. The administrative and intellectual shape of first-year writing courses has everything to with "what we do around here." By shining a light on writing practices as embedded in situations, undergraduate courses can focus on the rhetorical features of language use. This perspective supports academic writing as well as writing in the many contexts we expect students to become competent in. When a university redefines itself as an engaged institution, the debate over what this means should occur in disciplines, majors, and most certainly, in first-year writing programs.

To make my point, I examine briefly the work of urban planners, which, in a perhaps unexpected way, parallels the current concerns of English studies. As part of the evolving disciplinary investigations of the contemporary university, urban planners have begun to rethink their professional relationship to the city. In a chapter called "Making Space: Planning as a Mode of Thought," David Perry, who directs UIC's Great Cities Institute, describes a challenge for planners that maps onto the very same challenges for those concerned with producing text (Perry 1995). Perry's chapter argues that the work of urban planners is the work of "making space," which means conceiving of planning as a dialectically driven set of practices that depends on both participation and observation conducted at the same time. Critical for planners, as Perry points out, are the dominant relations of power always embedded in the making of space. The work of the planner, as described by Perry, bears a remarkable likeness to the work of the writer who must use the tools of language to construct a reality.

The sign at the top of one of the World Trade Centers that announced "It's Hard to be Down When You're Up" no longer exists. In his chapter, David Perry points out that before the terrorist attacks of September 11, 2001, this sign greeted visitors, as it greeted philosopher Michel de Certeau on his first trip to New York. This sign, intended to celebrate the view, provoked de Certeau's thinking about the way we interact with urban spaces. As he peered down at the vertical shapes through breaks in the hazy clouds, the tall buildings suggested monuments to urban development. At this moment, a tourist and no longer a pedestrian, unable to participate in the life below, de Certeau felt that something was missing. He wanted to be frustrated by the traffic, jostled by the crowds in the street, and tossed around in the gritty, everyday reality of city life. The sign valued "being up," while Certeau wanted to recapture, "being down."

The paradox that drove de Certeau's observation about the World Trade Center also drives the thesis of this chapter. Michel de Certeau rode the elevator back down to ground level and took a close look at the pedestrian, who, unlike the tourist above, walks in the city. To de Certeau, "[t]he act of walking is to the urban system what the speech act is to language or to the statements uttered" (1984, 97). Most literally, by placing the writer in the immediacy of city streets, she can focus on local decisions about language—about genres and about sentences—as they are formed in specific contexts. The writer can imagine consequences, intended and unintended, for her work. The writer, as does the walker, positions him or herself spatially: making decisions, choosing a path, moving nearer or farther, circumventing obstacles. As de Certeau says, "Walking affirms, suspects, tries out, transgresses, respects, etc., the trajectories it 'speaks'"(1984, 99). Writing lives in the immediacy of the situation, just as walking in the city depends on one's immediate context.

But wait. There is a further paradox. Many in composition studies have used these very words to argue that writing instruction must take students outside the classroom and into the city to teach rhetorical principles. I urge us away from this literal understanding of de Certeau's work. Rather, we should see de Certeau's notion of the writer-as-walker as an imaginative mode for the writer. What's important here is that the writer sees or imagines him or herself as an agent in a particular situation. I argue that writers need to see themselves moving through an imaginary landscape as well and not only walking through the grim reality of city streets. Even in later chapters where I describe the community-based writing activities of students in the Chicago Civic Leadership Certificate Program, I am not arguing that students must walk on streets outside of campus. With this caveat, we can now acknowledge the writer as an active participant who produces text through a variety of tactics, or what de Certeau calls "*bricolage*" (1984, xviii), an imaginative "making" characterized by the inventiveness of the artisan. The writer produces a text through moment-by-moment decisions, always flexible, always choosing the most interesting path. This feature of writing (or walking) doesn't exist in isolation and is difficult to bring into the composition classroom. The actor/writer is always walking through a particular context, which is created and defined by the vertical shapes of the surrounding buildings.

Both Perry and de Certeau want us to see that this geography is laden with values and defined by relations of power. Thus, while it is true that one is either up on top or down on the ground, both positions, with their inscribed values, have an impact on what we can write or where we can walk. The opportunistic pedestrian who walks among tall buildings employs tactics that respond not only to spatial constraints, but also to ideological constraints, questioning the meaning and value of specific discourses in specific contexts.

In the context of the university, the opportunistic pedestrian-student walks among the silos of disciplinarily and simultaneously participates in a variety of enclaves. Students, particularly first-year writing students, often feel inadequate as they look across a landscape of extraordinary authors who are seen as titans and whose writing they can imitate only inadequately. In some university settings, the learning process makes students feel like tourists or outsiders. This book argues for writing situations in which the student-pedestrian finds him or herself embedded in spaces that cut across the traditional disciplinary locations. This extended space allows students to study language use and how it inscribes power relations in particular situations. Remember here that these situations may be imaginary ones. The student/pedestrian, with her inventive tactics, can "inquire into the 'underside' of scientific activity" and ask further about the juxtaposition of the "theoretical ambitions of the discourse with the stubborn persistence of ancient tricks in the everyday work of agencies and laboratories" (de Certeau 1984, xxiii). Writing in composition classes should mean learning how knowledge is made in a variety of contexts.

Scholars have pointed out that while sciences develop through various methodologies, only sometimes do these practitioners examine the rhetorical nature of the knowledge they build, question the nature of facts, or review basic assumptions. Disciplines, J. S. Nelson, A. Megill and D. McCloskey maintain, wear a "mask of methodology" that hides the tactics and ordinary practices that contribute to building disciplinary knowledge (1987). Worried by how these somewhat hidden academic practices confuse students, Gerald Graff (2003) argues that "academia reinforces cluelessness by making its ideas, problems, and ways of thinking look more opaque, narrowly specialized, and beyond normal learning capacities than they are or need to be."

Graff's solution is to demystify for students the arguments that underlie academic work. In a recent textbook, *"They Say I Say:" The Moves that Matter in Academic Writing*, co-written with Cathy Birkenstein, students practice using key rhetorical moves that place them at the center of an academic conversation. By identifying these moves Graff and Birkenstein make clear to students the often mysterious relationship between what others (the "they") say or have said on a topic and what the student (the "I") might now contribute (2006).

Designing instruction that makes writing matter presents an enormous challenge. It asks us to do the unthinkable—to invest in *bricolage* as an academic practice.[8] Etienne Wenger claims that "Learning cannot be designed. Ultimately it belongs to the realm of experience and practice" (1998, 225). This chapter suggests that university-based writing instruction should jump its "well-worn groove" and provide opportunities for students to evoke a sense of participation even when they are in classrooms. However, the public discourse that drives learning both in and out of school and the complex literacy practices that support such learning should be part of the curriculum, not a back-channel strategy used by students and faculty members to make a space for unconventional approaches.

When students write in the context of an engaged university, they should be participating in new ways of learning. This sort of participation means seeing discourse in ways that they have not seen it before. It means seeing how current scenarios are informed by a variety of textual activities that can be tracked historically and spatially. Think back, for instance, to the work of Nick Hack, the student at California State University at Monterey Bay, who developed policy recommendations for undocumented migrant workers. His participation in a local organization complemented his historical research. This approach to writing, which emphasizes a writer's embeddedness, can bring university faculty and students together to create a space for learning that supersedes a narrow definition of both physical location and disciplinary content. This approach depends on seeing the university as a spatial entity, itself a participant, involved in solving important problems. Keith W. Hoskin described a new learner who wrote as our disciplines were forming; I'm proposing a new learner who writes as contemporary universities negotiate the meaning of engagement.

Chapter 2

<hr/>

Writing as Participation

The problem with the conventional freshman essay is that it has become a frozen and transparent genre. As such, it functions as a container for a certain kind of content usually characterized as personal experience. While this analysis is not new, innovative responses to it take place largely within the conventional institutional context of first-year writing programs where writing is seen as an exercise in illustrating learned skills. In these classrooms, situation and genre remain interesting ideas but not actions. My approach in this book is to involve student writers as participants in the larger institutional agenda of the engaged university. As faculty increasingly take up research opportunities in a broader, community-based landscape, their writing projects perform a wider range of tasks and achieve a wider range of results. This change in faculty activities provides exciting opportunities for student writers that illustrate how writing functions as situated performance.

I begin the chapter with two historical cases through which I examine how, even outside of the composition classroom, our expectations for particular genres result from a culturally driven acceptance of genre as a frozen and transparent container. What activates genre, I argue, is its delivery to participants situated in a public context by a writer with acknowledged or emerging expertise. To make this point, I illustrate an artist's project characterized not as a work of privatized, individual genius, but as the result of a museum's attempt to redefine its public engagement. We in English studies have a hard time seeing outside our disciplinary silo. Writing instruction, informed by the largely interpretive practices of English studies, teaches imitation to the novice writer. "Be like me," the student hears; or, "Write like this." In this chapter, I push for a greater acknowledgement of participation in communities of practice as a way to make writing matter for students. Understanding that we write in the context of larger institutional agendas, for good or for ill, will change our approach to instruction and alter the experience of students in our classes.

The Purloined Petition

Let's begin with a literary mystery. Katherine, known to us only as "Mrs. Russel's maid," recounted the terror of her trip to America and her religious conversion in a document that for many years was taken to be a diary. In this document, one of the many first-generation, colonial narratives collected by Thomas Shepard between 1673 and 1645, Katherine testified to her sins and told of her surrender to the Lord. She swore that she had "remembered the scripture" throughout the treacherous journey. Quoting Isaiah she promised, "I'll be with thee in the first waters," and drawing from Exodus, she found strength in the face of disaster, "when ready to be cast away, stand still and see salvation of God." Finally, sensing a call from the Lord, she affirmed, "So I came hither."[1] Conversion narratives such as Katherine's were originally taken to be confessional diaries, intended to explore one's feelings and thereby present an authentic account of the writer's experience (Caldwell 1983, 6).

We now know that writers produced these confessional narratives for a purpose other than self-expression. Patricia Caldwell's adept literary sleuthing uncovered this fact while investigating a work published in 1669, prior to Katherine's, titled *The Experiences of God's Gracious Dealing with Mrs. Elizabeth White*, which had been taken, not only as a diary, but which had been incorrectly cited as the diary of a colonial settler and was thus taken to exemplify an important autobiographical genre of that period (Hall 1987, 220–222). Caldwell did not begin her investigation for the purpose of disengaging Mrs. White's identity as a colonial settler; instead her close attention to the historical context of the text and to the writer's rhetorical aims led to her realization that documents like Mrs. White's and Katherine's were not diaries, but "relations," testimonials produced as part of a petition for church membership.

Even though Caldwell characterizes her investigation as a literary one, I argue that her analysis reaches far beyond studies of colonial American literature. "How," Caldwell asks, "shall we explain the past misunderstandings about the provenance of Mrs. Elizabeth White's memoir (1983, 35)?" In other words, how was it that so many historians and scholars of literature continued to read these works as diaries (39)? The same veil that obscured both Katherine's and Mrs. White's documents as petitions for church membership from scholars obscures the social uses of writing in the contemporary writing classroom. In spite of the well-documented rhetorical turn that emphasizes the contingency of language, the literacy narrative and its service-learning partner, the reflective essay, are often seen as diaries—authentic renderings of the writer's experiences, knowledge, and feelings. Even though we profess to know better, the words that compose the literacy narrative are often seen as a conduit or pipeline through which authentic ideas and feelings are conveyed to a reader. Students, themselves, however, understand the rhetorical impact of these essays; at some tacit level they know that they will purloin these essays and construct them as a petition for a grade.

Caldwell's focus on the way these documents fulfilled a socially driven purpose moves our inquiry directly into a rhetorical realm. If we define rhetoric as "the use of language to produce material effects in particular social conjunctures," we can see how these confessional documents responded to social initiatives (Bernard-Donals, and Glejzer 1998, 3). Caldwell's research drew on both circumstantial evidence as well as stylistic analysis. Whereas the colonial New England conversion narratives contained numerous mentions of the treacherous journey to America and were filled with specific historical references to people and places, Mrs. White's *Experiences* contained none of these details. From Caldwell's research emerges the startling fact that Mrs. White had never stepped foot in America and thus was not a colonial settler. Caldwell pursued the mystery further, "even if we knew nothing about Elizabeth White's life her written narrative alone should tell us that she never crossed the ocean" (1983, 5).

Most important to Caldwell were patterns of specific symbolic treatments that differentiated the Puritan, colonial narratives from the English ones, further confirming that Mrs. White's document was not a diary and beyond that, not a diary written by a New England settler. As a confessional diary, Caldwell expected that Mrs. White's *Experience* would offer a "free-form, running chart of the writer's spiritual temperature" rather than enact a rhetorical pattern found in many other narratives (1983, 6). However, Mrs. White's narrative strategy was not idiosyncratic; it characterized her conversion in a manner common to that of other similar documents produced in England at that time in which "dreams, visions, or just a sudden inexplicable realization of being personally saved" offered an identifiable rhetorical pattern" (30). By contrast, the narratives of the New England Puritans, like Katherine's above, typically featured a diminished self that travels in a "vast geography, both physical and spiritual, as well as through an expansion (at least momentarily) of the private person into the public figure of Israel" (30).

Caldwell's scholarship illustrated that these narratives—some written in England and others written by colonial settlers—were purposefully designed to display characteristic literary strategies. Petitioners submitted these narrative petitions (or delivered them orally) to church members who determined whether or not the candidate had attained spiritual maturity and might be admitted as full members to the church. Caldwell's literary analysis also convinced her that these petitions were the product of the "creative organization of materials . . . that comes about in order to fulfill—in its peculiar way and in no other possible way—an aim, an end, a need" (41). Thus, Mrs. White's diary functioned as a rhetorically crafted, situated performance and not as an authentically expressed personal narrative.

I contend that the epistemological certainty that allowed scholars to persist in reading Mrs. White's *Experiences* as a Puritan diary underlies the teaching practices that unwittingly champion a reified, school-based genre called the literary narrative that composition teachers frequently want to believe functions like a diary. Narratives that appear to be confessional are often assumed to be diaries that evoke an authentic experience from a reader who wants to enjoy such an intimate transmission (Felski 1989, 101). On the other hand, feminist scholar Rita Felski argues that confessional narratives can also be seen as a Foucaldian construction of subjectivity in which any attempt by a diarist to seek self-knowledge becomes an alienating recognition of one's inability to construct an identity out of the telling of experience (103). Felski wants to problematize attempts to define diaries as a narrowly conscribed genre or as the product of women's lives which "have until now been largely defined by their location within the private sphere, . . . [a] realm [that] necessarily constitutes the starting point for critical reflection" (115). Felski wants to resituate what had been seen as confessional writing for feminist scholars and others interested in identity politics and, in particular, in oppositional or marginal, identities.

The colonial petitions were seen as diaries for so long because such apparently confessional writing is often judged outside of its social and material circumstances. If we can get beyond the oversimplified "one-dimensionality" by which such confessional writing projects are frequently prejudged, we can, according to Felski, re-situate such texts as an "instrumental force in the creation of a feminist 'counter-public sphere,' an oppositional discursive space within contemporary society" (Felski, 121). Thus, Felski moves confessional writing out of its seclusion in a feminized private sphere and offers it as a tool for rethinking an identity politics grounded in specific situations.

The next illustration concerns the narrative of a successful petition that might be taken by some as a diary, defined by its expressive authenticity. Here, too, an unexamined or easy acceptance of conventional genres belies the complexity of the circumstance in which writing is produced. Susan Miller's book, *Assuming the Positions: Cultural Pedagogy and the Politics of Commonplace Writing*, examines the commonplace books collection of the Virginia Historical Society (1998), which displays a variety of everyday genres: copied verses, accounts of work, records of local visits, letters, slave records, diaries, speeches, and documents such as wills or deeds. Miller defines these texts as ordinary writing for their ability to "simultaneously appropriate and mutate an expanding range of human identities that become available in specific cultures over time" (1998, 39, 1). Even with the elevated class status of most of the writers of commonplace books, and with their presumed identities as former slave owners and defeated southerners, these texts offer a "radically textualized writing subject" that uses ordinary texts as a way to embed one's self in particular discursive situations (5–6). In the book's coda, she focuses on the divorce petition of Evelina Roane, the writing of which created an opportunity for what Miller calls, "homemade local authorship," which is neither a part of high or low culture, nor is it a part of our contemporary understanding of the public or private sphere (9). Like the case of the colonial diaries above, Roane's local authorship, "manipulates commonplace identities in specific exigencies" (12).

Evelina Roane's divorce petition, written in 1823, told in the third person and cast as a story, might be read as a compelling personal narrative, but must instead be understood as a carefully constructed argument intended to persuade her readers. Through her petition, Evelina Roane pleaded with the Virginia General Assembly to release her from her abusive husband.[2] As Susan Miller suggests, one might suppose that Evelina Roane won her divorce by telling an exceptionally powerful story and thus prevailing through the force of narrative truth (Miller, 264). As we will see, her divorce petition is not a diary even though it tells a personal story. Instead, Evelina Roane wins her divorce, not by telling a sympathetic story, but, by structuring the petition's argument to *sustain* the powerful nineteenth-century conventions of an authoritative patriarchy.

Miller explains that the Virginia State Assembly seldom heard divorce petitions, in part because no legislation supporting divorce had been written and in part because spousal issues were taken care of by legal separations. Evelina Roane's divorce was the only one granted of the sixteen that were proposed and the three that were finally heard that year. Evelina's husband, who beat her regularly, on one occasion causing a miscarriage, had moved his common-law wife, a slave, into their home along with their two biracial children and insisted that Evelina serve the new wife as a domestic servant. While some might argue that the court's granting of a divorce illustrated their outrage at this unacceptable relationship between a white man of privilege and his slave wife, similar situations had not resulted in the granting of divorces. Even if these historical circumstances did not assure a divorce, some might suspect that an emotionally charged narrative offered as a diary of the events of her life, might have convinced the Assembly to grant her a divorce. Not so, Miller explains (258).

What allowed the members of the Assembly to arrive at the unlikely decision to grant a divorce was an argument based on a rhetoric of sincerity aimed at upholding the existing patriarchal mores and providing a means for the Assembly's support. Roane constructed a vivid and compelling narrative that functioned as an argument. It allowed the members of the Assembly to see themselves sustaining and strengthening the patriarchal rule that could protect her. Roane described in stunning detail the indignities of her removal as wife and subsequent installation as servant, a life-threatening beating after visiting a family funeral, and, most important, a conflict between her father and her husband, that served, perhaps more than anything, to call into question the abusive husband's endorsement of the existing patriarchal order. Evelina Roane reminded the courts that because her abusive husband had forbidden her from seeing her father, she now must plead that the court provide "valid patriarchal nurturance" (Miller 1998, 262). In this way, she argued, the conventional patriarchal norms would be upheld, and she begged the court to protect her by upholding their very standards.

Evelina Roane won her petition, but not because she offered an authentic reflection on her experience. Quite the opposite, Roane complicates the notion of an "experiential discourse" with an argument that relied on personal experience as a rhetorical proof (Miller 1998, 264; Scott 1991). The judge's decision was based on the claims that she presented and supported. Evelina Roane's writing resulted in a rare decision: a divorce in the Virginia of 1824 as well as the custody of her son. To achieve the consequences she desired, Roane had to construct a provisional identity in support of fathers—her own and her husband as father—and more broadly, the patriarchy. In doing so, she could not rely on a sympathetic response to the ugly facts of her situation but rather on an argument that turned the patriarchy back on itself, forcing it to grant the divorce in order to sustain the local power structure.

Both the commonplace writing at the center of Miller's book and the divorce petition contained in the coda, were produced, Miller argues, outside of the educational institutions that were just beginning to be formed. As such, these texts complicate the distinction between public and private writing that would eventually separate writing in school-based settings from writing in public settings such as work, politics, or law. School-based writing would become a private or gendered sphere, while public writing would be elevated to literature and would be produced by recognized authors (Miller 1998, 73, 256). Further, Miller argues, the wide variety of writing produced in commonplace books was lost to this bifurcation between private school-based writing and the public authorship of literary texts. After the institutionalization of writing instruction in separate classrooms alongside the English department's classes, which would focus on interpreting literature of value, the lessons of the sort of texts Susan Miller describes become lost. According to Miller, such ordinary writing creates a visible "cultural signature" that highlights a writer's particular sense of self in a particular context at a particular moment of writing (1998, 2). It is this cultural signature that I wish to recapture in my argument for redesigning writing instruction in the contemporary engaged university.

In the two vignettes I have offered thus far, Katherine (Mrs. Russel's maid) wrote to gain entrance into a community while Evelina Roane wrote to escape a socially sanctioned relationship. What's important here is not the particular sociopolitical character of their activity but the way in which the activity of writing offered an opportunity to change each writer's material circumstances. As self-contained texts, these documents both look like personal narratives and in one case, a diary. However, when returned to their contexts and examined for how their writers shaped them in particular rhetorical situations, we see how, to paraphrase M. Bernard-Donals and R. R. Glezner, the writers crafted text to produce particular material effects in particular circumstances (1998).

Both Evelina Roane and Katherine were overwhelmingly concerned with the delivery of their texts and how they would function in a "particular social conjuncture" (Bernard-Donals and Glejzer 1998, 3). Delivery, in these situations, is much more complex than the oversimplified view of audience that populates most writing classes. Delivery works hand in glove with what are typically seen as its precursors—invention, arrangement, and style—to build toward what cultural studies and composition scholar John Trimbur calls professional expertise and the production of socially responsible knowledge (2000). Invention, arrangement, and style cannot exist apart from the writer's aims. Trimbur relies on Marx's *Grundrisse* to frame the contradictory relationship between use-value, a commodity's ability to respond to a human need, and its exchange value, the economic value ascribed to that same commodity. The tension between use-value and exchange-value can also be applied to the teaching of writing by linking it to the means of production. In his examples and in the examples that make up this section, what gets distributed, "is the productive means to name the world, to give it shape and coherent meaning" (2000, 209). Making writing matter depends on a heightened understanding of delivery in the first-year writing class.

Continuing this focus on delivery, let's move to a contemporary context to take a look at the writing of a grant proposal. Such writing is frequently seen as merely transactional: a request for funds that is either granted or denied. Called "vocational writing," for its ties to the world of work, teachers assume that these are the texts produced by filling in the blanks of standardized formats. Vocation writing, then, is disqualified from the work of writing in the classroom, which is seen to be about generating important ideas. What's missing in the teacher's quick dismissal of so-called vocational writing and in the embrace of the classroom essay is attention to delivery, which brings context back into play.

Let's take a look at a grant proposal written to obtain funds for a graffiti mural. From an article that appeared in the *Chicago Tribune*,[3] for example, we learn about a community organizer who wrote a grant proposal to the Chicago Community Trust, requesting funds to buy paint for a mural that would be painted by thirty graffiti artists on a south side retaining wall to depict moments in Chicago's history. As the project organizer worked on his proposal, we can be sure that he thought about the readers who would review the grant proposal and who would decide whether or not to fund it. Certainly, the community activist thought about the opportunity this project would provide for the graffiti artists who, interestingly, think of themselves as writers—graffiti writers. He would have thought about how Chicago's efforts to clean up graffiti could influence those evaluating the grant. He needed the money to complete this project, but more than anything, he wanted the proposal to communicate the complexities of this situation: the project was not intended to distract the youth from unlawful vandalism but to provide a venue for "one of the few indigenous forms of art for urban youth" (quoted in Feldman, et al. 2005, 6). This proposal writer hoped that readers would see how painting the mural could contribute to the city's cultural landscape rather than only provide a deterrent to vandalism. In producing the grant proposal for potential funders, the writer understood the complex and contradictory functions of graffiti. He hoped that in granting his proposal, the funders had signed on to his argument for graffiti's use-value as a contribution to Chicago's cultural landscape.

Katherine, Evelina Roane, and the community activist all wrote to reshape their worlds in some way. What's important for students to understand is that the rhetorical lessons emerge not only from an evaluation of the end product's worth but from a study of the way, according to Trimbur, the production of knowledge is tied to its circulation. Knowledge production is not internal, as is suggested in the writing of literary narratives, but "tied to the cultural authorization of expertise, professionalism, and respectability" (Trimbur 2000, 210). Here is where the engaged university enters. As a social institution, it has redefined the use value of its knowledge-making activities and in so doing heightened its responsibility to produce writing and knowledge that matters. As I argued above, the grant writer, although presumably most interested in obtaining the grant, is also interested in complicating graffiti for his readers as a form of indigenous art rather than a form of vandalism. When we evoke our rhetorical criteria to analyze how language is used to "produce material effects in particular social conjunctures," we see how writing proposals offers an opportunity for a student to examine how to use language to create effects in the world (Bernard-Donals and Glejzer 1998, 3).

Institution, Genre, and Social Action

Without the startling new information provided by Patricia Caldwell's research, scholars would have continued to assume that Katherine's narrative was a diary. Genre is frequently invisible, living in our heads at any moment as a sociocognitive given, providing a container for particular images or texts. Traditionally, genre has served to categorize the many creative and intellectual products of our culture—fiction, prose, drama, music, art, film, photography, and more. When producing work in a particular genre is seen as an act of imitation, the stability of the genres is emphasized. Over the past twenty years, however, genre theory has shifted its emphasis away from imitation and toward the dynamic and complex social interactions that undergird genre use. For Charles Bazerman genres are, "forms of life, ways of being. They are frames for social action (1997, 19)." In the illustration below, we observe how a museum's initiative provided an opportunity for an artist to consider the act of creating a portrait as a frame for social action.

The National Gallery in London had commissioned contemporary artists to "redo" a painting of their choice from the museum's permanent collection. I attended the exhibit and was particularly fascinated by the redo of contemporary artist, R. J. Kitaj, who had chosen to re-imagine the classic *Van Gogh's Chair*. The "redo," or genre transformation, is also a popular writing assignment in which students are asked to write their own version of a poem or essay. When this assignment is seen as an imitation, it assumes the stability of the genre and focuses on the internal composition of meaning without looking to the context or situation. However, a more sophisticated response takes broader concerns into account and imitation quickly becomes impossible. For example, figure 2.1 is a parody of the film review, written by Pete Franks, about the English 555 seminar in which we train new graduate students to teach a writing program (see chapter 6). As this piece illustrates, playing with genre can highlight the link between the conventional expectations for that genre and the new situation it is being applied to.

Figure 2.1. Parody of a Film Review

Film: *Making Writing Matter*

Director: Ann Feldman

Grade: ¤ ¤ ¤ ¤

Making Writing Matter, the new movie from UIC's First-Year Writing Program, is as gripping as it is daring. Highlighted by dramatic twists and turns throughout, the film features a host of UIC English teachers bringing academic writing out of the ivory tower and onto the streets of Chicago. The brilliance of the actors is underscored by Diane Chin's provocative script. What begins as mediocre, ineffectual student writing becomes dynamic, engaging writing with a clear social purpose. Blending the psychodrama of Hitchcock's *Rope*, the intensity of Peckinpah's *Wild Bunch*, and the romance of Hawks' *Only Angels Have Wings*, this film delivers more for the money than anything in recent memory. Watch for the unexpected cameo appearance by Dean Stanley Fish in the cafeteria scene. Highly recommended.

Source: Pete Franks.

Modern artist, R. J. Kitaj (pronounced Kit-eye), eschews imitation and refuses to be held captive by a traditional generic form; rather, he plays with genre by subverting it to his own social purposes. Kitaj calls himself an identity artist. To some, particularly students and teachers in the freshman writing classroom, writing about identity means creating narratives that capture personal experience. For Kitaj, however, the identity artist positions himself as a participant in a broad cultural context and uses his art to intervene in that context. Kitaj's aim reaches beyond aesthetics to change the way he can use an established genre such as the portrait.

Rather than see the well-defined genre of portrait and its subgenre, the self-portrait, as a specific type of painting, defined by the visual representation of a head or a body, current thinking about genre helps us to see how this representation emerges from a social context and, in particular, from the artist's relationship to that context. Consider Vincent Van Gogh, who carried with him, in his artist's mind a schema for the genre of the self-portrait. Van Gogh painted many portraits and self-portraits, each different, each a rearticulation of this familiar genre. A quite traditional self-portrait, *Portrait de l'artiste* (1998, 95), painted in 1887, hangs in the Musee d' Orsay in Paris and offers a fairly conventional rendition of the artist's face. Over time, through subsequent self-portraits, Van Gogh used the genre as a way to move his art forward and felt strongly that portraiture offered direction to modern art (Morphet 2000, 211). As Van Gogh proceeded to work in this genre, his self-portraits increasingly represented the despair that was overtaking him. *Worn Out*, for instance, shows him sitting on a chair with his head in his hands in utter resignation; the face, icon of the self-portrait, covered by his hands, cannot be seen (2000, 211). The next year, in 1888, he painted *Van Gogh's Chair*, a lone chair on a tile floor, a small pipe and bag of tobacco on the chair's seat, and the painter's signature on the onion box in the corner (2000, 202). Some might say that with *Van Gogh's Chair*, the artist had used the genre of the self-portrait to illustrate not his presence, but his disappearance from the scene. In this way, Van Gogh played on our cultural expectations for the genre of the self-portrait. His empty chair, the elided self-portrait, speaks to us about how he interpreted his relationship to artistic traditions; it illustrates how one can upset genre by working against these expectations.

Let's widen the lens to include a discussion of the National Gallery where *Van Gogh's Chair* hangs. The National Gallery, in celebration of the millennium, had invited contemporary artists to choose a painting in the museum's collection and "redo" it. Modern artist, R. B. Kitaj, not only known for contributions to the Pop Art movement in Britain in the early 1960s, but also for his semi-abstract expressionist bent, chose to redo *Van Gogh's Chair* and produced *The Billionaire in Vincent's Chair* (reproduced in Morphet 2000, 204; see figure 2.2). Kitaj, who grew up in the United States and studied art in New York City as well as Vienna, nourished a deep and years-long connection with Van Gogh's legacy as an artist and as a person.

Figure 2.2. *The Billionaire in Vincent's Chair*

As an expatriate and a Jew, living, teaching, and painting in Britain, Kitaj writes frequently about what he calls "his role" as a Diasporist painter. He feels connected to Van Gogh, who also felt himself an outsider in Auvers, near Paris, and who dreamed of returning to the comfort of his hometown in Holland. Kitaj's *First Diasporist Manifesto*, which announces his artistic agenda, says that his Diasporist approach is "enacted under peculiar historical and personal freedoms, stresses, dislocation, rupture and momentum" (1989, 19). This view of painting, a way of working out one's not-at-homeness, allows Kitaj to articulate his connection with Van Gogh, whom he names in his manifesto as a "related alien type" (1989, 99, 101). Kitaj wasn't interested in imitating the Van Gogh piece in homage to the original work. Rather, it was his close connection to Van Gogh, based on an imagined synchronicity that prompted Kitaj to take on the National Gallery project. Kitaj painted to make a change in his world rather than to express his feelings or to produce an aesthetic object.

Kitaj's composition plays on the idea of portraiture by filling Van Gogh's empty chair with the bold presence of a large, black-skinned man slouching casually against the chair. The two paintings share obvious motifs—both artists inscribe their first names and make reference to smoking. Yet Kitaj fills Van Gogh's empty chair with an imagined character to make a point about what has happened to the value of his work over the past century. Kitaj's redo of *Van Gogh's Chair* emphasizes the use-value of the original painting rather than its aesthetic qualities.[4] Rather than think of Van Gogh's painting as a universal example of fine art to be imitated, Kitaj builds on his connection with Van Gogh, the person as well as the artist. He creates for himself a situation, which gives rise to the painting he creates. In a letter to the author of the exhibit publication, Kitaj explains:

> Whenever I see a Van Gogh picture I quickly think of them stacked around in the dust of his little rooms unsold and unwanted. It's quite hard for me to divorce what I know to be their visual "aesthetic" from their other lives as forlorn, largely disliked things in a very humble room, and now as priceless trophies of vast wealth. (Morphet 2000, 210)

By filling Van Gogh's empty chair with a brazen, self-impressed billionaire whose physical body more than fills the canvas, Kitaj makes a point about the psychological and economic contexts in which Van Gogh worked. The billionaire, Kitaj quips, is "the only one who can afford it!" (Morphet 2000, 207).

This redo helps us understand how genre can contribute to social action. The genre of the portrait acts as a portal through which the *Billionaire in Van Gogh's Chair* makes a statement about Kitaj's perceived relationship with Van Gogh and the use-value of his works. Kitaj's redo of *Van Gogh's Chair* illustrates how the activity of painting (and writing) occurs as part of a broad social context. Paintings and texts share their contexts with institutions which, through their historical evolution and habitual practices, provide structures for shaping art and language (Miller 1994). It is true that while Kitaj could have produced this painting in many other contexts, this particular opportunity resulted from an institutional initiative and offered the opportunity to consider what difference that context might make.

In the introduction to the museum catalogue, Neil MacGregor (2000, 7) the director of the National Gallery, situates this contemporary initiative in the context of the museum's original purpose, which was to open the royal art collection to artists who could study and imitate the Old Masters. In fact, MacGregor admits that in many ways these millennial redos eschew imitation—striking out to create new representations and new relationships connected only by the thinnest of strings to the original work. However, this exhibit had another purpose beyond engaging contemporary artists in conversation with the past. Museums, as institutions, look forward as well as back and this exhibit aimed to renew its presence in its metropolitan context. One could imagine that this exhibit aimed in some small way to destabilize the National Gallery's identity as a "repository of artifacts" (Dector 2001, 84).[5] The museum might have been motivated to create some energy—as did many other institutions during the millennium season— by creating new relationships and inviting new patrons to visit. Perhaps by putting contemporary artists in conversation with the past and by inviting the public to witness this event, the museum aimed at strengthening its relationship with its public.[6]

The *New Encounters* exhibit suggests an institutional agenda focused on connecting the past to its contemporary context. Universities, like museums, have been rethinking their presence in urban centers and developing new relationships. This illustration, which connects the individual artist (or writer) to the institutional context through the possibilities of genre, provides a backdrop for further discussions about how writing instruction can establish a more focal position in the context of engaged universities. More specifically, it provides a way of looking at the role of imitation in writing instruction, which I introduce in a later section.

This Container Isn't Big Enough

I had been struggling to describe this book project to a friend and was surprised by a phone call from her a few days later. Excitedly, she told me, "Look in the *Sunday New York Times*, there's an art professor working with students to put up exhibits in the city. Isn't that like what you're trying to do?" The article, indeed, captured some key features of my project. Art critic Mia Fineman had written a travelogue, of sorts, describing her day-long tour of a unique art exhibit sponsored by the Whitney Biennial in 2004.[7] Harrell Fletcher, artist and part-time faculty member at Cooper Union worked with a group of art students who would find free sites around New York City where eleven little-known artists could exhibit their work. Fletcher wrote a guide to the off-site exhibits which was available at the Museum.[8] He called the exhibit, "This Container Isn't Big Enough."

What interested me most was the back story to M. Fineman's article. Fletcher told me that he had, in fact, brought one of his students, Einat Imber, along on the tour with Fineman, but that her presence was never acknowledged in the *New York Times* article.[9] Fineman's choice to leave out the student reflected, I surmise, her interest in how Fletcher's personal and political approach to art had prepared him to launch such an exhibit and what the Whitney's support of the exhibit said about the economics and circulation of art. Fletcher's work is, according to my parlance, engaged scholarship. By collaborating with previously unexhibited artists, by writing a guide to these artist's off-site exhibits, and by naming the show, "This Container Isn't Big Enough," Fletcher expanded the traditional space of the museum and commented on that activity through a rhetorically savvy approach to scholarship. The Whitney, by sponsoring his exhibit, had hoped to redefine its engagement to the city.

I became fascinated by the role that Fletcher's student must have played in establishing the off-site exhibit. Why did Fletcher ask students to do what he could have done himself quite easily? What would his students learn? Imagine for a moment, Fletcher's student, Einat Imber, as she set out to find a free space for Cleveland Leffler, whose "crudely drawn pictures of Mars and imaginary interviews with astronauts," according to Finemen, "read like Becket in outer space" (Fineman 2004). Certainly Imber had to determine what setting would provide the best frame for Leffler's work. When she found a possible location, what happened next? What sort of conversation did she have with the librarian at the Roosevelt Island Branch of the New York Public Library, where Leffler's work would eventually be displayed? Imagining this student-librarian conversation, I hear Imber describe the Whitney exhibit, explain why art should be exhibited in neighborhood settings, and discuss Leffler's unique contribution. I hear her answer the librarian's concerns about whether or not the art fits with the library's theme for that month, or about whether or not exhibiting Leffler's art is the best use of their limited display space.

This imagined, discursive moment captures the energy that should be at work in first-year writing classes. It's true that the art student isn't writing—she has no pen in hand—and she may not have planned her dialogue in any conscious way. Nor did she produce the artwork she is advocating for. Yet, the exigency of the situation drives her discourse; she is Quintilian's rhetor, embedded in real space and in real time. When this art student finds a site for Leffler's art work, she has done more than exhibit her skills at persuasion; she has participated in changing the traditional relations of power that define the museum. She has learned an important lesson about the development of expertise, and about the circulation of art that parallels important lessons about the circulation and delivery of texts.

Einat Imber has contributed to Fletcher's larger agenda, which shouts out to the Whitney Museum: "This container isn't big enough!" This moment connects us to the core issues that drive this book. What would happen if we looked at the metropolitan research university and proclaimed "This container isn't big enough!" What would happen if students walked the city, taking writing outside the classroom as Fletcher's students did? How would we teach differently and what would our students learn? What new understandings about the way language and rhetoric works would students acquire?

Fletcher's exhibit critiques the traditional museum by climbing over the walls of the container. His critique, however, depends on students who take responsibility for placing art outside the walls of the museum. Fletcher and his students create what curator and writer, Peter Noever, calls the discursive museum, a space where various discourses come together and where a particular reality is shaped through language. As Noever explains: "The encounter between art and its viewer results from a desire to establish a discourse. One could even say that the museum is a specific configuration of discourses" (Noever 2001, 8). Thus, when Einat Imber presumably spoke to the librarian about displaying Cleveland Leffler's work, she was, according to Noever, contributing to the idea of the discursive museum. Our challenge will be to reconsider how the education of undergraduate students, and particularly students in first-year writing classes, can become part of the "discursive university."

Writing About What Others Have Written

The English teacher who appears in film often captivates students with his or her compelling presence, drawing them into an emotional lair. Consider *The Dead Poet Society* in which an eccentric, self-involved teacher wields enormous psychological power over young, impressionable students. Such films say, "If you want to learn to write, imitate me." Cinematic invention aside, imitation has provided a powerful motivating force for student learning. David Bartholomae's 1985 study, "Inventing the University," challenged us to think about the subtleties of imitation in the context of the university with his oft-repeated characterization:

> Every time a student sits down to write for us, he has to invent the university for the occasion—invent the university, that is, or a branch of it, like history or anthropology or economics or English. (1985, 134)

In the 1985 study, placement essays not only provided the data for Bartholomae's study, but also illustrated the struggle of students to "take on the role . . . of an authority" (136) and imitate what they imagined to be the language of the powerful, authoritative professor. To achieve this academic voice, the student must leave behind the familiar, "naïve" commonplaces and try on a new, less familiar set. These discipline-based commonplaces, the "peculiar ways of knowing, selecting, evaluating, reporting, concluding, and arguing" define what students write in a university context (1985, 134). Bartholomae sets these academic-based ways of knowing apart from the "naive codes of everyday life" (157). For instance, the student who simply rehearses familiar commonplaces about creativity in his writing has not learned the "distinctive register" of university discourse. On the other hand, a student who can position him or herself in the context of a sophisticated discussion of the meaning of jazz improvisation can attempt or at least mimic an academic conversation.

Students, of course, are well aware of this strategy. Several years ago, a student suggested to me that she had adopted this sort of strategy—imitating a teacher—to facilitate her entry into the academic environment. She said, "There is a sort of game we play when we enter a classroom. We listen to the teacher. We wait to hear his views. We notice the words he uses and then we incorporate them into our writing"(cited in Feldman 1996, 2). Such behavior reflects the dark side of the time-honored academic tradition of quoting an authority as well as the much-valued rhetorical tool of learning through imitation (Boyd 1991). This student's imitative act carries with it, Susan Miller (1998) explains, the mark of an institutionalized American composition studies. Quoting the language of an authority, Miller argues, whether a teacher or a text, has dominated humanistic study and made us think about writing exclusively as an interpretive act rather than a productive one. When we think of writing as something produced in response to another piece of writing, we limit our uses of writing to a largely interpretive realm.

Nearly a decade later, in the published proceedings of a 1993 conference, *Composition in the Twenty-First Century: Crisis and Change,* David Bartholomae (1996) begins not with student placement essays as he did earlier, but with an excerpt from an award-winning student essay. He argues that the essay is not only good; it is *too* good. The student produces a flawless narrative that traces the relationship between management and labor in the American steel industry that illustrates his skill at academic writing. This student is not the entering freshman experimenting with an academic voice, but a mature undergraduate who has learned the lesson Bartholomae set out to teach: how to invent the university through his writing.

This "too good" student writer has taken up imitation on a grand scale. He develops an argument by reproducing a master narrative of how the steel industry evolved drawn from "disciplinary boundaries and disciplinary authority" (Bartholomae 1996, 13). He accepts this master narrative without asking questions about how particular choices might have contributed to the construction of this narrative. Let's take a look at an excerpt of the award-winning student writing Bartholomae includes in his essay:

> Initially, such early steel entrepreneurs like Andrew Carnegie and Henry Clay Frick used the technique of vertical integration to control all factors of steel production. This necessitated the construction of massive bureaucratic organizations to take advantage of economies of scale in the procurement of the required natural resources and the subsequent production of the steel itself. Each organization was a textbook bureaucracy, with its fixed areas of managerial jurisdiction and supervisory hierarchies, consisting of numerous layers of management personnel. At the same time, in order to achieve strict control over these new, huge bureaucratic operations, management adopted techniques which minimized human variability and uncertainty in the production process. Most of these techniques were derived in large part from Frederick W. Taylor's philosophy of "scientific management." (1996, 24–25)

Bartholomae argues that while this student's success has been validated by the university-wide committee that awarded his prize, he wants us to consider the essay that might have been written by another University of Pittsburgh student who might have been the son or daughter of an unemployed steel worker or management-level employee.

Bartholomae suggests that the child of an unemployed steel worker would write a different sort of essay. Maybe—maybe not. This assumption confuses a student's writing with a purported identity—either as a successful academic, as in the prize-winning student, or as a marginalized identity, as in the child of an unemployed steel worker—and it further assumes that the student's identity drives the writing. What's missing from the "too good" writer's essay is a sense that his argument derives from an ongoing conversation. He doesn't anticipate how others who disagree with his portrayal of the steel industry might characterize this history. It's not that the child of a steelworker might write a different essay, but that this writer needs to anticipate the arguments that might cast his story in a different light. This is precisely the point made by my colleagues Jerry Graff and Cathy Birkenstein in their new textbook, *"They Say/I Say": The Moves that Matter in Academic Writing* (2006). What matters most in academic writing, they argue, is that the writer sees him or herself taking a position (the *"I Say"*) in the context of a larger conversation (the *"They Say"*).

Bartholomae's antidote for the "too good" student is to authorize student writers as practitioners of what he calls "practical criticism": Students in his writing course will suggest revisions for a "not too good" student essay. The unedited student paper that Bartholomae provides tells the story of a church mission to St. Croix, the largest of the U.S. Virgin Islands, to aid in the cleanup of damage from a hurricane. The essay begins with the student's arrival at the island met by suspicious residents who wonder what the students want in return for their service. The writer tells us that by the end of their visit,

> ... the islanders came to realize that we did not expect anything in return for our work, except their friendship. In the beginning, this concept was hard for them to understand, but as they watched the changes occur, they learned to appreciate our help. (Bartholomae 1996, 24–25)

Bartholomae includes this student's essay, with her naïve rendering of noblesse oblige, in the readings for an introductory writing class on travel narratives along with scholarly material such as Mary Louise Pratt's *Imperial Eyes* (1992). Students will revise this essay by rethinking the centuries-old tradition of the travel narrative genre. Many such courses, offered as cultural studies writing courses, in fact, elide student writing and focus instead on how students read, interpret, and critique the missionary narrative (Bartholomae 1996, 26). Bartholomae's approach to revising the student-written St. Croix essay will steer students away from a writing-process approach that has traditionally asked students to write from personal experience through a recursive process of planning, drafting, revising, and editing. Revising, in this approach, asks students to add detail or reduce redundancy—that is, to enhance the written product through internal changes. Whenever an essay is written largely out of personal experience, we assume that the writer has all the information available to improve the writing through revision.

In sharp contrast, Bartholomae broadens the sociocultural context by asking students either to revise based on their growing understanding of the historical context of U.S. relations with St. Croix, or by contemplating the options available in travel genres and how the missionary genre fits or doesn't fit with these genre expectations. This sort of revision, Bartholomae explains, constitutes practical criticism. As expected, classroom activities would also involve a close reading of Pratt's scholarly text. In revising the St. Croix essay, students might try nonchronological approaches, imagine other perspectives, or consider other documents, such as historical tracts or advice given to the students prior to their trip to St. Croix.

Clearly, this is an innovative and exciting plan for bringing student writers into the scholarly work of criticism. But is this what we should be doing? Unfortunately, Bartholomae has stopped just short of characterizing the student writer as an actor in a situation. Students revising the student-written St. Croix essay still function as interpreters of texts—albeit they interpret a wider range of texts, including student writing, than they might in other classes. Writing about what others have written—even when that writing challenges personal constructions of knowledge—has largely been conceived of as the intellectual work of the humanities. However, setting out to write travel narratives to a public audience—not the professor—gives the faculty member a new way to make use of his or her authority and disciplinary knowledge by helping the student work out the differences that writing to a public audience makes. Imagining a public audience, the faculty member can incorporate issues of delivery into the student's practical criticism, helping to avoid the unspoken dicta of the professor to the student to "be like me."

Writing for Participation

A young Latina student writes an opinion piece in support of the civic contribution of street corner vendors, *eloteros*, who are under attack by the city's alderman. Does she write out of an internally driven authentic voice? No. This student, I argue, writes as a participant in a public space, drawing on a range of materials, each chosen for its particular and contingent purpose in this writing context. I met this student on the first day of a first-year writing class as I began reading from the class roster.

"Mohammed D'Keidek?"

"Here."

"Nancy Li?"

"Yes."

"Carissa Zill?"

"Here."

"Tiffany Smith?"

"Yo!"

"Berenice Salas?"

"No, It's Be-re-níce. Please say it like this: Be-re-níce."

"Certainly," I replied, unsure of just how to roll her name over my monolingual tongue. "But you're going to have to help me."

And so I met Bereníce Salas, who told me she intends to major in elementary education and who has a strong commitment to community projects. She volunteers at Chicago's Latino Film Festival and assists a local labor activist with translation and other projects. Bereníce had enrolled in my English 160 class called "Writing on Location." Just as she expects me to pronounce her name correctly, she also expects that writing instruction in this class will support her interest in changing her world. Not all students, perhaps not even most students, enter college with her perspective on writing. Yet when a university announces its commitment to engagement and when faculty increasingly study issues related to its metropolitan context or conduct research collaboratively with community partners, these activities should have an impact on undergraduate education and in particular on writing instruction.

Let's look at an opinion piece written by Beneníce Salas (see figure 2.3). For this particular writing project, students took a position on an issue currently under discussion in their neighborhood and wrote an opinion piece that could be published in a local paper. Asking students to write about something going on in their

Figure 2.3. Beneníce Salas' Opinion Piece

Delicious Culture in a Pushcart

Elote is Spanish for corn; *eloteros* is Spanish for corn vendors. *Eloteros* are typically Mexican immigrants who sell corn, pineapple, and other foods in a pushcart on the street. They promptly prepare fresh foods with your choice of condiments. I would refer to the *elotes* as culture on a stick with a pinch of authenticity. To the Little Village neighborhood these micro-entrepreneurs create jobs for themselves in order to support their families. They can be found everywhere in Little Village, especially in the parks during the summer. Chicago's *eloteros*, a valuable part of our city's culture and street life, contribute to the ethnic mosaic that makes Chicago a great city. Most importantly, these food vendors provide a needed service to the community.

In the late 90's Alderman Bernard Stone began banning street vendors in the 50th Ward. Alderman Burton Natarus, whose 42nd Ward now includes most of downtown, quickly followed by sponsoring a law that forbids street vending anywhere in the Loop (with the exception of city-commissioned fruit stands on State Street). The Park District added its own citywide ban that summer. Shortly after, Aldermen Mell and Burke also contributed to an ordinance against these vendors. In support of this ordinance, Burke told the story of how his aide's dog got sick and died after eating a popsicle purchased from one of these street vendors. Health inspectors went to Little Village and ticketed all street vendors. The inspectors' unjust actions included a case in which they poured bleach over a vendor's food. This unreasonable act not only cost the vendor a day's work, but also insulted the hygiene of Mexicans.

I lived in Little Village and I have eaten food from *eloteros* all my life and have never known of anyone who ever got sick from a street vendor. If anything, *eloteros* sell the best tasting fruits and vegetables in all of Chicagoland. The variety of fruits and vegetables that the *eloteros* offer help improve my eating habits. It takes skills to prepare mouthwatering food in less than a minute. They offer a convenient service, provide nourishing snacks, and promote wholesome nutrition. When one buys from a street vendor, one sees what is going on; however restaurants are another story. I feel confident in the hygiene of the vendors, but much less confident about the hidden violations that occur in the backrooms of many Chicago restaurants.

(*continued*)

Figure 2.3. *(continued)*

> So where does this ordinance leave the people of my community? Street vending is a long-standing tradition in Mexico, and the Mexicans of Little Village are expressing and sharing their culture with the city. When I observe that the city is overzealously attempting to restrict street vendors from creating legitimate means of work, my intuitive reaction is frustration. Chicago's success has come from waves of immigrants to its shores. These Mexican immigrants have to make their own jobs.
>
> Chicago attracts tourists because of its diversity: Greektown, Little Italy, Chinatown, etc. What about Little Mexico? It is to the City's advantage to have *eloteros* add their culture to the diversity of Chicago. Mexican people come from other places because they like the corn; this is the tradition of La Veintiseis, of 26th Street. When my family moved from La Villita to my current neighborhood, I missed the *eloteros*. They have become part of my heritage and I try to travel back every weekend to eat authentic *elotes*. *Eloteros* also make people feel safe and prevent crime; they are like street police stationed on each block. Police can't be everywhere so they depend on informal social control. *Eloteros* as well as other street vendors increase safety on the street.
>
> For many reasons, I believe that the city officials should not allow heavy-handed forces to over regulate the humble but important Mexican *eloteros*. This may be a class clash or a case of racism that has ignited from fear of a minority's success. One thing that these officials must realize is that Latinos are a part of mainstream society and should not be shunned. Perhaps some see this as one way of weeding out undesirable elements that conflict with the rapid gentrification occurring in Chicago. How can it not be? Just look at who it directly affects. This ordinance is immoral and unprincipled. It completely disregards many of those that will be affected, including customers, and is a direct attack on the Mexican and minority communities at large.

Source: Berenice Salas, February 13, 2003.

neighborhood locates the subject matter for writing outside of the readings students will do in the class and creates the possibility that writing will be understood as consequential. The final draft of the paper I include here and Berenice's comments about her work help us to see how a writer can negotiate between the need to be situated as well as the need to respond to written conventions.[10]

In writing this piece, Berenice, intended to intervene on behalf of the *eloteros*. This opinion piece exposes a fierce energy that comes from Berenice's sense of participation in the community she writes about. Cast in the conventional form of an opinion piece, however, Berenice must negotiate between the pull of participation on the one hand and the pull of conventional genre expectations on the other. Certainly she drew on her memory of the *eloteros*' bicycle horn that sent her racing to the kitchen counter to reach for the change jar. This writing project, however, did not ask her to reproduce her childhood experiences through a personal essay. In sharp contrast, Bereníce was aware that this school-based writing assignment asked her to develop a thesis-driven argument that could function as a petition for a grade. However, the driving force behind her writing was her wish to change the situation for the *eloteros*.

Bereníce's class prepared for this assignment by reading a case study from my textbook, *In Context*, that included a variety of documents surrounding a particular civic issue. Latina author, Sandra Cisneros, upon painting her house a bright shade of purple, found herself cited for a code violation by the preservation committee that supervised the historic suburb of San Antonio where she lived (Feldman, et al. 2005). The local preservation committee argued that purple was not an approved color for the King William historic district where Cisneros lived. Cisneros countered that purple was indeed a historic color, prevalent in the homes of her Latino ancestors. The case study included portions of guidelines from the community's preservation committee as well as transcripts from a talk show on the issue, as well as a sampling of the opinion pieces and letters to the editors that appeared nationwide as the events around the Cisneros' issue unfolded. Overall, the case study materials illustrated a situation in which Cisneros felt compelled to speak out and in which writing played an important role.

Typically, students in writing classes read model essays by excellent prose stylists and then write in response to those essays. The genre typically doesn't change: an essay by an expert writer begets an essay by a novice writer. For instance, students might read Gloria Anzaldúa's "Chicana Artists: Exploring Nepantla, el Lugar de la Frontera," an essay describing Anzaldúa's struggle to sustain her identity as an artist, a lesbian, and a Mestiza in the face of overwhelming pressure to create commercially successful art (Anzaldúa 1993). Writers such as Anzaldúa produce some of the most important ideas our contemporary culture has to offer: they engage us in challenging conversations about important issues, they illustrate stylistic acumen, and they may even help us give the boot to stubborn opinions. Indeed such readings introduce students to the tapestry of ideas that contribute to the liberally educated student.

Gloria Anzaldúa makes writing matter; the student typically does not. Anzaldúa didn't, I'm sure, write to be included in a composition anthology. She wrote exquisitely and provocatively, hoping to launch her readers into action or at least to see the world differently. As students read such landmark essays and write about them, they can easily lose sight of the initial exigency that compelled these authors' work. Anzaldúa's essay was, most likely, a response to a specific situation. Because we want our students to have an originary writing experience, writing classes ought to place students in situations through which, they too, can see writing as a way to participate and to intervene. A renewed sense of engagement at the institutional level should create situations in which both faculty and students can intervene through writing.

The tension between Bereníce's years-long experiences of writing highly structured school assignments based on conventional genres and this relatively new experience of engaging with her context embodies a duality that learning theorist Etienne Wenger says defines all learning. Wenger wants us to ask what it would mean if we "placed learning in the context of our lived experience of participation in the world?" (1998, 3). Wenger's emphasis on lived experience injects more energy into the participatory side of this duality. By looking at learning as it occurs outside of the classroom, we get a picture of what he calls a "community of practice," which refers to an informal coming together of groups to get things done. Communities of practice are assembled *as needed* in everyday life and provide opportunities for learning, participation, and identity formation, all of which occur as a back and forth struggle between the needs of the group in a specific context and the needs of the members. This characterization of learning has been applied in a variety of settings and offers a rich lens for seeing the ways in which institutions, historical practices, everyday life, and conventional knowledge come together in the context of learning. When we look at how writers participate in a community of practice, we see how learning grows out of particular situations.

Communities of practice thrive on the tension between participation and reification. Even though participation is sometimes given insufficient attention in the educational process, it is easy to understand. It includes the experiential side of negotiating meaning—living in the world, participating, acting and interacting, defining one's identity through membership in communities; and recognizing the mutual engagement of participants in any given situation (Wenger 1998, 62–65). Participation tugs at reified knowledge—knowledge that has been turned into a thing. Much knowledge that is transmitted in schools is considered reified—facts, conventions, frozen genres. Yet it's fair to say we can't live without reification—we couldn't function without being about to depend on some conventions, even while remaking others. Reification gives form to our experiences. Features of writing, like syntax, genre, and organization can easily become "things."

It often seems that the only way we can teach writing is to turn it into a thing and depend on it's "aboutness" for negotiating meaning. Wenger (1998, 59) reminds us that everything from ". . . recipes to medical procedures, from flashy advertisements to census data, . . . from the evening news to national archives . . . depends on the "aboutness" of language. A recipe provides the conventional procedure for making a roux, but we may innovate later in the process with the herbs we happen to have on hand. In the composition classroom, the "aboutness" of writing often emerges through our use of familiar genres such as the personal essay or the academic argument, which have become reified and lost their lively

Figure 2.4. Bereníce Salas' Draft of First Paragraph

First Draft: *Elotes!*

    Elotes is Spanish for corn: *Eloteros* is Spanish for corn vendors. *Eloteros* are typically Mexican immigrants who sell corn, pineapple, and other types of foods in a pushcart on the street. To the Little Village neighborhood they are micro-entrepreneurs who create jobs for themselves in order to support their families. They are found everywhere in Little Village, especially in the parks during the summer. Chicago's *Eloteros* are a valuable part of the city's culture and street life. They are part of the ethnic mosaic that makes Chicago a great city and also provide a needed service to the community.

Final Draft: Delicious Culture in a Pushcart

    Elote is Spanish for corn; *eloteros* is Spanish for corn vendors. *Eloteros* are typically Mexican immigrants who sell corn, pineapple, and other foods in a pushcart on the street. They promptly prepare fresh foods with your choice of condiments. I would refer to the *elotes* as culture on a stick with a pinch of authenticity. To the Little Village neighborhood these micro-entrepreneurs create jobs for themselves in order to support their families. They can be found everywhere in Little Village, especially in the parks during the summer. Chicago's *eloteros*, a valuable part of our city's culture and street life, contribute to the ethnic mosaic that makes Chicago a great city. Most importantly, these food vendors provide a needed service to the community.

Source: Bereníce Salas.

connection to real situations for writing. Looking at writing through the lens of this duality—participation versus reification—helps us to see how writers negotiate meaning in the context of a community of practice. Let's look at the first draft of the opening paragraph in Bereníce's essay (see figure 2.4) and compare it to the revised version that appeared in her final draft included above.

    In the first draft, most of Bereníce's sentences weakened the paragraph: the *eloteros*, the subject of almost every sentence, performed no action. Rhetorically based grammar texts typically advise writers that filling the predicate slot with forms of the verb "to be" weakens the critical agent-action relationship that gives prose its energy. To make my point, I offered a brief lesson on verbs, defining and giving examples of transitive, intransitive, and linking verbs. I asked the class to reread their drafts and circle the verbs in the main clause of each sentence. Students were surprised that the overwhelming number of verbs they had circled were forms of the verb to be. I asked them to choose three sentences, revise them to replace the linking verbs with action verbs, and turn them in at the end of class. This grammar exercise illustrates the powerful necessity of reification: the teacher's lesson directed students to revise to enact a reified notion about sentence structure.

However, Berenice's revision of key sentences in this paragraph depended on more than a reified convention; it depended as well on her participation in the *eloteros'* world, which offered the much needed content for the new verbs. Once the linking verbs were replaced with action verbs, the *eloteros* now had actions to carry out. Even so, Berenice appropriately retained a linking verb to define her terms, "*Elote* is Spanish for corn; *eloteros* is Spanish for corn vendors." During her revision, Berenice began to see her project differently, in a fuller context, and thus added the sentence, "I would refer to the *elotes* as culture on a stick with a pinch of authenticity." This still-clumsy sentence, while ignoring my lesson about strong verbs, nonetheless generated the new title for her opinion piece, "Delicious Culture on a Stick." These revisions illustrate how Berenice navigated back and forth between the knowledge offered by both participation and reification as she worked on her draft.

Proponents of expressivist pedagogy would argue that Berenice's writing results from an authentic personal voice: a young Latina driven by her sense of identity to defend the *eloteros*. She cares deeply about her ethnic heritage and the well-being of her community, but like Evelina Roane, discussed earlier in the chapter, Berenice writes to enact a rhetoric of authenticity rather than to express her personal voice. She explained how she used conventional rhetorical strategies to rethink her initial anger at the Alderman whose dog died, presumably after eating a popsicle purchased from an *elotero*. She followed up by asking, "First of all, why would you feed a popsicle to a dog?" In the final draft, she removed her question and told me, ". . . I am angry at this alderman . . . I feel like saying, 'You're stupid; why would you do that?' . . . I think I got a little too personal in my opinion piece there and that would be too much for my audience. I should sound neutral but persuasive at the same time." In this context, Berenice draws on reified knowledge as well as her lived experience.

Revision or Social Action?

In an opinion piece in College English, Joseph Harris (2003) argued that we need to see writing as a practice. Harris opens his article by comparing his classroom to a classroom described by Ira Shor in his 1996 book, *When Students Have Power*. Both Harris and Shor are scholars who are not afraid to roll their sleeves up and get down to the hard work of teaching writing. You will see that each of these teachers identifies one important part of the puzzle but misses another. Harris wants us to focus on writing as an intellectual practice through the close work of revising one's text, while Shor wants students to understand what might be involved in creating a more democratic classroom. Some might see these two approaches as irrevocably distinct, but I will argue that their approaches are complementary.

Here's how the comparison begins: Harris reports that Shor prompts his students to develop critical consciousness through democratic choice in the writing classroom. Students in Shor's classroom read B. F. Skinner's novel, *Walden Two*, which, within a fictional context, offers a dialogue of ideas on solving society's problems (1948). They also read *Ecotopia*, in which the author proposes a fictional society based on radical environmental principles (Callenbach 1975). Students write two proposals, one to improve the College of Staten Island and one to improve New York City. To bring us along in his argument, Harris points out a disconnect in Ira Shor's classes between the writing assigned and the pedagogy undertaken: although Shor quotes often from his students he doesn't focus on the students' writing *as writing*. He doesn't, for instance, suggest examining revisions or how a piece might have been approached differently.

I see a different disconnect in Shor's democratized classroom: students read provocative humanistic works that help students understand what a Utopia is: what works, what's broken, and what needs fixing. They read novels, but they are assigned proposals. It's likely that most students have never written a proposal and only have a vague sense of how to proceed. Students need to learn several things: how to identify a specific aspect of their college (or city) that could change; how to gather information that will support the proposed change they argue for; and more important, students need to learn the conventions of the genre and how they might be adopted or altered.

The settings for these two scholars' work could not be more different. Ira Shor teaches at the College of Staten Island, which draws from local, working-class students; Harris began the article while he was on the faculty of the University of Pittsburgh and finished it at Duke University, both highly selective institutions. Harris characterizes the Staten Island students as "guys with baseball caps" and as "girls and women with big hair" (2003, 579). Harris reports that Shor's students approve of their class's orientation because they are interested in learning about how they can improve society's problems. This worries Harris. He recounts the complaint of one Staten Island student who wanted to continue the close reading of texts she had begun at the elite, private college she had attended until her parents were unable to pay the tuition.

Harris worries that Shor is turning his Staten Island students into lunch-bucket kids, who, because of their social class, get what they are entitled to—in his opinion, an education in civics. When Shor dismisses his student's complaint that the class is not a proper English class, Harris rushes to her defense, unwittingly revealing his own attachment to a writing class defined by discipline-centered readings of literary texts. Harris articulates his concern, accusing Shor of dividing writing instruction into two camps:

> I am alarmed at his two-tier imagining of higher education, which has the mass of students talking about "civics" while reserving the close "unraveling and interpretation" of texts for an elite. (2003, 581)

So, while the big-haired girls and the baseball-capped guys learn how to improve their world by writing proposals, Harris's students—who are described merely as students with no particular class affiliations—are doing what students should be doing at an elite institution: engaging in close analysis of literary or popular texts.

Harris argues that writing students should become disciplinary critics who write about texts in the context of ongoing disciplinary discussion of these texts. To do this, students need to see writing as a practice in which instructors and students focus their attention on the doing of academic work. Students become involved and participate, rather than remain spectators, looking on at the experts who conduct the disciplinary activity of English studies. I applaud Harris's attention to the practice of writing; in his view careful revision in the context of ongoing conversations will teach students how to write. I am concerned, though, with the extent to which this practice, as he demonstrates through student examples, illustrates a narrow conversation, in which students write about and revise a narrow diet of essays on popular or literary topics. What students do not learn is that these texts and their conversations about these texts are situated in broader institutional and social contexts.

Disciplinary blinders can, once again, encourage students to imitate faculty. Harris doesn't see the extent to which his writing instruction is locked into his own disciplinarity nor does Shor see that his interest in critical pedagogy and creating activist citizens has usurped his interest in writing. Students in Harris's class focus tightly on the text and their response to it, and Harris is right that this practice is at the core of effective writing instruction. Students in Shor's class focus on the democratic practices involved in the classroom community and achieve a sense of participation in a larger agenda as well. These two classrooms, each isolated from the other, have between them what's needed to make writing matter. Had Harris and Shor somehow been able to collaborate—I fantasize about locking them in a room together unable to leave until they produce a jointly designed syllabus—students would benefit immensely. Assignments like Shor's proposals would focus more on the underlying features of argument and on a rhetorical analysis of the proposal genre. Harris's revision assignments would now ask students to consider possible audiences for their work outside the discipline and to consider as well consequences for their written work.

Harris emphasizes writing as revision, while Shor emphasizes writing as participation. On the one hand, Harris is right that students need to be able to engage in close analysis of texts and that teaching should focus on this practice. His approach offers numerous benefits: students see how other writers handle problems of genre, of situation, of syntax, and of reasoning. Shor, on the other hand, is also right. When students see themselves as committed participants in a democratic society, their writing becomes an important tool. Shor's students are more likely to see themselves as actors in a public context. Writing courses need to provide students with opportunities for both revision and participation.

Writing in a Community of Practice

Making writing matter offers a pedagogical challenge whether students leave the classroom or whether the physical classroom, itself, becomes a liminal space where action is simulated in a life-like context. An interesting writing project by Candice Rai, a PhD student in the University of Illinois at Chicago's English department, offered students an opportunity to consider how writing can contribute to an ongoing public issue. More important, this project created for students the experience of working in a community of practice in which learning depends on a lived experience of participation. The writing project and the pedagogy that drove Rai's classroom enacted the hoped-for connections in which students found themselves engaged in an important civic issue, wrote in appropriate genres, and focused on producing clear and effective prose. Further, the Wilson Yard writing project, described in figure 2.5, brought students into an actual situation being written about in newspapers at the time of the class and as such, it positioned students as participants in a community of practice.

Figure 2.5. Candice Rai's Wilson Yard Writing Project

Wilson Yard Proposal—Synthesis/Argument (4–5 pages) Due March 7.

In 1996, a fire destroyed a Chicago Transit Authority repair shop in Uptown. The building was demolished, leaving an empty space known as Wilson Yard. The dialogue about what to develop at Wilson Yard has engaged people who do not normally work together—Aldermen, city planners, various organizations in Uptown, economically and ethnically diverse residents, researchers, and professionals from various fields. Your role in this assignment is to write a detailed proposal for the type of development you believe should take place at Wilson Yard. Your proposal should entail extensive consideration of the social, economic, logistical, and other various factors associated with your decision.

The Wilson Yard writing project focused on an investigation of a community planning process that occurred in Uptown, an economically and ethnically diverse neighborhood in Chicago that was feeling the effects of advanced gentrification. It gave students a heightened sense of participation in an ongoing, consequential situation; the writing they produced had the potential of making a difference in the situation. Ms. Rai's freshman course, "Communities in Transition: Defining and Redefining Urban Space," facilitated an archeology of sorts that allowed students to unearth their school's history. Students explored the role that the University of Illinois at Chicago (UIC) played in urban development during the 1960s when it moved from the drafty, corrugated steel structures that had been a Navy outpost located on a pier extending into Lake Michigan to a new, hotly debated location just west of the busy downtown Loop.

Ongoing debates pitted the powerful momentum of the university's eminent domain against the values of an ethnic, working-class community that fought valiantly but unsuccessfully to retain its neighborhood. The writing class next explored a recent controversy—UIC's south campus expansion, which replaced Maxwell Street, a historically significant open-air market, with a housing development called University Village. The class then turned to the Wilson Yard case study to examine a situation currently unfolding in the city that brought to bear many of the issues the class had been concerned with.

Students read three key books from different contexts—critical theory, sociology, and community organizing—that provided background knowledge on urban issues and that illustrated a range of arguments and methods. Robert A. Beauregard's (1999) edited volume, *The Urban Moment*, included essays exploring the idea of a good city, the language we might use to represent the city, and its possibilities for civic engagement. In *American Project: The Rise and Fall of a Modern Ghetto*, Sudhir A. Venkatesh (2000), a sociologist, reported on several years of fieldwork at Chicago's Robert Taylor Homes, illustrating how efforts to provide low-cost public housing resulted in housing projects teeming with gangs, violence, drugs, and no sense of a viable community. And, William Petermans's *Neighborhood Planning* (2000) offered students a professional guide to community organizing that included case studies and practical tools for those involved in grassroots organizing. Rai also assembled a group of documents that emerged directly from the ongoing Wilson Yard deliberations. These texts included public planning documents, a variety of proposals, survey results, oral comments from residents and city officials, and relevant newspaper articles. These additional documents helped students piece together the evolving debate, analyze its language and its rhetoric, observe argument in action, identify their particular position in this public context, and thus prepare to write a proposal that could contribute to the ongoing issues. This project's emphasis on urban planning is not crucial to my argument. Such projects can also be designed based on issues at home in an English department. David

Bartholomae, for instance, might have asked his class to go beyond reading and revising the student-written travel narrative to produce their own travel narratives. Similarly, we see how an imagined syllabus produced collaboratively by Joseph Harris and Ira Shor could engage students' sense of participation in ongoing public concerns while paying close attention to the texts they read.

Situating writing projects in local contexts, even university-based or disciplinary contexts, changes how students see writing, thus teaching the larger lesson that all texts, even classroom essays, are situated and shaped in specific contexts. The engaged university regards itself primarily as a social institution. As I argue in chapter 1, its core knowledge-making activities increasingly urge disciplinary specialists toward collaborative partnerships with people and organizations outside the university.[11] The problem is this: engagement with community partners, while often articulated at the institutional level through policy institutes, research centers, and economic incubators, rarely connects to the daily practices of educating undergraduates. On the other hand, when engagement is articulated at the undergraduate level through service learning or volunteer activities, students typically write classroom-based reflective essays about their experiences. Students in the soup kitchen, the food pantry, the daycare center, or the women's health center typically do not see themselves as writers, nor do they see ways that writing can change that situation. This book argues that students, as part of their first-year writing class, should make use of the resources available in engaged universities.

What difference should it make for writing classes that a university reinvents itself as an engaged institution? Consider this: At the same time students in Candice Rai's first-year writing class deliberated the fate of the Chicago Transit Authority's Wilson Yard, faculty at UIC's Center for Urban Economic Development participated in meetings with representatives of the Illinois Department of Commerce and Community Affairs to prepare a document that outlines goals for regional transportation development and for local land-use plans. In both situations, students and faculty are working in communities of practice that make writing matter. Unfortunately, the students and the faculty aren't talking to each other. What if these faculty, working on urban transportation issues, met with Rai's writing students as part of, perhaps, an undergraduate research forum, described their work, and invited the freshman to participate in the project. Suppose, further, as part of a group project, students were asked to draft a portion of a proposed agreement and in addition write a cover letter arguing for their proposal. If students and faculty worked together on this project, they could talk about the subject matter of their research as well as attend to the rhetorical concerns of the writing project. This imagined connection between faculty and students in the context of an engaged institution allows me to highlight the shaping of discourse and focus on writing as part of a challenging undergraduate education.

Chapter 3

—————⟫•◦⟪—————

Telling Tales Out of School

When Is a Diary Not a Diary?

In the previous chapter, we learned of a document that was taken for many years to be a diary because its narrative told the story of the writer's religious experience. Only later did scholars learn that the purported diary was really a petition, crafted specifically for admission to the church. Because the document looked like a diary and sounded like a diary, its genre was never questioned until a literary scholar investigated the text's social function. This chapter experiments with genre to illuminate how a writer's situation contributes to decisions about the shape of the text.

Most scholarly work is conducted through argumentative prose situated in an ongoing intellectual conversation. This chapter, while scholarly, is an exception. Its narrative mode contrasts sharply with the book's other chapters. What follows is a *faux* diary containing dated entries that detail some of the events that occurred as I began this book. These events are now part of a personal and an institutional past. It's important to note that, while I didn't keep a diary during the events I narrate, if I had, I would have commented on the very events that I focus on in this chapter. To provide anonymity, I have, of course, changed the names of students and assistant deans, and created composite characters from several individuals. I have retained only the names of well-known academics and participants who are clearly recognizable.[1]

This *faux* diary functions differently than the diary intended for self-expression and personal exploration; instead, it provides a "back story." Increasingly, the term "back story" has been used in the media to enhance news stories through commentary posted on blogs or Web sites. The back story constructs a narrative of the event to support the argument being made. As

71

such, the back story functions as a rhetorical device, a tool that uses narrative to explain a given situation or event. It builds on our expectations that there's a story behind the argument. Another way to think about the diary-as-back-story is like the dramatic device of the play-within-the-play. Recall how the play within Hamlet, the Murder of Gonzago, reveals new insights about events in Hamlet and thus provides a back story for the murder of the king.

These *faux* diary entries complicate our assumptions about genre by illustrating the radically embedded nature of writing: the situation drives the writing. In this chapter, the resources of genre allow my evidence to mimic a diary but function like a back story. As such, these diary entries provide evidence for my argument. With this understanding let's begin.

Down the Elevator

Fall 2001. Getting onto the elevator at the twentieth floor of University Hall, I checked nervously to make sure I had my folder with our latest survey data, copies of well-designed syllabi, and a few pieces of exemplary student writing. I wondered why I had been called down to the fourth floor college offices and why they were keeping me in the dark with this too-familiar power play: a secretary informs me of the meeting, but has no information about the meeting's agenda. I had learned by now to ask who would be attending the meeting. Okay, not Dean Fish himself, but two associate deans. Surely, I could handle whatever questions they had for me.

I had often traded e-mails with Kathleen in her role as Dean of Students about particular students—did this student need English 161 to graduate, or had another student received a waiver for English 160? But why was Robert attending? Over the years, he'd been involved in retention issues and had written a major report proposing an overhaul of the undergraduate program, which, of course, took its place on the shelf of good ideas. Hmmm, two against one.

I slipped into the hardback chair while Kathleen and Robert each took one of the two small sofas cornering the coffee table. I had perched myself opposite them, just erect enough to look down at Kathleen's thighs spreading across the sofa's seat and Robert's pear-shaped middle sinking into the green mottled fabric. To be ready for whatever they had in store for me, I began the slow deep uj-jayi breathing that I had been practicing in yoga class, inhaling to lengthen and expand my ribs, followed by a long, slow exhale that led me to the power in my abdomen. Let's see what a seated warrior pose could do for me now. The chatter in my head told me the writing program was in danger; my steady breathing told me I was ready to respond.

I waited. They began. It didn't seem as though they had a clear plan, which was reassuring. Kathleen offered, in a rambling kind of way, that the college was worried about how many lecturers we had been hiring to cover composition classes; almost in the same breath, she added that many universities like ours offer only one required composition class.

Robert joined in. "Don't you think the second required class could be converted to a writing-in-the-disciplines class and handled by individual departments?"

Thank God they hadn't planned for the meeting more carefully; I was all over them. This half-baked proposal had been floated in hallway conversations over the past year, and I had been rehearsing my response with colleagues in the English department who sat on various college committees. Here at UIC, most students are required to take two writing classes. Since I took over as director of the program in 1995, I had been developing a conceptual framework for each of the courses. The first course, English 160, introduces students to public and academic discourse by asking them to consider how a writer shapes a text as a way of participating in a particular situation. I had moved away from assigning the ubiquitous personal essays that respond to other nonfiction essays and toward assigning writing with heightened attention to context and consequence. But, to Kathleen and Robert, English 160 was still a basic writing course. With English 161, I had been at it a bit longer. My textbook, *Writing and Learning in the Disciplines* (1996), had been passed around and even Robert and Kathleen understood that the ways of knowing in particular disciplines could be important for students to understand. Yet they had no problem suggesting that we jettison English 161 into some-as-yet unknown orbit if it meant saving money. Composition was, at this moment, a cost center, not a learning center.

They were looking at me, waiting for me to respond. Still nervous, still fighting the feeling of being in the principal's office, I blurted out: "I understand that you are worried about how much adjunct lecturers cost the college, but shouldn't our discussion focus first on the pedagogical consequences of eliminating one of our two required writing courses?"

They both looked at me blankly and said nothing. I sucked in some more air and went on.

"First of all, our students need a full year of writing. You know the data—over 60 percent of them have been raised by a parent who doesn't speak English. We're not like other universities filled with suburban white kids who can at least fake the academic talk we expect of them."

I knew I sounded angry. I should be more reasoned, more collegial—a good woman speaking well—but I couldn't stop myself. At retreats, we had agreed that writing instruction was an important component of the undergraduate curriculum, but those noble thoughts were quickly forgotten when the budget drove the conversation.

"Do you really want to tell the faculty that students won't get a course in academic research until the start of their junior year? Further," I kept going, "this strategy of converting first-year writing courses into WID courses can't succeed without a carefully developed plan for the faculty who will teach them."

Then I simply stopped talking. There was a lot I didn't say, but I figured I had said enough and I was afraid that I would say too much. The conversation just sort of drifted to a close with Robert and Kathleen doing a lot of shrugging. On the one hand, I knew that they were sounding me out, seeing if I'd cooperate in the gutting of the freshman writing program. Deep down, I knew this wasn't the end of the conversation. Ill-advisedly perhaps, I put the meeting behind me, shutting it out as the elevator door closed behind me on the way back to my twentieth floor office where I busied myself with the daily demands of training new teaching assistants and observing classes. Nothing came of our meeting and things were quiet for a while. I should have seen, however, that this conversation was just the start of several skirmishes that would continue to challenge the existence of the first-year writing program as I, perhaps foolishly, concerned myself with imagining ways that first-year writing could become a more important part of the undergraduate curriculum.

Both Ends Against the Middle

Spring 2002. Seated around the long oak table in the conference room on the twentieth floor of University Hall, about twenty-five lecturers, all teachers of first-year writing, talked among themselves. Joe Travers said something barely audible about Dean Fish and those within hearing distance guffawed loudly with a hollow bravado. Others sat quietly, grading papers or marking texts with yellow hi-liters. Erin McLellan—the self-appointed spokesperson for the lecturers—hunched over a pad scribbling what I guessed would be a series of pointed questions for the new head who would soon enter and take the empty chair at one end of the long, wooden table. A few latecomers slipped into chairs against the wall. Faculty who walked down the hallways on either side of this fishbowl peered through the double glass doors. Seeing the lecturers amassed in one group, they picked up their pace and scurried down the hallway to wherever they were going. Staff members sauntered by more slowly, peering into the room, curiously taking in the scene.

I, too, waited for the new head to appear. I had seen him around but hadn't insisted on an appointment with him immediately after his arrival, nor had he shown any interest in the department's efforts to teach writing to the freshman class. So now I sat in the back of the room against the wall, ignored by the lecturers who believed me to be in cahoots with the head. Sitting next to me, unsure of what was going on, was Tom Moss, who had just been hired a month before. No one spoke to either of us. You could have cut the tension in the room with a knife.

Word had gotten around about the budget crisis and that a large number of lecturers might be cut. These money problems hadn't existed two years before in the fall of 2000, when Dean Stanley Fish invited Walter Benn Michaels to visit campus and enticed him to join the UIC faculty. Michaels, then the chair of English at Johns Hopkins, was one of many scholars attracted to UIC as part of Fish's grand project to provide world-class faculty to students who might be seen as lunch-bucket kids. Still, the world-class salaries and the increasing drain on the budget made the recently appointed Chancellor and the even newer Provost very nervous. Neither of them had been in place when Fish was hired by Betsy Hoffman who left soon after to assume the presidency of the Colorado system. By the time Michaels arrived on campus as the new head of English, trouble was in the air. Now, within days of moving into his large corner office, he found himself facing down angry lecturers who feared for their jobs and he found himself considering, possibly for the first time in his career, what it meant to teach writing at an urban research university.

Michaels, tall and slightly stooped, entered the room with his executive assistant, Sandra Begoun, who sat, lips pursed, to his right and took notes on a yellow pad. Michaels began softly, exuding a somewhat disarming boyish charm by welcoming the staff and talking about how pleased he was to be at UIC. He must have been nervous because he continued talking for nearly half an hour without a break. As he spoke, his energy level picked up; hands flying, fingers snapping to punctuate his drawn-out clauses, he somewhat hypnotized the group with his monologue. He was aware, he explained, of the untenable labor situation at work here in the English department, and he had pledged himself to respond to the lecturers' situation.

"I cannot say that all of you will be here next fall, but I will work my hardest to develop a transparent process by which lecturers will be evaluated and considered for rehiring next year," he explained.

He went on to tell the tense but still quiet group that he had ideas for not only how to raise the lecturers' salaries, but also how to plead their case to the dean. On the other hand, he countered, the budget crisis was real and everyone would have to suffer. Finally, he slowed down having said everything he could think of to say.

Erin saw her moment and jumped in. With both palms pressing firmly down on the conference table, she pushed her wiry torso up, cocking her forehead's wedge of silver hair toward Michaels. She matched his highly subordinated and elaborated clauses with her own heavily embedded accusations. Had she not, she demanded, glaring through narrowed eyes, gotten her PhD from this very department nearly ten years before and had she not devoted herself to teaching the arts of expression to our local youth?

She pleaded, reminding him that she had not asked for much over the years, "I have a mortgage to pay and even scraping by with few amenities does, alas, cost some money."

She did, however, have a solution in mind, which she went on to explain, "If cuts are to be made, you should support those of us with the highest academic credentials, that is, the PhD, which marks achievement in the academy. Those of us with PhDs, especially those earned from this department, are owed a debt that must be paid."

I was finding it harder to remain quiet, but I reminded myself that this meeting was between the new head and the lecturers; he was their employer; I was their supervisor and an observer at this meeting. Nonetheless, it was becoming clear to me that a dangerous division was developing among the lecturers. Several of the lecturers had earned doctorates in English Literature from our department. On the job as lecturers for more than a decade, they had effectively hidden themselves away in the privacy of their classrooms. These lecturers were stuck. They had ignored the First-Year Writing Program's evolving approach and had doggedly perpetuated whatever pedagogy they had practiced in graduate school. Most had let go of their scholarly ambitions in the face of mountains of papers to grade. By now these lecturers had families, connections, and Chicago felt like their home. Of course, all the PhD students in Composition and Rhetoric had gotten jobs almost immediately after finishing their degrees and were working somewhere else in tenure-track jobs.

Erin's solution was meant to secure her position and alienate a group of newly hired lecturers. These new teachers were using this job to supplement their careers as freelance writers. They brought fresh energy to the program and were quite willing, if not entirely convinced, to try out the situated approach I argued for. The meeting deteriorated as some lecturers, predictably, those with PhDs, supported Erin's position. Others pointed out that when it came to teaching credentials, a PhD in literature didn't contribute much at all. The lecturers ignored the head as the verbal melee escalated; comments became increasingly personal and sarcastic. Clearly, the lecturer's listserv would be flaming with PhDs lining up against the newbies, and, from the few rumors that drifted down to my office, that is exactly what happened. I sat silently next to Tom Moss wondering what would become of the first-year writing program. Walter Michaels shifted around in his seat and cleared his throat to signal that he wanted the floor again. The tumult subsided and bodies turned once again to face Michaels. Speaking softly, Michaels closed the meeting by saying that he planned to meet with the associate deans of the college to work on the budget situation. Perhaps he had not intended to let it slip, but he offered that one of the alternatives they were considering was cutting English 161, the second required writing course. But by then all the lecturers were so exhausted and depressed by the hour-long ordeal and the continued uncertainties that they could only look at each other in pain and disbelief. They knew what that meant but no one said a word. If English 161 was eliminated, everyone in the room would be gone by the next school year. One by one, each of the lecturers filed out of the room. No one spoke to me and they said little to each other.

The University in Ruins

Taking a break for fiction. I ordered *The Lecturer's Tale* (Hynes 2001) right after that unsettling meeting with the lecturers and began reading it with my morning coffee as I wondered how fiction might map a version of my own reality. The blurb on the book's cover—a "devastatingly satirical portrait" of academic life—prepared me for the cast of stereotypical characters that populated the fictional English department of the top-ranking University of the Midwest: the undergraduate chair, lesbian and feminist theorist, Victoria Victorinix, whose "bloodless manner" had survived several shifts in theory as well as the "genteel bigotry" of deans and department heads (2001, 4); the hirsute Eastern European theorist, who dressed like a Hong Kong action film star; and the tough-talking department chair whose working-class persona propelled him onto the talk show circuit to subjugate truth and beauty to " the etiology of *powah*," as they said it back in Hoboken (2001, 80). Amid these colorful personae, the protagonist of the novel, Nelson Humboldt, ungainly son of a high school teacher from Maytag, Iowa, who blushes at the use of the term "phallocentric," finds himself first demoted from the rank of assistant professor and then ignominiously fired from his job as a composition instructor.

J. Hynes' portrait of the feelings-first writing classroom provided comic relief as I struggled with the day-to-day events of my own academic drama. At University of the Midwest, learning to write seemed to Nelson like participating in a twelve-step program:

> Students were encouraged to mine each literary text for a lesson in their own personal growth, no matter how foreign that text might be to the experiences of a generation of privileged young Minnesotans. They were also encouraged to express their feelings on any topic without fear of contradiction and Nelson was under orders not to use a red pencil on their papers lest he intimidate them. (2001, 36–37)

This satiric image of expressivist pedagogy provided a comfortable distance between this fictional composition program and the one I directed at UIC. I left my comfort zone behind, however, when I came face-to-face with Hynes' analysis of the economy of composition, and its predictable hierarchical structure so familiar to my daily life in the academy:

> They [the lecturers] combined the bitter esprit de corps of assembly-line workers with the literate wit of the overeducated: They were the steerage of the English Department, the first to drown if the budget sprang a leak. . . . they were the colonial periphery, harvesting for pennies a day the department's raw material—undergraduates—and

shipping these processed students farther up the hierarchy, thus creating the leisure for the professors at the imperial center to pursue their interest in feminist theory and postcolonial literature. (2001, 63)

Now I registered a galvanic skin response, thinking about the immediacy of the ongoing budget issues and the meeting we'd just had with the lecturers. The budget was about to spring a leak and I was determined to do more than plug the hole.

While initially taken in by Hynes' arch characterization of familiar types, I began to see that the novel follows, as Peter Sands points out, a Utopian plan in which the lowly lecturers, and in particular the sincere but untalented Nelson, come out on top in the end (Sands 2007). This gothic tale begins on Halloween Eve with young Nelson getting his pink slip from Victoria Victorinix. Dejected, Nelson leaves her office and walks toward home when a ghoulish figure pushes Nelson into a bicycle's spinning spokes that severs his finger tip and sends it rolling out into the middle of the road. As Nelson will soon discover, the finger tip, recovered and reattached in the emergency room, is endowed with supernatural powers. He does not need to write memos or academic books; all he needs to do is point his finger or touch his subject and his will is done.

Nelson pays a call to the "petite, wide-eyed," Linda Proserpina, who, with only a master's degree and a three-year contract directs the composition program and assigns sections of Composition 101 (64). She cannot, she explains, assign him sections without Victoria Victorinix's written permission. Exiting the elevator and heading toward the head's office, Nelson tries to ignore the deprecating murmurings of the favored young men working toward their graduate degrees clustered around her office door. Trembling with fear, he confronts her and grabs her hand, asking her to approve the composition sections. His throbbing finger does the trick; her eyelids flutter, her lips twitch (71). The next day, Linda Proserpina takes two sections of composition away from someone else and gives them to Nelson.

This unlikely supernatural power is foreshadowed in the early pages of the book when Nelson's father, near tears, offers his son, as a guiding principle, a line from a Robert Browning poem, "A man's reach should exceed his grasp. Or what's a heaven for?" (15). Nelson's reach surely does exceed his grasp. Through a series of ruinous events, most prominently, the burning of Thornfield Library, the emblem of this elite university, the tenured faculty members flee and the lecturers take over, cooperating fully with the new corporate management that solicits and enrolls a new clientele.[2] Now this formerly elite university will attract and enroll racially diverse students who could not have afforded to attend the University of the Midwest in its former instantiation. The University of the Midwest now becomes an "urban university." This newly constituted urban university, however, has lost its scholarly agenda, and capitalizes, instead, on teaching basic skills to large numbers of urban students who never could have attended the University of the Midwest in its glory days.

This tale—a "revenge of the lecturers," if you will—does not leave us much hope. This dystopian novel succeeds only in substituting one set of problems for another. The lecturers now control the university, reaping the salaries of the former faculty for teaching hordes of students instead of publishing scholarly work. Hynes' satiric portrayal of the university as an ivory tower in ruins is too formulaic, too seamless, and too determined. From the time we hear the father's advice, "A man's reach should exceed his grasp" and Nelson's finger is severed, we can anticipate the novel's path. The destruction of the ivory tower doesn't come about through a collaborative revolution. Instead, it is instigated by one young man—a pudgy, Caucasian graduate student—whose reattached finger can bend the world to his will.

What's missing at the University of the Midwest and what would have complicated things enormously is a graduate program in Composition and Rhetoric. What might have happened if the "favored young men," clustered around the head's door, had been working on dissertations, studying rhetoric or literacy, and planning to pursue careers in this area? The presence of such an academic specialization with a research focus on discourse and literacy might have forestalled the complete and inevitable reversal. But at the University of the Midwest, its elite, theory-driven English department became the enemy; the department had to go. Thus, Nelson, the lone lecturer, must act as an army of one, armed with only his powerful finger. Our protagonist must use his powers as an individual to bring the university to ruins and then to reassemble it with, himself, as its leader—or, at least, as the head of the English department. Hynes' *The Lecturer's Tale*, it turns out, did more than provide a busman's holiday; it got me thinking about how the stories we weave, in fact, limit the way we can imagine the teaching of writing.

What's a Writing Program For?

Back to Spring 2002. Had Nelson Humboldt been a lecturer on our staff, he could have ignored that contentious meeting and the issues that drove it. To secure his yearly appointment, he needed only shake the new head's hand and invoke the bizarre power emanating from his reattached finger. Our group of lecturers had no such powers. While Michaels clearly felt sympathy for this group of lecturers as undervalued teachers and wanted to respond to their precarious employment situation, he had been, to my mind, a little too glib at the end of the meeting about the possibility of eliminating English 161. He was new here and probably familiar with only the sort of English department caricatured by Hynes in *The Lecturer's Tale* where faculty taught theory and where nobody thought much about first-year writing.

As the last lecturer filed out of the conference room, I rapidly reviewed my options. I knew I had to get to Michaels and fast. I turned to Tom who was digesting Michaels' comments as well and said, "I have something to do. I'll meet you back at the office."

I took off after Michaels as soon as he left the conference room. Wedging myself between him and Sandra in the middle of the hallway, I grabbed his hand, knowing that I had none of Nelson's powers, and shook it hard, introducing myself as the director of the first-year writing program,

"I know we haven't met, but I must speak to you. I won't take much of your time, but I do think you ought to know something about this program if you're going to be making decisions about lecturers and courses."

A bit startled, he replied, "Sure, I've been meaning to talk to you, but it will have to be tomorrow. I'll stop by your office just after my class at 2:00 PM. I won't have much time because I'll be heading off to another meeting on the other side of campus."

"All I need is a short half hour," I said, knowing that I would not sleep that night.

I was ready at two o'clock the next day at the long conference table, when Michaels rushed into my office. He threw his long, wool gabardine overcoat on a chair next to him. On top of it, he tossed the Wolford paper shopping bag that had once held pricey panty hose but which now held his class's papers. As he leaned over the table, his long fingers poked out from the sleeve of his black cotton jersey and stubby wool jacket.

I sat next to him and said, "I need to tell you about the writing program and in particular how we train the graduate students who teach in the program. I can't imagine a worse way to introduce you to the first-year writing program than yesterday's meeting. I want to take you in through another door. The lecturers are angry and rightfully so, but they are part of a much bigger picture. Unless the first-year writing program contributes to the teaching and learning that goes on at UIC—and I mean in a bigger way than through basic skills—it will always be on the chopping block. Look at it this way: you're here to build the graduate program in English and this department can be enriched by a focus on language and discourse rather than by being dragged into economic battles over poorly paid lecturers."

Michaels looked at me curiously. He pointed out, "You know, at Hopkins there was hardly a writing program; I never had to think about lecturers or about a course required of all students." Then he nodded, signaling me on.

I didn't know how interested he was in first-year students, but I knew that he would be intensely interested in graduate students since they are the heart of any English department. I figured I had get him to see that there was real intellectual work going on in preparing graduate students to teach writing.

Michaels' approach at the lecturers' meeting had been to talk and keep talking for at least a good portion of the meeting, but now he was sitting quietly, allowing me to go on, so I did. "Look," I said, "I am trying to rethink the role of a first-year writing program and what it should be, here, at UIC. How can the writing program contribute, intellectually, to a research university in an urban context?

Michaels, unusually still and uncharacteristically quiet, continued looking at me.

"This is, at heart, an epistemological question," I threw out, figuring I'd just go for it. "If we see ourselves, as an institution, producing socially useful knowledge—that is, not functioning in the isolation of an ivory tower—then how does that change the way we conduct our research, the way we teach, and specifically, the way we teach writing? You've probably heard the term, engaged university, by now. Even if some think it's an empty cliché, consider what it would mean to take the term seriously. You came to this department to do something different. In redesigning the first-year writing program I'm asking what sort of writing instruction is warranted by this thing we call the engaged university."

I looked at him just to make sure he wasn't spacing out. He was actually listening and craning his neck over my arm to get a look at the thick pile of syllabi I had picked out to show him.

"I want to show you the syllabi that English graduate students produce in English 555. It's a seminar that new master's and PhD students take each fall before they teach." I figured that the details were going to make or break my appeal. "Here's a 160 syllabus written by Cindy Yamagata—she's that graduate student who's just been hired at Iowa to teach in their PhD program."

Pointing to a bold-faced heading about halfway through the document I said: "Look at this project. This one is really cool. Students write a talk show dialogue about school architecture by developing characters who represent differing positions. And, of course, they have to participate by taking a position themselves. They look at a sampling of the discourse—spoken and written—that surrounded the design of a new elementary school in Pilsen. You know, Pilsen is the Mexican-American neighborhood just south of here. Students look at scholarly articles, at talk show transcripts, at requests for proposals, at Web sites, at Board of Education specs, and at letters-to-the-editor. In the class, students analyze these texts for their rhetorical features and to see how a particular genre works in a particular situation. I also pointed out the evaluation criteria Cindy had designed for the writing project, explaining that an imagined dialogue would look very different from an essay and so would be evaluated on the basis of different criteria.

Michaels was still very quiet, following along, peering closely at the syllabus. I wondered what he was thinking but I didn't dare ask. I probably now had fifteen minutes left; I didn't want him to get up and leave before I made my case for English 161, whose life support was apparently about to be terminated.

"Okay, okay," Michael's said, "I'm getting it. In fact, I hadn't ever thought about it in that way before." Michaels was clearly a quick study. "But I'm going to have to leave soon, so give me your spiel on 161."

"Right. English 161 is quite different," I said, quickly changing course. "Here we want to engage students in what, to them, is the mysterious activity of scholarly inquiry. To do this, instructors choose a scholarly or trade book that illustrates an inquiry; the single-author book invites the students to read deeply in their area while tracking an exemplary inquiry. In addition, students read a range of discipline-based journal articles, book chapters, and popular treatments to see how inquiries proceed in a variety of disciplinary and public arenas."

I stopped suddenly, realizing I had been talking at him as though he was a graduate student, so I quickly pulled out the next syllabus. "Take a look at this syllabus," I pressed on, "This graduate student has chosen a book called *American Project: The Rise and Fall of a Modern American Ghetto* by Sudhir A. Venkatesh published by Harvard in 2000. Venkatesh, a sociologist, studies Chicago's Robert Taylor Homes, a model public housing project that declined in the midst of urban poverty. His study builds on multiple methods—surveys as well as ethnographic fieldwork—but it also models reference and citation; it illustrates how an academic argument can be carried out, and, more important, it presents a rich and well-developed inquiry into an important cultural and academic question. But this book is just the starting point. Students read news articles, academic journal articles, examine public policy, look at Web sites and, day by day, become a part of a conversation about what makes a viable city. When students write what you might think of as a research paper, they are really tracking their evolving understanding of the issues they've been reading about. The whole point is to get the student to take a position on these issues and defend it."

He was still very quiet, listening, and thumbing through the syllabus. I tried one more angle: "Walter, it's just as important that we think about what graduate students, themselves, are learning in order to teach these courses. They can't convey the conceptual machinery of inquiry unless they experience it themselves as writers and as scholars. That's the connection between teaching first-year writing and being in graduate school. These graduate students have to see themselves engaging in the same sort of intellectual work that they are asking of their students."

The half hour was coming to a close. Walter picked up another syllabus and thumbed through it, and then he did the same with another. He said to himself, quietly, almost muttering, something like, "My graduate students at Hopkins couldn't have produced syllabi like these."

He shook himself out of his reverie, grabbed his coat and bag of papers. "I've got to go. Thanks for this." And he was gone, loping down the long corridor toward the elevators. Exhausted, I exhaled slowly as I watched him disappear around the corner. Whatever happened, I had given it my best shot.

The Mountain Makes Its Own Weather

Fast forward to Spring 2004. The reception honoring Stanley Fish for his five years service as Dean of the College of Liberal Arts and Sciences at UIC was clearly a watershed moment for everyone involved—certainly for the Chancellor and the Provost, neither of whom held their current positions when Fish arrived at UIC, as well as for those faculty hired by Fish and those, like me, who had been at UIC for many, many years. Standing there, alongside the trays of mushroom tarts, pinwheels, and a whole poached salmon (no cheese-drenched nachos today), I wondered if we would learn Fish's plans for the next year. Would he leapfrog into a president's chair at another large public university or would he return to his faculty appointment in the English department as my colleague? I wondered, too, how the Chancellor and the Provost would craft their goodbyes. Would they employ reverence and tact, stepping lightly over the budget wars, or take a more adventurous approach, playfully acknowledging the fierce battles of the past three years as the budget had disintegrated.

Much to the delight of those present, they chose the latter approach. Chancellor Sylvia Manning admitted sportively to the group that years before they—Fish and she—had known each other's marital "ex-es," making for an unsteady start as administrative colleagues. Manning, a scholar of Victorian literature rewrote Edgar Allen Poe's dark poem, "The Raven," as a way to honor their uneven relationship. The familiar, rhythmic opening, "Once upon a midnight dreary, while I pondered weak and weary," drew us in as Manning read from her script. Like an orator of ancient times, Manning must have sensed the immediate results of her spoken poem as she looked at the broad smiles around the room. Figure 3.1 provides her version of Poe's poem.

The Chancellor had clearly captured her complex relationship with Fish and had, perhaps, even achieved catharsis through her transformation of this classic poem. Standing among the English faculty, some of whom were still in the department and others who had moved on to become associate deans and vice chancellors, I sensed equally complex emotions: loss of a compelling leader with no sense of what might come next and no budget relief in sight.

Our newly appointed Provost, Michael Tanner, straightforward and terse, not given to poetic transformations, took quite a different approach to mark this occasion. He began slowly, cautiously, reminding the audience that he had arrived from the West Coast just that year. Going further, he told us that he had brought with him a vivid memory of Alaska's landmark, Mt. McKinley, appreciatively known as Denali, Athabascan for "the high one." He talked about its hold on the imaginations of those who lived near enough to see the mountain and the challenges it presents for climbing—how one never knows what the sudden changes in the weather will bring. Suddenly, a turn in the trail and

Figure 3.1. Upon the Retirement of Stanley Fish as Dean of LAS, May 2004 (with apologies to Edgar Allan Poe)

The Fish

Once upon a midnight dreary, while I pondered, weak and weary
O'er the budget and its problems, abstruse, arcane and yet a bore—
While I nodded, nearly napping, suddenly there came a tapping
As of some one gently rapping, rapping at my office door.
"'T is some visitor," I muttered, "tapping at my office door—
Only this and nothing more."

Ah, distinctly I remember it was in the bleak December;
And each separate dying ember wrought its ghost upon the floor.
Eagerly I wished the morrow;—vainly I had sought to borrow
From my work surcease of sorrow—as budget bleeds at every pore—
As that budget bled so badly, I was swamped in red-ink gore,
Hopeless now for evermore.

Entered then the deanly Fish, just the man that I should wish,
Slight of stature, lightly stooping, book in hand but nothing more.
Not the least obeisance made he; not a minute stopped or stayed he;
But abruptly sit he bade me, perched himself beside my door.
Perched upon a small high table, just beside my office door.
Perched, and sat, and nothing more.

Then this awesome dean beguiling my sad fancy into smiling
By the oddly fitting clothing and the winsome smile he wore,
"Say." I said, "though I be sour, what brings you here at this strange hour;
Thou of deans the very flower, your advice upon me pour,
Advice that is so badly needed in this budget's awful gore."
Quoth Dean Stanley, "Evermore."

"Evermore," I shrieked inanely, at his speaking so insanely,
With an answer that so little relevance or meaning bore;
For we cannot help agreeing that no living human being
Ever yet was blessed with seeing Fish beside her office door,
Dean like Fish upon a table just beside her office door,
Saying only, "Evermore."

Then Dean Fish, smiling slowly, hands in pockets, nothing lowly,
Forward came to stand before me, I hoped his wisdom to outpour.
But nothing farther then he uttered—not an eyelash then he fluttered,
Till I scarcely more than muttered, "Other deans have flown before—
On the morrow he will leave me, as my Hopes have flown before."
Then said Dean Fish, "Spend some more."

(continued)

Figure 3.1. (*continued*)

> Startled at the stillness broken by reply so strangely spoken,
> "Doubtless," said I, "what he utters is his only stock and store
> Caught from habits formed at Duke, or perhaps formed just by fluke,
> That make him here seem like a kook, as I drown in budget gore,
> Income falling, costs still growing, colleagues angry, trustees sore,
> And Stanley saying, "Spend some more."
>
> And then my spirit newly struggling, with Fishian counsel bravely juggling,
> Feeling a new-found sensation my sad gloom now spreading o'er,
> Rememb'ring too his sage advice, not with authorities to be nice,
> But rather hit 'em hard and strong, demand our budgets they restore,
> Return, sustain to its true glory, our full support from days of yore,
> Which can't be gone for evermore!
>
> Now soon to be, Dean Fish is flitting, as our dean no longer sitting,
> Nor upon the small high table set beside my office door;
> And his eyes will have the seeming of a seer who is dreaming,
> Elsewhere the lamp-light o'er him streaming, shadow not upon my floor;
> And my soul without that shadow, with Fish no longer at my door,
> Shall be lifted nevermore!

you're buffeted by cold winds and rain that prompt you to zip up to keep your body temperature stable. The mountain, Tanner explained, creates its own ecosystem; that is, it makes its own weather. Just as in those rare moments when Denali pops through the clouds, visible for miles and miles against the blue sky, Tanner's point suddenly became clear. Stanley Fish, too, makes his own weather. The audible gasp throughout the room suggested that the same light bulb lit up in each person's head.

I was not the only one who suddenly appreciated Tanner's point. At that moment, I saw how I had been navigating for the past five years in a complex weather system generated by Stanley Fish. Some might say, quite reasonably, though, that Fish, himself, operated in a weather system not of his own making. The post 9/11 economic downturn had hit everyone hard: corporations, nonprofits, city and state governments, individuals and families, and certainly state-supported universities. Yet Fish's response to these circumstances created mini-squalls peculiar to UIC that defined the day-to-day life of every faculty member and every department during the last half of Fish's deanship.

Learning to Spell Rescission

Back to Fall 2002. The articles in the *Chicago Tribune* that had chronicled the arrival of Stanley Fish as Dean of the College of Liberal Arts and Sciences at UIC in 1999 and that had continued to follow his exploits now turned to the worsening statewide budget crisis. Illinois's brash new Democratic Governor, Rod Blagojevich, elected in the fall of 2002, wrote close scrutiny of higher education into his action plan. In his first policy speech, Blagojevich cited the "utter lack of accountability" of public colleges and universities; he called for increased transparency in spending—no more fancy dinners, no more charter flights for administrators, and no more free tickets to Urbana-Champaign football games for state legislators (Becker 2003). At the weekly staff meetings of the first-year writing program, we chuckled at the plight of administrators who had had their hands slapped. These threats to curtail the misbehavior of a few, however, escalated into the far more frightening demand that state universities give back a portion of their existing budget (Becker 2003). Rumors circulated wildly as news of the budget crisis grew louder, and we all learned how to spell "rescission."

During previous years, the Chancellor had publicly held that budget cuts would not affect the undergraduate program. But she could no longer make this claim. Everyone would suffer, as Walter Michaels had proclaimed, although, as we in composition expected, some would suffer more than others. All soft money that departments had in discretionary accounts was appropriated by the College of Liberal Arts and Sciences, leaving individual departments no say about how to use these funds. Every penny, every purchase, every stipend—yes, even the purchase of paper clips—was reviewed by the college. An attempt was made to cancel any graduate course with fewer than six students, but those highly paid faculty whom Fish had hired away from elite universities protested that PhD students would be unable to finish their degrees if their key courses were cancelled. At the most heavily attended faculty meeting in the college's recent history, Fish proclaimed that he would not consider raising the two-course-per-semester teaching load and thus, compromise this university's mission. But no faculty members received raises that year.

Walter Benn Michaels had gradually come to see the value of the First-Year Writing Program for both UIC undergraduates and the graduate students who were the lifeblood of the English department. Lecturers, too, played a crucial role in carrying out the department's teaching responsibilities. We had just begun to talk about the teaching of writing and its intellectual role in the department of English when we were thrust into the vortex of this budget-driven storm. The College of Liberal Arts and Sciences was told that they must "give back" six million dollars from its existing budget. Working with Michaels and Moss, I was responsible, finally, for proposing a plan that would squeeze cash from our composition program as its contribution to the rescission. We had to make the best of a bad situation.

I knew that the college would ask us to reduce the number of lecturers we had been hiring yearly. This was happening in every undergraduate program that used lecturers to teach large numbers of first-year students. Math, Spanish, and psychology were all holding meetings and constructing worst-case scenarios. Our memory of the difficult meeting with the lecturers prompted us to put in place a process to evaluate their performance. A senior member of the department agreed to observe each lecturer and write an evaluation of his or her teaching. These letters, student-written teaching evaluations, and copies of syllabi formed the basis for an evaluation process that would be applied at the end of the school year to make the hard decisions ahead.

We knew that the greatest proportion of First-Year-Writing teaching was being done by lecturers who could be assigned up to four courses a semester and by graduate students, who taught three courses a year. Our first-year writing class size had swollen to twenty-four students while graduate seminars might have as few as three students but never more than twelve. Even though the lecturers were paid very little, they were on yearly contracts that, once cancelled, could be converted to a cash contribution to the college. The provost's office had prepared and distributed to department heads a bar graph illustrating university expenses that showed, predictably, that the largest proportion of costs was in faculty salaries. Tom Moss worked up various spreadsheets for the department that illustrated how the English department faculty's typical two-course load of small graduate seminars taught a very small number of students. Michaels quickly realized that even with a two-course teaching load faculty could teach much greater numbers of students. Faculty soon were shifted from graduate seminars into freshman literature classes. The PhD teaching assistants, many of whom had migrated to the more desired literature classes were shifted back to composition. With these changes, we were able to teach writing to greater numbers of first-year students and, we hoped, retain more of our lecturers. But these adjustments were not enough.

The dean's office was determined to find ways to reduce enrollment in the First-Year Writing Program as a way to generate cash. Michaels, Moss, and I realized that we had to develop a list of options for the dean's office and then argue for the one we were most able to live with. Daily, through e-mails, phone messages, quick meetings in the hallway, longer meetings in the department head's office or in mine, we brainstormed possible cost-cutting measures and then tried to imagine their long-term consequences. Another department had decided to eliminate their remedial courses, but we did not consider that an option. The dean's office favored eliminating English 161, the second required course, which we felt spelled pedagogical disaster.

The specter of *The Lecturer's Tale* stayed with me throughout these deliberations. The university certainly seemed headed for ruin. But here, instead of the burning of the research library, it was the First-Year Writing Program that would be going up in smoke. On one hand, I saw myself as research faculty, defending UIC's mission as a research university and wondering how I would ever get others to see that writing courses play a critical role in the university's intellectual agenda. On the other, the administrator in me fumed about these shortsighted plans to eliminate English 161. I found myself looking at the data and wondering what stopgap measures could prevent the inevitable carnage. "What will the dean's office do with the ever-growing number of new students who would begin school here next fall? They've made no plans for additional courses to replace the ones they want to cut! . . . Arghhh!"

Then I would turn the angry wheels of my mind to the faculty, forgetting for the moment that I, too, was faculty. I'd confront Michaels, "Why do we have to engage in this ridiculous exercise? Why can't the faculty take some re-sponsibility for this giveback? Why shouldn't faculty teach three courses a se-mester?" Michaels responded, playing out the rest of the scenario for me. "We are pressing the faculty to teach more students within the two-course load. You know, Ann, if we increased the teaching load, the faculty would stream out of here in droves. I, for one, would leave."

"Hah!" I thought angrily, "he never really left Hopkins." But then, it began to sink in that I couldn't have written this book without that same two-course load and that a balance between teaching and research was part of the attraction of a re-search university. I drifted back to *The Lecturer's Tale*, where the library burned, the faculty left, and all that was left were lecturers and underprepared students.

I must say that there were also moments of opportunity throughout this process. This was the first time in decades that everyone around me was talking about first-year writing. Michaels, having just left behind the headship at Johns Hopkins, could not have anticipated that his first year on the job would be con-sumed by these discussions. Throughout the crisis, my daily work went on. I continued, of course, to train new graduate students in English 555. But I also initiated two new projects. That January I submitted a proposal to UIC's Great Cities Institute for a fellowship that would support a leave during the next aca-demic year to work on this book. At the same time, I had begun working with the Office of Academic Affairs on a service-learning grant that would be funded the following year. Stanley Fish would publish "Say it Ain't So" in the *Chronicle of Higher Education*, and we would wrangle over the role of grammar in first-year writing classes. Jerry Graff would publish, *Clueless in Academe: How Schooling Obscures the Life of the Mind*, and we would consider letting students in on the academy's dirty little secret that argument drives the way we think and write in the university and further, that "the argument game" is not so different from the language games we play outside the academy (2003, 3).

In the eye of the budget storm, however, we faced hard decisions. With Michaels' support, I argued, through a series of e-mails to the dean's office, that faculty members across the campus would oppose eliminating English 161, which, in their view, prepared students to conduct academic research. We reminded the group of associate deans, who were managing this complex "give-back," that university-wide academic committees would have to make this decision. Sharing the decision to eliminate writing courses with university-wide governance committees did not sit well with them; they could not afford the time that such a decision could take, nor did they want to let the decision out of their hands. Instead, we reluctantly agreed to what seemed like the least grievous option: to lower the ACT score that would allow more students to waive English 160, the first required course.[3] This could reduce the number of students taking first-year writing courses and the changes could be made simply by the head of the English department and by me—under protest. I was responsible, finally, for delivering a memo outlining our proposed plan to the head who would transmit it to the dean. At the end of this episode, faculty had returned to the freshman classes, graduate teaching assistants had moved back into composition, fewer students took English 160, and ten lecturers were not rehired for the next fall, allowing the First-Year Writing Program to make its contribution to the rescission.

The Grammar Sessions

Spring 2003. My struggle with Stanley Fish over the role of grammar in the First-Year Writing Program began with a quick kiss on the cheek at a department reception. Fish then got right to the point. He was appalled at the lack of syntactic dexterity in his graduate class and wanted to know what we could do to teach grammar to our graduate students and to our undergraduates. He had announced his commitment to grammar instruction nationally in the *Chronicle of Higher Education* (June 2002) and locally at UIC by teaching a ten-week mini-seminar to new freshman on grammar. He had struck on an innovative project in which students create a private language that includes grammatical rules and a lexicon. Students produce a page long text in their newly designed language, translate that text into English, and explain how the translation proceeded.

Now, at this departmental reception, he was intent on expanding his influence. Without wasting words, he told me he wanted composition classes to focus on grammar. I had had a sense this was coming and had begun to think about how to respond. I agreed with him that it was unfortunate, indeed, that grammar instruction had fallen away from composition pedagogy over the past twenty years as interest grew in the composing process. But, I went on, while it was all well and good to demand that graduate students and lecturers teach grammar, I doubted that many could.

He was incredulous, "What do you mean, they can't teach grammar?"

"They can't." I said simply. "They don't know it well enough themselves." Further, I reminded him, we just fired a group of lecturers. "You can't train a staff when they come and go on one-year contracts." Fish left my side with a curt nod and a pointed comment to the effect that we weren't done with our conversation.

The next evening, when I returned to English 555, the graduate training seminar that I describe in chapter 6, I reported on my conversation with the dean. I asked the new teaching assistants what they thought about adding an emphasis on sentence-level grammar and syntax to the first-year writing classes they were planning. An uncomfortable silence spread throughout the usually gregarious group. After waiting through the requisite but lengthy silence I asked for a show of hands. Who felt they could add a strand of grammar instruction to a writing class? Only two of our new crop of PhD students felt they could do so. Asked to explain how they had gained this expertise, one described a self-study program she had undertaken to learn grammar in order to pass a test required of new high school teachers. The other new graduate student described a parochial high school English class taught by a rigorous, unrelenting nun.

I listened, realizing that these new graduate students all had been in high school during the heyday of composing process pedagogy, which had pushed aside grammar instruction in favor of a pedagogy that imagined writing as an externalizing of inner knowledge through a process of prewriting, drafting, and revising. This approach had seemed new and exciting to teachers at that time, perhaps because it constituted a radical swing of the pendulum away from a traditional focus on correctness and because it took up exciting new advances in psycholinguistics and cognitive psychology. I had, in fact, unwittingly contributed to this composing process pedagogy through my early research in cognitive processes in writing (Matsuhashi née Feldman 1981).

I was just thinking what a "teachable moment" this situation provided when Luke Zamacheck broke the silence and simply started talking to me and the group, "It's my fault; this is all my fault. I just feel sick about it."

"What do you mean?" I said.

"I'm the one in Fish's graduate class who doesn't know grammar and he's right!" Luke went on, "I had always thought I could write until I took his class. He marked up my whole paper and gave it back to me to redo. Thank God he didn't grade me on the paper; I would have failed. It wasn't exactly grammar that was the problem, it was the way I didn't—or couldn't—use my sentences to push the logic of the paper forward. I had no argument—just loosey-goosey sentences, one after another. I don't know how to fix this paper. It's the grammar, sure, but it goes beyond that. I can't believe I thought I belonged in graduate school."

Luke put his head down and covered it with his hands. Another student came to his defense and said, "No, Luke, it wasn't only you. It was me, too. He did the same thing to my paper. I feel like I can't write. I don't know grammar and I certainly can't teach it."

"Well," I asked the class, genuinely not knowing the answer, "What are we going to do about this?"

At our next meeting, I asked the same question of Walter Michaels and Tom Moss. The dean's interest in grammar posed a fascinating problem. Tom Moss and I were still reeling from the horror of telling ten lecturers that they would not be hired back. We wanted to find a new, broader role for lecturers that could provide shelter in the next budget storm, which surely, we felt, must be right around the corner. I realized, too, that I simply had not given enough thought to how grammar fit into the first-year curriculum. Asking first-year students to write for academic and public situations, rather than writing essays to demonstrate knowledge to the teacher, brought grammar and syntax into clearer focus.

The new Provost, who had come on board just as our budget troubles hit, had been given a certain sum of money to initiate new programs. We knew that he would focus broadly on undergraduate education and that he was concerned about retention. Perhaps as an olive branch extended to the college after the severity of the budget cuts, he had granted funds for our college to launch a freshman "Links" program. First-year writing courses would be linked with sections of history, or philosophy, or biology, or criminal justice.

Tom Moss, Walter Michaels, and I knew this was an important opportunity. Perhaps there was a way, we ventured, to leap out of our well-worn groove, and connect with faculty teaching other first-year classes. Once again, I took the elevator back down to the college offices on the fourth floor—this time with Tom Moss—to meet with Sarah Peaceman, a faculty member from the sociology department who had come on board to work with Stanley Fish and was now in the role of associate dean charged with designing this new links program for first-year students. We sat in frayed modernist chairs placed around a chrome-and-glass coffee table on one side of her office. This associate dean, newly installed in her office, laid out the preliminary plans she had made for the next year's linked classes. Tom and I knew that an opportunity existed, here, in this largely unformed plan, for tying together our lecturers, the dean's interest in grammar instruction, and our hopes for first-year writing classes. The conversation meandered a bit as we brainstormed ways to make this new program work. Then Tom Moss hit on a solution.

"How about," Moss asked, "if we appointed our best lecturers—our most energetic, successful teachers—and paid them an additional $8,000 a year as a special stipend? They could design special sections of first-year writing that would be linked to the other first-year courses. In this way, we could work closely with a staff of eight who would teach three courses each rather than try to organize twenty-four graduate students teaching twenty-four courses."

"How, then," Peaceman asked, "can we justify paying these lecturers this extra money?"

Tom Moss smiled as the solution tumbled out of his mouth, "Well, they'd have to take a grammar seminar with Stanley Fish to prepare to teach these linked classes. Further, they'd have to revise their syllabi to include grammar instruction and to develop the topic of the linked course. Everybody wins: we can pay some lecturers a better salary, the lecturers will integrate grammar into their courses in a pedagogically appropriate way, and the new links program gets a committed group of teachers who want it to succeed." The three of us sat back and admired the shining new plan that had materialized in the midst of what had become habitual desperation. The plan was approved by Dean Fish, as we expected it would be, and a schedule was determined for the seminars, which would be held during several weeks in the spring semester.

The eight anointed lecturers, a few additional writing instructors, Tom Moss, and I were seated around the same long conference table of the year before when the lecturers had met with the then-new head, Walter Benn Michaels. Everyone was nervous; but it was a giddy and hopeful sort of apprehension, nothing like the anger and fear of previous years. Fish arrived a bit late and asked playfully, but with a bit of an edge, whether we were ready. He passed a thick pile of handouts around the room and asked that all the participants identify themselves and say something about why they were attending the sessions. Several admitted that they were woefully deficient in grammar but eager to learn. A few others said that they were curious about how Fish's approach would differ from the way they had been taught. I said that I wanted to use these sessions to rethink the role grammar instruction should play in the rest of the first-year writing program. Fish nodded approvingly. But, for the most part, our comments constituted the obligatory niceties that would get the ball rolling. Only after the session got going would anyone offer anything that sounded like a challenge or an objection.

Stanley Fish launched into his lecture and held sway for a long time, arguing his point from a number of different angles but always coming back to the crux of the argument he had published in "Say it Ain't So" in the *Chronicle*: teach grammar and nothing else. He shared anecdotes about his students' work on their "private language" project, about talks during office hours, and about insightful moments that arose during class. And, he offered a definition from one of his handouts: "A sentence is a logical structure of (causal, temporal, spatial) relationships between agents (subjects), actions (verbs), and objects (objects)."

Looking up at us, he paused and announced with an air of finality, "That's it. It's all about structure and relationships."

What he said made a lot of sense to me. He explained that the focus on parts of speech doesn't help us teach writing because it ignores the rhetorical function of those structures. He wanted us to focus in our classes on the structure; teach the logical relationships between the parts of a sentence, he implored, not the rules. These ideas all seemed, in fact, quite exciting.

The group began to shift uncomfortably, however, as Fish extended his argument to explain what he thought was the appropriate pedagogical approach.

"Aim low," Fish instructed, using the title from the piece he must have been preparing for the *Chronicle* (Fish 2003). He made it simple: "First, do your job. Second, don't do someone else's job. And, third, don't let anyone else do your job. The structure of language is an inexhaustible subject and that's what you should be teaching. You are teaching students only what you can teach them; you cannot teach them to be good people, and you shouldn't try."

Janet Weistill couldn't stand it any more. She raised her hand and asked Fish how could this approach help empower students. This was the question Fish had been waiting for. With fresh energy, he launched into a verbal assault, "Is it necessary to be a good man in order to speak well? We do ourselves and our students a grave disservice if we conflate the two." He went on something like this, "We empower students when we teach them how to craft an effective sentence. If what you mean by 'empower students' is this thing called 'self-expression,' you are forwarding ideas that have no value whatsoever. The notion of self-expression, and the purported empowerment it brings is entirely false and pernicious because it means no correction to the student's writing will ever be accepted. Students say 'I know what I mean' but they don't realize language has its own structure and meanings. When students are allowed to express themselves, they'll fail to communicate what they want to communicate."

Brian Robinson decided to jump in and try a different approach, "But how do you know that students' writing is improving? Do students actually do any writing of pieces longer than sentences in your class?"

Fish had no answer to Robinson's question. It was clear that from the materials Fish handed out that all his classroom work focused on language structure; students were not writing the traditional essays or arguments found in most composition classrooms. But this exclusive focus on grammar, he claimed, was where we needed to start. "We should not," he insisted, write about content." Fish was incensed about a particular version of cultural studies writing classes in which graduate teaching assistants committed to a particular idea, say, postcolonialism, designed courses in which students read about, discussed, and wrote essays on postcolonialism. For Fish, the only acceptable content was sentence-level grammar. "Content, Fish reiterated, is the structure of the relationships of language. Or to put it another way, the only error is a failure of logic."

The group was quiet for a while as each considered on the one hand, his or her willingness to return a portion of their classroom activities to a focus on the structure of language. Elsa Nikopolis, a graduate student in literature, spoke up, "I am a second language speaker and so I appreciate all that you have said about the structure of the language and how critical it is to making meaning. But frankly, I'm a little confused. I agree that the composition classroom shouldn't be a site for political action. Where I got my master's degree, we had to use a course pack that worked out the composition director's Marxist commitment. We called that composition class "Oppression 101." I hated teaching in that program. But look, on a more basic level, aren't we always, as Austin points out, doing things with words? I mean, your publications are always meant to do something. *They're not just sentences.* Can't we focus on the structure of the language and *still* teach that writing is a way to do things with words?"

Fish looked at her. "Perhaps," he admitted, "Students need to learn the structures of sentences first, then they can move on. Your job is to teach that structure."

Getting What You Wish For

"Sam Cassidy is on the phone," my husband shouted up from his basement office.

"Okay, Okay! What does he want now?" I muttered as I looked around for the phone.

I picked up the phone to hear Sam shouting, "You won't believe it; you just won't believe it. Are you sitting down? We got the grant!"

"Oh, no! We didn't," I protested, hoping that this was his idea of a joke.

Summer 2003. Our newly funded grant program resulted from a second try; an earlier submission had been turned down by the Corporation for National and Community Service. This time, the grant-writing team, headed by Sam Cassidy, relied on feedback from the earlier effort. We had developed a joint approach— Sam worked with both Academic Affairs and Great Cities to redesign the grant proposal. Both offices had an interest in seeing the idea funded. The Vice-Provost, Pradhi Kerala, was eager to develop some sort of civic engagement program at the undergraduate level, which coincided with Great Cities' Director David Perry's interest in expanding the work of Great Cities Institute.

Sam knew it was critical to get faculty involved. He had me; I had been very involved in the first proposal submitted by the Great Cities Institute and could see the connections between the first-year writing program and this new version of civic engagement. However, Sam was having trouble getting other faculty to come on board. He had been talking to Marietta Rodriguez in Criminal Justice, who was interested, but who had been told by her department head to do nothing until her tenure book was finished. Folks in political science and Latin American Studies had also expressed interest, but could not be cajoled into coming to meetings. Sam was sure that Dean Fish's article in the *Chronicle* (2003), critiquing *Educating Citizens* (2003) and warning against service learning was frightening faculty who might have otherwise been interested in the project. Nonetheless Sam had forged ahead, muttering all the while that we would get the grant, but the proposed program would never be implemented.

As soon as Academic Affairs received a notice that the grant was awarded, Pradhi and I began to meet weekly to plan for a starting date the following fall. The first year of the grant was built on our two required composition courses,

English 160 and English 161. Our next task was to identify the specific general education courses that students would take in the second year of the program and, in order to do that, we would have to work through a particular college. Pradhi suggested I call Sandy Gorelick, an associate dean in the College of Liberal Arts and Sciences, to ask how general education courses might contribute to the second year of the grant project and how we might obtain academic credit for students doing fieldwork with community agencies. I called, and as the conversation proceeded, I realized that this phone call had been a mistake. No, I told myself, it had been a mistake of *huge* proportions. Sandy became increasingly alarmed as I explained the grant and she started wondering, aloud, "whether or *not* the college could facilitate such a grant." She asked for a copy of the grant application and, as it was copied and distributed, a furor arose about what was telegraphically referred to as "the grant," or variously "that goddamned grant."

The associate deans in the College of Liberal Arts and Sciences argued vigorously, as did Stanley Fish, that service learning, seen largely as volunteerism or political action was inappropriate as a core academic activity. I did not disagree. Fish had staked his reputation in editorials in the *New York Times*, at a Great Cities conference on engaged research, in a speech at the Honors college convocation, and at Cornell's School of Criticism and Theory on upholding and justifying the university as a place apart. Tempers flared, and Fish and I had an angry conversation about the process of approval for the grant and its "provenance." Fish and his group of associate deans presumed that service learning had little connection to focused academic work. Our program officer didn't help. In trying to explain the sort of language needed for our performance measures he offered, "You could, for instance, indicate how many lots the students will clean up." The cleaning-up-lots example, proposed in the context of developing performance measures, hit the Vice-Provost hard. This was his worst nightmare—that he would be responsible for godfathering at UIC a program that seemed to promote volunteerism and service, not academic excellence. I spent more than one sleepless night going over the ways I might intervene and what I might say or write. Here I was, finally able to develop a project that could push the first-year writing program to the next level, and I found myself yet again in the eye of a storm.

I understood the anger that circulated throughout the administrative offices of the college: the grant application, as written, confirmed some of our worst fears about service learning. Sam Cassidy had imagined a developmental growth model in which students mature as moral beings over the three-year period of the civic engagement program. As he wrote and showed me drafts, I tried, unsuccessfully, to turn his focus toward situated learning. I had been working for some time in the first-year writing program to dissuade teaching assistants from designing courses in which writing was viewed as a medium for expressing, or reflecting on, inner self-knowledge. In my version of the proposal, students would write in the field for community agencies. Rather than contribute to moral development, this activity would teach students how writing could make a difference in the reality of particular community agencies. This service-learning grant would evolve into the Chicago Civic Leadership Certificate Program (CCLCP) and would provide opportunities for students to apply their academic learning in public settings through writing projects. Now we would have a chance—if only in a pilot project—to see how writing, as part of the ongoing scholarship of both teachers and students, could play a role in undergraduate education.

Reflecting on Experience?

You have just read a chapter composed largely of narrative that sounds like a reflection on my experiences as a composition director at an urban research university. Reflective writing is enjoying a resurgence in composition and rhetoric as a way to provoke discussion of disciplinary issues. Jessica Yood argues that "self-conscious, reflective prose" is emerging as a new genre for examining our profession and that this genre depends on recognizing "experience . . . not as a category of knowledge but a genre, a discourse and an activity (2003, 526, 538). I'm concerned that such a position, validating reflection as a genre, makes the same mistake as the scholars I report on in the opening of chapter 2 who, for many years, took a colonial settler's narrative prose to be a diary. Experience does not speak for itself (see Scott 1991). Any report of experience—a faculty member writing about the profession or a student writing about a service-learning experience—emerges purposefully from a specific situation to take shape in a hybrid or traditional form of genre. By elevating reflection to a genre, I believe, we cut off an important discussion about what sorts of evidence, experiential or otherwise, allow a writer to pursue a particular representation of reality.[4] Rather than consider these diary entries as a reflection, then, I ask the reader to consider them as a petition for this book's thesis.

Part Two

---◆---

Designing Instruction
to Make Writing Matter

Chapter 4

—————————➤•◀—————————

Rethinking Reflection in Community-Based Writing

A New Space for Teaching and Learning

Bathed in the light from floor to ceiling glass walls, Candice Rai, Megan Marie, Tom Moss, and I relaxed into four new chairs richly upholstered in a tapestry of orange, tan, and burgundy geometric shapes, and spread out our lunches and notebooks on the black oval coffee table. We might have been the first to sit in these four chairs. The Rebecca Port Coffee Shop had finally opened that summer day in June 2004, allowing me to buy the cup of coffee that I had been tasting ever since construction had begun. This new space had been deftly retrofitted into a second-level exterior overhang at the base of University Hall, our modernist twenty-eight-floor high rise. The floor to ceiling glass façade offered a welcome contrast to the rest of the building, derisively called the "the big house" by faculty who felt trapped in their offices by concrete verticals that left only slivers of glass through which to view the busy city below. Our task that day was to take the next steps toward planning the first year of a five-course, community-based certificate program that would ask students to complete writing projects as part of their fieldwork in local communities.

Sobered by the challenges ahead, we appreciated the revitalizing energy of the bright new workspace provided by the Port Center Coffee Shop. Megan, who was new to UIC, looked around and asked what had been here before. We tried to explain that, in fact, nothing had been there before; it had been an open space under the third floor, an overhang that now provided a concrete ceiling. Well, *almost* nothing had been there before. I stood up with my arms stretched parallel to the floor trying to map the path of the second-level external walkway that once traversed the very spot on which we now sat. At one time University Hall elevators had stopped here, at the second floor, to discharge students and teachers out onto the external, elevated walkways. A campus renovation project had removed the massive outdoor walkways that spanned the campus and provided an elevated track for moving students around the campus. While these walkways must have looked fascinating in the architectural drawings, in reality they added to the grim concrete weight of the campus and turned out to be a bad idea: walking on the upper level exposed students to the wind and the rain, but worse, walking beneath these horizontal behemoths exposed them to the rainwater and the melting snow that wormed through the disintegrating caulk and dripped, dripped, dripped as students hurried from one class to another. I stretched out my left arm pointing with my index finger toward the Art and Architecture Building where the blunt, rough cut edge of the walkway still jutted out from a shuttered entrance to the second floor. Then I swiveled my head in the opposite direction and stretched my right arm and finger at the other craggy edge of the now dismembered walkway which had provided a transit route through this space and across the plaza to the Behavioral Sciences Building. Megan looked each way and nodded as she connected in her mind's eyes the phantom walkway to its second-floor entrances.

The campus, especially the walkways, had been designed to move students from one place to another, regulating them on the one hand and keeping them moving on the other. The faculty would be housed in the campus's tower, University Hall, and would come to the students who waited in classroom buildings (Haar 2002, 157). The newly installed glass walls of the coffee shop disrupted University Hall's brutalist architecture and upset the rationale used to design this urban campus. Architect Walter Netsch had applied a utilitarian approach developed from the then-current notions of urban planning. Students would travel from the outer rings of the city toward the campus where, upon arrival, they would enter a micro-city complete with walkways that transported them to classes (2002, 157). Once on campus, the students—blank slates to be imprinted—entered classroom buildings to be taught by the faculty members who had descended from their offices in the tower. Times had changed, however, and the purity of architectural design had given way to the need for spaces in which faculty and students could meet and connect with each other.

The new Port Center, where we sat, is one of several renovated spaces sponsored by Project Oasis, a campus improvement plan initiated by Jane Tompkins, a name that will be familiar to many in English studies and in composition and rhetoric. In her earlier work as a literary critic, Tompkins focused our attention on women's novels of the nineteenth century as worthy contributions to the literary canon, and then studied classic westerns, such as Zane Grey's as important cultural artifacts. Most recently, however, Tompkins had turned to examine her own teaching and published *A Life in School: What the*

Teacher Learned in 1997 just before she and her husband, Stanley Fish, arrived on our campus. We all wondered how her new interest in teaching and learning would imprint our campus. To our surprise, Tompkins's interest in the life of classrooms evolved into a desire for better spaces for learning—which, on further thought, was quite understandable given the rapidly deteriorating classroom spaces of our architecturally significant campus. Over the past several years, while Stanley Fish held the deanship at the College of Liberal Arts and Sciences, Jane Tompkins worked on a very different sort of institutional change by taking charge of classroom renovation as Assistant to the Provost for Campus Environment. This new coffee shop was one of her key efforts, and we recognized that Project Oasis's motto "Learning doesn't stop at the classroom door" could have been the motto of the project we were planning as well.

We were designing a new space for writing instruction in a concrete institution. To build the Chicago Civic Leadership Certificate Program, we would have to clear away some heavy debris. We would then imagine a space for learning that allowed students to move inside and around the tall buildings of disciplinarity while learning how writing depends on embeddedness and is motivated by exigency. Instead of seeing the campus as a transportation hub where students arrived to be regulated and taught, we hoped that students would see the campus as a base camp as they designed writing projects with partners in nearby communities.

This chapter introduces the work we did that summer through two strands that thread through and around each other. The chapter's first strand provides a back story, if you will, that argues for the importance of genre and the dangers of reflection for teaching writing. I begin with a memoir by Vivian Gornick taken by many writing teachers to be an authentic account, a literacy narrative, of her growth as a writer. Then, I chronicle the events that occurred when angry journalists questioned the veracity of Gornick's memoir. The journalists insisted that the memoir should reflect—that is, mirror—the facts of Gornick's experience; while Gornick, as a writer, knew that this genre required a literary and rhetorical rendering of the content. This divide between the deep rhetorical function of the memoir to shape reality and a too-easy conception of language as a vehicle for facts is at the base of much confusion about the role writing about personal experience plays in the classroom context. Both the reflection essay and the literacy narrative embody contradictory rhetorical and generic aims; students are asked by teachers to produce an authentic account of an experience and, at the same time, convince their teacher that the expected learning has occurred. What starts out as an essay based on personal experience—which itself is problematic because experience is always mediated—becomes a petition to the teacher for a grade.

I want to be sure that the reader does not hear this discussion as a diatribe against personal writing. Much interesting and exciting work has been done in composition and rhetoric on how narrative and personal experience might be incorporated into a variety of alternative genres and contexts. Margaret Willard-Traub, for instance, points out that

> increasingly, in fields ranging from English studies to anthropology to law to medicine, approaches to writing that incorporate autobiography and personal narrative are being used by scholars not simply as a means for meditating on lived experience, but also as methods of scholarly analysis and argumentation. Such autobiographical, multivalent, and multivoiced texts have attracted much critical attention within their fields, especially for their ideological challenging of traditional disciplinary discourses that some would argue privilege certain kinds of knowledge—and certain writers and readers—over others. (2006, 424)

Indeed, the previous chapter in this book takes up Willard-Traub's challenge to engage autobiographical material in the service of scholarly argumentation. This complex view of personal writing influenced our CCLCP team as we planned for our first writing classes and deliberated about the shape and purpose of writing projects. We wanted to consider the complex issues that surround the range of genres in which personal experience might find its place (see also, Schroeder, Fox and Bizzell 2002; Trimbur 2001). More important, we decided not to assign the troubled genres called reflection essays and literacy narratives.

These classroom genres depend on two assumptions deeply embedded in our culture. First, as illustrated in the story of Vivian Gornick's memoir, writing is often falsely seen as a neutral or invisible technology that translates personal experiences into a written representation of those events. Further, reflective essays, when used in a service-learning context depend on writing as a translation tool that can display learning. This popular claim locates learning in the activity of writing the reflection essay after the student has returned from a community-based experience. I claim that what happens is quite the contrary; the learning actually occurs as the student immerses herself in the social context as a participant in a community of practice.

The second strand in this chapter describes our start-up activities for the first-year writing courses in the Chicago Civic Leadership Certificate Program (CCLCP). That summer in 2004, we recruited students and developed community partnerships. At the same time we undertook our greatest challenge, which involved imagining and designing writing projects that fulfilled both community and classroom needs. The curriculum for CCLCP's courses would, we knew, build on the existing first-year writing courses at our university. But once we started thinking about how writing instruction would proceed in CCLCP, we ran smack up against service-learning's strong and widespread commitment to reflective writing. As this section suggests, curriculum development that summer involved difficult and complex deliberations that continue to engage us. But now, I turn back to the chapter's first strand and to Vivian Gornick's memoir.

Tales of Becoming a Writer

Fierce Attachments opens with a telling vignette (1987). Vivian Gornick, at eight years old, a keen observer of her neighbors' quotidian interactions, listens in the tenement hallways as intimate lives become the stuff of casual conversation. Mrs. Drucker, smoking a cigarette in her open doorway, explains to Gornick and her mother: "He wants to lay me. I told him he's gotta take a shower before he can touch me" (3). Gornick, fascinated by this coarse declaration, banks it for the contribution it will make to her evolving sense of self. She can anticipate her mother's ready response—if not the precise words, the intensity of it—for these two women and the others in the building shared a "shrewd, violent, unlettered" connection (4). Without a pause, Gornick's mother announces that Mrs. Drucker is a whore and that's why her husband—always "he"—feels dirty to her. It's not him—Gornick's mother asserts—it's her. The implication, left hanging in the thick hallway air, is that she, Mrs. Drucker, who doesn't work and is thus beholden to the breadwinner, has struck a bargain with the devil and now must pay. Shrugging, Mrs. Drucker says, "I can't ride the subway," a euphemism, Gornick tells us, for being unable to work. Scenes like this provide a petri dish for Gornick as she grows from an observer to a full-fledged participant in this rough life.

Attending New York's City College changed things. It divided Gornick from her mother, who lived self-righteously with her depressed but romantic longing for her deceased husband. Attending college also divided Vivian from Nettie, the neighbor across the hall who lived famously for sex with any available man. Gornick's allegiance to City College, a home away from home, provoked, "an unshared life inside the head that became a piece of treason. I lived among my people, but I was no longer one of them." Gornick reports:

> I think this was true for most of us at City College. We still used the subways, still walked the familiar streets between classes, still returned to the neighborhood each night, talked to our high-school friends, and went to sleep in our own beds. But secretly we had begun to live in a world inside our heads where we read talked thought in a way that separated us from our parents, the life of the house and that of the street. We had been initiated, had learned the difference between hidden and expressed thought. This made us subversives in our own homes. (1987, 105)

Her mother had wanted Vivian to attend college even though she had her own doubts about this enterprise. She snapped back at an uncle who recommended marriage by pronouncing: "This is America. The girls are not cows in the field only waiting for a bull to mate with." Gornick's mother defended school because she saw it as a route to a teaching job, however, she became enraged at the thought of her daughter reading novels for their own reward.

She hadn't understood that going to school meant I would start thinking: coherently and out loud. She was taken by violent surprise. My sentences got longer within a month of those first classes. Longer, more complicated, formed by words whose meaning she did not always know. I had never before spoken a word she didn't know. Or made a sentence whose logic she couldn't follow. Or attempted an opinion that grew out of an abstraction. It made her crazy. Her face began to take on a look of animal cunning when I started a sentence that could not possibly be concluded before three clauses had hit the air. Cunning sparked anger, anger flamed into rage. "What are you talking about?" she would shout at me. "What are you talking about? Speak English, please! We all understand English in this house. Speak it!" (1982, 108)

School was only part of the picture. The obvious schism created by school drew on the deeper emotional pathways traveled by each of the women who passed each other on the stairs and who heard the battles and the dramas that played themselves out behind the paper-thin walls. Gornick will ride the subway and will travel far, but not before she relives the lives of the women, such as her mother and Nettie, who she thinks she is leaving.

Later, Gornick attended graduate school at Berkeley and saw in the English Department other versions of the men and women she had left behind in the Bronx: the professor interlocked with the protégé, the ambitious male graduate student who seduces the brilliant young woman into marriage, and those, like Gornick, who keep clear of that swamp she called "love." Until, that is, Gornick, "the fierce moralizing Jewess" succumbs to Stefan, "a lapsed Catholic endowed with a missionary zeal for painting" (1987, 133). This brief marriage and the subsequent attempts to sustain other relationships are developed alongside evocative descriptions of her trials as a writer.

As relationships came and went, Gornick learned that writing required a steady, daily rhythm: thinking about the problem at hand and working toward solving it with diligence and patience. She chronicled her writing process and described an image that appeared to her when the writing was going well. This image, a vision of a rectangular space, captured the dynamic impulse of her writing:

The sentences began pushing up in me, struggling to get out, each one moving swiftly to add itself to the one that preceded it. I realized suddenly that an image had taken control of me: I saw its shape and its outline clearly. The sentences were trying to fill in the shape. In that instant I felt myself open wide. My insides cleared out into a rectangle, all clean air and uncluttered space, that began in my forehead and ended in my groin. In the middle of the rectangle only my image, waiting patiently to clarify itself. I experienced a joy then I knew nothing else would ever equal. (151–152)

The rectangular image offered an orgasmic depiction of the inner landscape of the writer. The hovering rectangle, a simulacrum for the blank page or perhaps a more erotic space, is the source of all energy, all words, and all joy. This moment defined her fully. When the writing goes well, men move into the shadows as the rectangle pulls her into language and frames an idea; the idea takes hold and pages of manuscript appear. Gornick's coming of age as a woman and as a writer draws us in and works its magic on us. Rising from the ashes of a working-class family, a failed love affair, a broken marriage, her writing process gathers momentum and becomes the defining feature of her life.

Writing teachers have been taken in by Gornick's memoir and by ones like it that tell the story of one's release into language. The extraordinary writing draws us in making us feel like we are reading the pages of her diary. We want to believe that this talented writer has laid bare the story of her life. As writing teachers, we want students to see how Gornick's writing process emerged. And, we want to provide an opportunity for students to learn how writing can teach us who we are. But we are fooling ourselves and we should know better. While a memoir should not engage in an intentional reconstruction of the facts—more about this below—it always performs a shaping function situating the writer as a self under obligation.

Memoirs are written as writing that matters. Too frequently, though, teachers take them as the simple, veridical story of one's life, spilled from memory onto the page. They then become literary models for an essay assignment called the "literacy narrative," or the "reflection essay," in which students are encouraged to spill memory onto the page. When this happens again and again in the institutional isolation of the composition classroom, students learn, mistakenly, that one's writing process is bound to one's personal experience. The memoirs that students read are crafted by authors who speak to consequential public issues, but the literacy narratives that students write read like diaries. Worse yet, an unspoken pact between teacher and student, values highest those diaries characterized by emotionally laden, confessional materials or stories of rebirth and conversion (Faigley 1989). This sort of writing has been characterized as writing that matters *to me*. Planning for instruction in the Chicago Civic Leadership Certificate Program required a pedagogy that corrected for the confused rhetorical purposes that drive the literacy narrative assignment.

Performing in Writing

Vivian Gornick tells us that *Fierce Attachments* is not a mirror-like record of what happened to her, nor is it an identity story. After years of teaching graduate students in MFA programs how to write memoirs, Vivian Gornick articulated what she had learned about writing memoirs in *The Situation and The Story: The Art of Personal Narrative*. She argues that writing a memoir means understanding how the subject—the self—becomes a persona, obligated to shape the story in the context of a particular situation. Gornick looked back at the writing of *Fierce Attachments* and described her task as finding a syntax, a sense of control, a persona who could speak about the situation at hand. She discovered during the process of writing that "this point of view could only emerge from a narrator who was me and at the same time not me" (2001, 22). She wasn't searching for her real voice, but a different voice, a voice that could engage in a self-investigation. This other voice must create a dynamic dialogue that implicates the self in a particular situation (35–36).

Gornick opens *The Situation and The Story* by describing her difficulties writing *Fierce Attachments*. She tells of her many attempts to characterize her difficult relationship with her mother. The whiny, grating, accusatory voice she came to the project with wouldn't do; neither would the girlish self-pity found in an early diary. In order to write the memoir, she had to correct for herself, wading through a tortuous process filled with self-doubt until finally she had created a situation and a persona—not an identity—who could write the memoir out of that situation (22). This persona could respond to the "commonplace need, alive in all of us, to make large sense of things in the very moment, even as experience is overtaking us" (24). Gornick wrote, resisted, fell back into confession, pulled herself out of the abyss, and returned day after day to the persona she had found. What she learned was that she needed to cling to this persona who could pull her "out of . . . her own agitated and boring self to organize a piece of experience" (25).

What Gornick makes clear in *The Situation and The Story* is that she is passing as someone else. Gornick is performing in writing, as she puts it, a "self under obligation" (91). The writer's obligation, she argues, is to engage with the experience, the particular context that holds the raw stuff of experience. What emerges from this process is not a report of experience, but the wisdom drawn from that experience that is used to shape the particular piece of writing. The need to shape and tell a story emerges from that situation and not from the self.

The voice Gornick speaks of is neither the "inner voice" of Willa Cather's "inviolable self," a coherent self to whom things have happened and about which that self might write, nor is this voice a confessional voice. Rather, we might think of the writer as composing a screen play in which one maps a dramatic event. Kenneth Burke, proponent of the twentieth century's new rhetoric, which sees language as a form of human action, created a tool called the "pentad" that could be applied to Gornick's performative approach. This rhetorical formulation captures the writer's project quite accurately: a narrator investigates the scene; considers the act, or what is taking place; identifies the agent or agents involved; studies by what means, or agency the act is carried out, and finally, determines why the event is taking place (Burke 1962a). In identifying these elements and this dramatistic method, Burke holds that language has, embedded within it, a motive that drives it.

There is no essential self at work here pouring out experience into a diary, rather words and syntax crafted in obligation, in response to, a particular situation. Further, Burke argues that his notion of rhetorical purpose or motive is not a feature in one of the five angles of the pentad; rather, it's a function of "language itself, a function that is wholly realistic, and is continually born anew; the use of language as a symbolic means of inducing cooperation in beings that by nature respond to symbols" (Burke 1962b, 43). Gornick recognizes this rhetorical function of language when she tells us that the writer of personal narrative must create a dynamic that can provide "motion, purpose, and dramatic tension" (Gornick 2001, 34). The narrative is written by a writer who can make sense of her own participation in this dramatistic situation and who can draw on motive to shape a narrative that will deliver its wisdom (Gornick 2001, 91).

The Memoir and Its Truth or Consequences

In July 2003, about two years after the publication of *The Situation and The Story*, Gornick spoke at Goucher College to an audience of students, writers, and journalists. Terry Greene Sterling, a journalist who was attending a two-week seminar at Goucher, attended Gornick's talk and wrote about what happened in *Salon Magazine*, setting off a series of criticisms and inviting a rebuttal by Gornick. After noting that Gornick is considered by many to be "the grande dame of memoir and personal narrative" and after reviewing her work as a journalist for the *Village Voice* and her many critical essays and book reviews, Sterling pointed out that the *New York Times* had "hailed Gornick's memoir as a 'fine, unflinchingly honest book'" (Sterling 2003). It would appear that Sterling chose her words carefully, because in the very next paragraph, after briefly summarizing *Fierce Attachments* and setting the scene at Goucher College in which Gornick answered questions from the audience, she offered her memory of the event speaking as a reporter who was offering a factual account of the question and answer session:

> Then she answered questions from the audience—and shocked her listeners by describing the liberties she'd taken with the truth. Her revelations transformed the session into a debate seminar about truth vs. creative license in the post-Jayson Blair era. (2003, 1)

Sterling went on to report that Gornick "admitted that she had 'composed' some of the walks and conversations with her mother in the memoir and had also invented a scene that involved a street person and her mother" (Sterling

2003). Gornick's comments had caused quite a stir. She had not intended any of her responses to that tough-minded audience of journalists as confessions, but the journalists took them as such. They heard "composite character" and "invented a scene" and began to grill Gornick pointedly about whether or not she had fabricated information. In her report on the event in *Salon*, Sterling characterized the contentious question-and-answer session as a culture clash, "a sophisticated New York memoirist facing off against a crowd including highly regarded journalists" (2003, 1).

The journalists demanded factuality, insisting that a memoir is the story of what happened, while Gornick struggled to explain that the point of a memoir was to compose a *telling* of the actual facts and events to which the journalists were so wedded. In her rebuttal, also published in *Salon*, she repeated the point she made in *The Situation and The Story*: "what actually happened is only raw material; what the writer makes of what happened is all that matters" (Gornick 2003).

Maureen Corrigan, well-known book critic on National Public Radio's *Fresh Air*, who was not present at Gornick's talk, read Sterling's piece and jumped into the debate. She added her perspective on talk radio and then wrote in to *Salon*, agreeing with Gornick that a narrator of a memoir is not the same person as the person who actually lived the life written about (2003). Corrigan, however, took a legalistic tack, advising Gornick that she should have included a prefatory note telling the reader that some of the content had been fictionalized. I agree with Corrigan on this point and have added such notes in this project where I included fictionalized narrative accounts. What angered Corrigan, it appears, was Gornick's comment that "memoir writing is a genre still in need of an informed readership." Corrigan thought Gornick was insulting her readers and translated Gornick's comment into the title of her piece, "You as a reader, are a dope."

Corrigan got it wrong when she accused Gornick of disparaging her readers; Gornick didn't intend to insult anyone. What she was trying to say, perhaps unsuccessfully, is that we really don't understand memoir as a genre, and as such, we don't know how to read memoirs. During that ill-fated talk she was attempting, as she says, to make "a definite distinction between what the writer of personal narrative does, and what the writer of biography, newspaper writing, or literary journalism does" (Gornick 2003). Her point, as I see it, is that a writer of personal narrative does not invent facts, rather, she composes her experience. The genre of memoir requires this. We, as readers, carry, perhaps unknown to us, rhetorical baggage that defines the memoir as a factual account. Gornick discovered at her talk the extent to which our understanding of memoir as a genre has become infected by the recent scandals caused by Jayson Blair, the journalist at the *New York Times* who created elaborately fabricated news stories, and historians, such as the late Stephen Ambrose who had plagiarized (inadvertently or not) the material of others.

When Vivian Gornick wrote her memoir, she built not only on a generic architecture drawn, of course, from years of writing, but also from teaching students to write memoir and from a close study of the past century's memoirs. In the *Situation and The Story*, Gornick explores the terrain marked by the memoir and makes the point again and again that memoirs are a *literary* genre, not a journalistic one. Over the past thirty years, Gornick asserts, those who have had a story to tell have begun to write memoirs rather than novels (2001, 89). This shift, Gornick suggests, follows a movement away from an essential Cartesian self and toward a self that is perpetually becoming. She quotes V. S. Pritchett as saying of memoir, "It's all in the art. You get no credit for living" (quoted in Gornick 2001, 91). More important for our discussion here is Gornick's assertion that "truth in a memoir is achieved not through a recital of actual events. . . . What happened to the writer is not what matters; what matters is the large sense that the writer is able to *make* of what happened" (91). Memoir, then, takes an imaginative turn and readers should understand this imaginative strategy as a core feature of the genre.

It is ironic that a journalist, such as Terry Greene Sterling, who wants Gornick to convey facts like a body on a gurney, also composed the experiences she reports. Sterling's piece in *Salon*, which purports to report on an event, is clearly composed for the purpose of dramatizing a particular perspective. Sterling titles the piece, "Confessions of a Memoirist" and tells us that Gornick's "revelations . . . shocked her listeners." Sterling herself adopted features of the commentary, while purporting to write a news article. She speaks of journalists as purveyors of facts and wants writers of memoir to be included in the same nonfiction club. For Terry Greene Sterling, the issue is that Vivian Gornick has left the broad category of nonfiction behind. For Vivian Gornick, the issue is that the memoirist ought not be handcuffed by a journalist's definition of nonfiction. What Gornick understands, but has trouble explaining, is that the genre shapes the text as much as do the actual events.

On Not Assigning Literacy Narratives

Back in the Rebecca Port Center, our notebooks and planning spreadsheets spread out before us, this story of Vivian Gornick's brush with "truth or consequences" echoed an ongoing debate in our field. Our first inclination was to ask our students to write literacy narratives as a way to use writing to learn about their writing experiences. However, this debate between journalists and memoirists about representing personal experience made us think twice. Often, writing teachers assign the literacy narrative or personal experience essay at the beginning of the semester as a way to open up a conversation about how students have learned to write. The literacy narrative and its service-learning cousin, the reflective essay, are also frequently assigned outside the classroom in writing centers as a way to train tutors, in teacher education programs, and in service-learning classes. The literacy narrative typically goes something like this: Students are asked to read model memoirs like Vivian Gornick's *Fierce Attachments* (1987), Victor Villanueva's *Bootstraps* (1993), *Mike Rose's Lives on the Boundary* (1989), or bell hooks' *Bone Black: Memories of Girlhood* (1996). Next, students are asked to write an essay in which they characterize themselves as the reader or writer they are today. By tracing events that occurred in the past, students are expected to gain valuable insights into their current literacy practices and how they compare to the literacies of others. Students are asked, as they draft, to consider their writing process, family histories, successful writing experiences, or painful realizations about their language education. Further, students are asked to reflect on what these memories mean for themselves as a reader and writer. Such essays are evaluated for whether or not they have a thesis, whether they are well-organized, whether the details and anecdotes illustrate the main point, and whether the writer reflects on the events' suggestions about the writer's evolving self.

School-based narrative assignments often misconstrue key features of the writing situation and subvert the ways in which writing can invite students into complex rhetorical contexts. Here's where the literacy narrative and the reflection essay go wrong. Gornick's memoir, which characterizes her development as a writer, belongs to a genre with a long and complex history. The detailed analysis conducted by Gornick in *The Situation and The Story* of the literary tradition of memoir attests to this fact. In sharp contrast, the literacy narrative is typically not memoir or even autobiography, which would present major challenges for a first-year college student. Students are assigned an essay characterized by narration, which is a mode of discourse rather than a genre. The modes—description, narration, exposition, and persuasion—were fixed in composition pedagogy by Alexander Bain in his mid-nineteenth-century *English Composition and Rhetoric* (Bizzell & Herzberg 1990) and have been the basis of countless textbooks. The modes are not genres because they do not articulate broad social motives; rather, the modes provide a textual technique that might contribute to any genre. Yet narration is frequently elevated to the role of genre for its purported ability to substitute for memoir.

Some composition scholars equate the writing of literacy narratives with establishing an agentive self. Mary Soliday described the writing of literacy narratives as an act of self-translation, where, she says, "writers can articulate the meanings and consequences of their passages between language worlds" (1994, 511). When a student tells his or her story of acquiring language through a literacy narrative, the student acquires what Soliday calls, "narrative agency," (1994, 511) which, in fact, doesn't refer to writing. Narrative agency, for Soliday, gives students a sense of their cultural identity and works to articulate difference and respond to the conflicts that students face when they enter college. This pedagogy, drawn from cultural studies, but also conflated with the self of expressivism, sidesteps writing in order to help students locate their cultural selves. I argue that students find out who they are by writing in particular situations; there is no single stable self that they will find by excavating memory and reporting on their dig.

Writing, when inflected with the personal voice, does important cultural work. However, the literacy narrative has been accepted as a mechanism for students to narrate a truth about their lives without recognizing the challenges this sort of writing involves. When we read Gornick's memoir as a literacy narrative, we are tempted to take her description of her writing process at face value. The memoir—translated as Vivian Gornick's experience—becomes proof for our theoretical construction of the writing process. In sharp contrast, when we understand that this memoir has been composed by a persona, someone who is performing in writing, the differences between *Fierce Attachments* and the literacy narratives we assign to students become more obvious.

The student who is assigned a literacy narrative in response to *Fierce Attachments* can only produce a piece that weakly imitates the power of the source text. This pedagogical sleight of hand frustrates students who hear "you can do this, too," but who are not given the tools. The "authentic self" who writes a literacy narrative in the first-year composition classroom is expected to be entirely self-sufficient. The student is told that the stuff of writing comes from the inside and suggests, as Joseph Harris puts it, "a self that stands outside or beyond language and culture," which, he goes on to say is "both its central appeal and flaw" (1997, 29). Just like the journalists who confronted Vivian Gornick, we desperately want to believe that students can be assigned literacy narratives that will prompt them to tell their own stories—that is, to translate their "selves" into a text through narrative.

Typically, we evaluate literacy narratives for the extent to which we sense that the student has been honest about his or her experience. Again, Vivian Gornick's experience with journalists who want facts is frequently replicated by composition teachers who most want to know that students have been honest in narrating a true story. In a landmark article published in 1989, "Judging Writing, Judging Selves," Lester Faigley demonstrated the extent to which "good writing" is defined by our expectation that the student will divulge a true expression of self. Working from Catherine Belsey's *Critical Practice* (1980), Faigley defines writing such as literacy narratives as expressive realism. This sort of writing, Faigley explains, purports to offer a window on reality that student writers can use to look inside and view the ideas and feelings they, themselves, harbor (1989, 397). Faigley looks closely at the contributions to a volume of student essays, *What Makes Writing Good*, edited by William Coles and James Vopat, that invited well-known composition teachers to submit their students' best work (1985). In reviewing these choices, Faigley found that the composition specialists overwhelmingly valued writing that seemed to present students' authentic representations of themselves.

Rather than see narrative as a mode or a vehicle for personal voice, I argue that we need to examine the ways that genre provides a lens for the resources of culture and context. Genres are an important resource that offers stable frameworks for texts, as well as the possibility of manipulating those frameworks. One way to engage students in writing that matters is to take up what Anis Bawarshi calls the "genre function" (Bawarshi 2003). Genres, for Bawarshi, connect individuals to social situations through writing. In so doing, we understand genres as "socially constructed, ongoing cognitive and rhetorical sites—symbiotically maintained rhetorical ecosystems, if you will—within which communicants enact and reproduce specific situations, actions, relations, and identities" (2003, 39). Vivian Gornick, we see, understood her participation as writer in a complex context and tried to present a nuanced articulation of her position to an audience who saw her memoir largely as a narrative report of the facts. Even though her response was largely unsuccessful, Gornick tried to explain to her critics that the cultural history of the genre had, in a sense, driven her writing of the memoir.

The argument that Gornick makes for the memoir as a genre supports the argument I have been making throughout this book that writing must be seen not as a translation of a writer's essential, inner self but as a tool for shaping reality. When we ask a student to compose a literacy narrative to explain to a teacher how he or she learned to write, the assignment creates a social context in which the writer is motivated to demonstrate to the teacher what has been learned. Asking the student to write a literacy narrative further suggests that writing is something that happens inside one's head exclusively and reinforces the metaphor that drove much early composing process research. Ironically, this interiorized view of writing is reproduced in Gornick's image of the rectangle that fills with sentences as the writer works. We should not assume that this representation is a factual account of how she writes. Rather, we should understand that the rectangular page-like image that fills with words in Gornick's memoir was carefully crafted, a performance. We see how she writes and speaks through a cultural and social lens and not through an authentic representation of her self.

Against Reflection

Our conversations early that summer convinced us not to assign literacy narratives to CCLCP students. And we knew, intuitively at first, that we would not assign reflection essays. This section lays out our thinking about why service learning's commitment to reflection did not support our approach to writing instruction. Most people will agree, ourselves included, that reflection, commonly understood as thinking or analysis, is a good thing. Most people will also agree that we want students to do more of it. However, when we move too quickly to solidify reflection as pedagogy or as genre, we lose our critical purchase and end up seeing writing as the too-easy translation of reflective thinking. In the list that follows I propose five stumbling blocks that convinced us not to assign the reflection essay during the first year of CCLCP classes.

1. Too much of a good thing? Written reflection is the sine qua non of service learning; it has become the near-universal pedagogical tool for community-based learning. Robert Bringle and Julie Hatcher delineate two closely related components of service learning as a "course-based, credit-bearing educational experience." First, students participate in a service activity that responds to a community need, and second, students "reflect on the service activity in such a way as to gain further understanding of course content, a broader appreciation of the discipline, and an enhanced sense of civic responsibility" (2003, 83, reprinted from 1999, and quoted from 1995, 112). Bringle and Hatcher go on to explain that the "community service does not necessarily, in and of itself, produce learning" (2003, 84). It is reflection that creates a connection between—a bridge, to use Bringle and Hatcher's term—the community-based experience and the course material. This imagined separation between the service experience and the classroom writing misrepresents the wide range of writing possible in civic activities. To solidify a move toward institutionalization, service learning scholars claim that reflection cuts across all disciplines while also contributing to particular courses' aims (Bringle and Hatcher 2003, reprinted from 1999, and quoted from 1995, 83). Even further, scholars have attempted to turn the reflection essay into a classroom genre. However, identifying a single pedagogical method that is expected to work across disciplines and across community-based activities works against the very institutionalization it was intended to achieve.

Reflection typically refers to a process of critical thinking, a metacognitive activity that allows students to think about thinking or to think about their service-learning experience (see Smit 2004, 98–118). After participating in community-based service activities, students return to the classroom to reflect on what they have learned. This back and forth between the community and the classroom is described as a "cyclical pattern" between thought and action through which learning occurs (Eyler & Giles 1999, 7, 175–176). Much reflection is conducted via writing assignments such as journal entries, research papers, case studies, and digital dialogues. In fact, Bringle and Hatcher go so far as to claim that "writing is a special form of reflection though which new meaning can be created" (2003, 85). While most academics understand that writing grows out of reflection, they do not equate writing with reflection.

Dan Butin argues that positioning service learning as a "coherent and cohesive pedagogical strategy" will backfire when the movement itself is "an amalgam of, among other things, experiential education, action research, critical theory, . . . social justice education, . . . community-based research" and many others (Butin 2006, 490). Further, positioning service-learning's reflection, its pedagogical method, as a grand narrative works against the ways of knowing that define higher education (491). Recent work by Diane Chin explores the ways in which pro-service-learning arguments can alienate faculty instead of persuading them of service-learning's contribution to the academic endeavor (2007). Although Chin's work critiques justifications for three approaches to service learning—building citizenship, supporting social justice, and inculcating moral character—its underlying message concerns how faculty conceptualize their core disciplinary activities. Which, of course, brings us back to engagement.

Engagement, as I argue in the book's introduction, means that a university commits its core intellectual agenda to pursuing a relationship with its metropolitan (or rural) context that depends on making knowledge as part of a reciprocal relationship with numerous stakeholders. In this view, inquiry and knowledge-making is still at the core of a university's work, but this work is conducted in partnership with others. Partners increasingly want a key role in shaping the university's research agenda and student's learning outcomes (Sandy and Holland 2006; Bacon 2002). If anything is to be generalized across disciplines, it must be these powerful concepts—inquiry and knowledge-making—that are transformed into the work of specific disciplines, or the missions of interdisciplinary research and outreach centers.

Service-learning scholars could take a lesson from compositionists, who, for decades, have made use of a pedagogy called "writing to learn." Much like reflection, writing-to-learn practitioners invite students to use writing to demonstrate that they have learned the concepts taught in a particular course. This methodology has survived precisely because it proved a useful and flexible tool for university faculty who wished to see evidence of learning in a particular course. Proponents of writing to learn did not attempt to universalize it or turn it into a new genre called the "write-to-learn essay"; rather, they recommended ways to tie it directly to the course content (See for instance, Anson 1997; Walvoord 1996; Fulwiler 1984).

2. Promoting participation not changed attitudes. Even though many service-learning scholars claim that reflection contributes to learning, much discussion of reflection ends up promoting changed attitudes when it should advance a sense of participation in a complex context for learning. Service learning can indeed be a transformative educational experience, but that transformation does not occur through the writing of reflection essays.

Here's a rather horrifying example of how reflection can go wrong: Bruce Herzberg, over ten years ago, in his critique of reflective writing, narrated an interchange in which one student said: "We're going to some shelter tomorrow and we have to write about it." Another student replied: "No sweat. Write that before you went you had no sympathy for the homeless, but the visit to the shelter opened your eyes. Easy A" (Herzberg 1994, 309). The student dispensing advice astutely had decoded this writing assignment as one aimed at changing attitudes and moral capacities and explained to his friend that the "before I was, but now I am," rhetorical formula will satisfy the teacher. The student was advised, in other words, to demonstrate a savvy response to the curriculum's hidden agenda.

In a note following his article, Herzberg reports that Edward Zlotkowski assured him that anonymous surveys reported high rates of changed attitudes. This response begs the question. Is changed attitudes what service learning should be about? Is it desirable to teach for specific moral capacities? Creating a student with a particular identity—the moral citizen—is a dangerous road to travel. It assumes a thinly veiled pedagogy of transmission which ignores recent work in both rhetoric and cognitive science that highlights the social and participatory aspects of learning. Thus, written reflection assumes learning to be an interiorized process in which attitudes and identities contribute to the development of a coherent and moral self. In sharp contrast, I argue that agile writers need to learn how writing shapes rather than reflects reality. Further, such interiorized views of learning do not fit with our emphasis on the mutuality of the service-learning relationship with community partners.

The reflection essay depends on a mirroring metaphor that grows out of a substantial, but varied, intellectual history. The simplest and most limiting metaphor depends on a physical process in which light bounces off a surface. Initially the surface is seen as a mirror but eventually our intellectual history transforms that physical surface to the mind or the inner self (Williams 1978). Marxist literary critic, Raymond Williams, finds that this metaphor for reflection contributes to a certain passivity in which the object of reflection—perhaps a pastoral scene—is reflected in a piece of art (1978, 99).[1] The activity of reflection positions the student writer as a self-contained, inward looking and coherent self, much as the writing process movement did, when writing was seen as an internalized cognitive process of planning, drafting, and revising. In composing reflective journals or essays, the student writer is supposed to become an author of him or her self, writing about what's inside through a process of introspection. This identity-based pedagogy has come under critique as part of a broad reconsideration of the role of rhetoric in making knowledge (Bowden 1999).

A small but growing group of service-learning practitioners have been grappling with the shortcomings of structured reflection by asking students to see writing as a way to participate in service-learning activities rather than simply recording the results of learning. Tom Deans, for instance, has identified a range of literacy activities in service-learning courses (2000). Students can, of course, "write about" their community experiences, but Deans identifies two other alternative approaches. Students could write "with" the community as part of grassroots efforts that include "activist research, literacy work, proposal writing, and collaborative problem solving (2000, 19). Or, students could write "for" the community, producing documents that contribute to the community's social capital. Ira Harkavy, as well, outlines an approach to service learning that derives from the "Deweyan tradition of democratic problem solving" and that involves students in "action research" that should be seen as a knowledge-generating activity (Harkavy, Puckett, and Romer 2000, 113.) In more recent work, Deans argues for studying genre in service-learning contexts as a way to contrast typical and innovative uses of form (2006). An emphasis on genre, which I discuss in greater detail below, helps the writer see how language and texts are designed to advocate for a particular reality through choice of words, syntax, and genre. Students learn how disciplines and communities can make knowledge together.

3. *Learning doesn't happen apart from the community-based experience.* Theories based on reflection typically characterize learning as an individual psychological or constructive mechanism. However, what makes learning happen is quite the opposite; it is participation in social knowledge-making contexts whether they are in the classroom or in the community. For instance, David A. Kolb, an educational theorist, who favors experiential learning, developed a four-stage model for experiential learning that can be drawn as a continuous circle linking concrete experiences to reflective observations, which evolve into abstract conceptualizations, and then promote active experimentation as the student reenters concrete experiences (1984). When service-learning scholars complicate this model, they typically create a larger number of boxes, circles, and arrows but do not reconceptualize learning as anything other than an individual process. Even in these updated theoretical models, reflection becomes a method for enhancing individual cognitive development. (For example see Cone and Harris 1996, and Rockquemore and Schaffer 2000, reprinted in the Campus Compact Service-Learning Toolkit 2003).

Learning, however, as I argue throughout this book, emerges from participation in deeply situated experiences (see also Cooks and Scharrer 2006). And that goes for teachers as well as students. The program I describe in this chapter and in the next (with co-authors Candice Rai and Megan Marie), the Chicago Civic Leadership Certificate Program, grew out of a scholarly approach to writing, situated in the historical, political, and intellectual contexts of rhetoric, composition, and English studies. We see writing as a social activity or a practice that depends on the context in which it takes place.[2] As a faculty member and program director, I have undertaken writing projects, this book included, that could not have been completed outside of the everyday practices and the ongoing interactions with my colleagues, students, and staff. Thus, when one sets out to theorize learning in this complicated setting, one sees the close connection between the knowledge made through disciplinary or community practices and the social interactions that undergird them.

The theoretical framework that guides our civic engagement activities is called a "communities of practice" approach (see chapter 2). This approach turns the internally motivated theories that support reflection inside out, but it does more than add an external component. Instead, the social theories that support communities of practice treat "relations among person, activity, and situation, as they are *given* in social practice itself, viewed as a single encompassing theoretical entity" (Lave 1993, 7; see also Kirschner 2004 for a similar approach referred to as enculturation). Learning in a community of practice is comprised of both participation and reification. Our students, for instance, as participants in a not-for-profit agency that conducts workshops on fair housing practices for recent immigrants, research and write summaries, or briefs, of recent court cases. Their learning depends on new knowledge about the typified, or reified, on the form of summaries needed by the agency as well as on the mutual recognition of and connection with their partners at the agency (Wenger 1998, 55–61).

Situated learning depends on shared histories in which participation and reification function as interdependent dimensions of the same learning enterprise (Wenger 1998, 68). This definition fits precisely with the description offered in chapter 1 by Stanley Fish for disciplinary scholarship. The work of a literary critic, a discipline-centered writer, depends on that scholar's grasp of "a coherent set of purposes . . . that inform an insider's perception" (Fish 1995, 21). The work of a writer—whether a literary critic or a student writing legal briefs—depends on his or her grasp of a community's ways of knowing and its histories, rules of thumb, vocabularies, narratives, politics, and customs.

4. Writing is not a neutral technology. Too often service-learning practitioners view writing as a neutral tool that can record or transmit learning. Writing is anything but a neutral tool. The student, teacher, or community partner who writes forwards an agenda that pursues a motive or desire. Writing works this way, even with such mundane tasks as writing a grocery list. Our goal in designing the Chicago Civic Leadership Certificate Program was to heighten students understanding of writing as an agentive activity.

Proponents of structured reflection claim it is the "hypen" in service-learning, "the link that ties student experience in the community to academic learning" (Eyler and Giles 1999, 171). In *Where's the Learning in Service Learning?*, J. Eyler and D. E. Giles, report on a large-scale survey of service learning in higher education that suggests a greater classroom emphasis on reflection, predicts academic learning, particularly subject matter knowledge, knowledge of social agencies, and greater problem-solving ability (1999, 173). Reflection, they say, offers an opportunity to get some distance on an experience and to "monitor one's own reactions and thinking processes" (1999, 171). Writing reflection essays, then, is characterized as a way to get what is inside the student's head and heart onto the page so that it can be transferred to the teacher. These views of reflection depend on an interiorized psychology of learning.

It's true that both reading and writing look like solitary activities that can be carried out apart from experience. Sitting slump-shouldered, plunking away at an old manual typewriter, ripping unsatisfactory pages from its roller, crumpling them and tossing them into a nearly full wire wastebasket, the writer at work offers a familiar cultural image. However, literary theorists, rhetoricians, and writing specialists imagine writers and readers differently. Literary theorist, Steven Knapp, argues that the act of reading, which seems a wholly interiorized endeavor, can create a sense of agency in the reader. The reader, he says, is caught up in an "irreducible oscillation between typicality and particularity," that is, between understanding broadly the possible forms of action, and noting how an agent moves through a particular fictive world (1993, 139). The interaction noted by Knapp between particularity and typicality is commented on again and again by scholars who study what it means to produce or consume texts.

Participation in any scene as a reader or writer may be likened to a two-faced Janus (Bakhtin 1993). Like Etienne Wenger's participation and reification or Knapp's typicality and universality, Mikhail M. Bakhtin identifies such opposites as mutually necessary components of the uniqueness of lived experience (1993, 2). What emerges from the mutuality of this two-faced Janus is action—or writing—characterized by what Bakhtin calls "answerability." Like Vivian Gornick's self under obligation, each act we perform and each word we write, "looks in two opposite directions: it looks at the objective unity of a domain of culture and the never-repeatable uniqueness of actually lived and experienced life" (1993, 2). But instead of pulling us apart, the answerable act or deed creates a sense of motivation and desire. And, as I continue to build my case for the non-neutrality of writing, motivation and desire become increasingly important. (So don't change the channel.)

Contemporary rhetoricians want to know what consequences decisions about language use have for the ways we communicate with each other. Kenneth Burke, too, contributes to our theme of opposites that pits particularity against typicality. For Burke, identification, the opposite of division, focuses us on the importance of reciprocity in our relationships. Our motives and desires direct us to act in concert with those we identify with and to remain divided from those we oppose (1962a, 21). These motives underlie Aristotle's classic definition that rhetoric is the art of persuasion. Burke gives the following example: two individuals collaborate, "in an enterprise to which they derive different kinds of services and from which they derive different amounts and kinds of profit. Burke asks, "who is to say, once and for all, just where "cooperation" ends and one partner's "exploitation" of the other begins?" (25). Resolving this dilemma will rely on language and one's identifications will be very important in defining one's position. But identification also implies division. Burke wants us to pay close attention to how the "wavering line" between connection and estrangement or in his terms, between identification and division, becomes an opportunity for language use by a human agent. Rhetoric, for Burke, "is an essential function of language." It, as I say earlier, offers a "symbolic means of inducing cooperation in beings that by nature respond to symbols" (43). Writing, then, is never a simple translational tool; it always functions as a way for individuals to enact particular motives in a complex setting fraught with division and expectations.

5. *The reflection essay is a vexed genre.* The reflection essay says two contradictory things to students: At first it seems to be saying, "Tell me about your experience and what you think you have learned." Students typically respond to this request with something that looks like a diary, a personal account of the event. However, it also says, in more or less explicit ways, that the teacher is looking for evidence of learning and will grade the essay on these terms, since he or she cannot know the student's experience or what the student thinks and feels about the experience. This conundrum recalls the event narrated earlier in which Vivian Gornick defended the writing of her memoir as a literary genre against the reporters who wanted facts. It also repeats the internal conflicts that increasingly occur around the literacy narrative, which seems to want a report on the writer's evolving literacy, but which inevitably becomes a petition for a grade. I argue here that faculty who assign writing should avoid the blanket approach that reflection provides and consider the uses and function of genre when designing writing projects for the classroom. Further, community-based writing projects offer a unique clinic in which students, community partners and students can apply important considerations of genre to particular situations that give rise to writing.

Let's consider genre a bit more closely. Increasingly, composition scholars have focused on how genres function to create meaning in specific situations.[3] The previous and limited view of genres as a particular sort of container that defines poetry as poetry or the short story as the short story has given way to an understanding of genre as a tool for shaping meaning. Genres function to regulate the relationship between typified situations and the unique circumstances described in the previous section that underlie particular motives and desires. Another way to view genre, as I say in chapter 2, is to focus on its delivery to participants situated in a public context by a writer with acknowledged or emerging expertise. Much attention has been paid to hybrid genres as a welcome and creative response to this new and more complex understanding of the forms writing can take (Bishop & Ostrom 1997). However, the reflection essay offers a hybrid form that confuses rather than clarifies the writing situation.

Genres enact cultural and institutional agendas. While each and every piece of writing responds to a very specific and unique situation, we carry in our heads typified responses that tell us how to respond to these situations. We have a script for the thank you note, the high school classroom's five paragraph theme, and the science fiction novel. We also have a script for the diary-like, school-based, personal essay that undergirds the written reflection. Both teachers and students share this vexed understanding of the reflection essay.

This list of five concerns suggests that we narrow our focus from a highly general view of student learning to specific learning situations. Further, since college-level reflection is almost always carried out through writing, our focus should be on writing instruction. As we planned writing projects for CCLCP students, we asked ourselves about what we wanted the writing to accomplish in a particular situation. We then asked what typical genres existed that might be put to use in a particular situation. These two centers of thought on situation and on writing created, as Kenneth Burke says, a wavering line between identity and division or as others have said, between particularity and typicality. We walked this wavering line each time we thought about writing projects for our students.

Recruiting Students for CCLCP

A curriculum alone, however, does not a program make. Even before we contemplated writing projects, we had begun the process of recruiting students. In May 2004, near the end of the previous spring semester, Tom Moss had obtained a list of all the students who had expressed intent to enroll at UIC. He culled the list for students with a 22 ACT English subscore or better, since, given the multiple demands of this program, we needed students who could move ahead quickly. Candice, Megan, and I stood around Tom's computer and held our breath as he pushed the button that would send our Web-based flyer to about 1,100 students. Would students respond? Would there be the interest we expected? Having pushed the button and set our initial plan in motion, we dispersed to continue other work. I sat in my office going through my mail and checking my to-do list when, about fifteen minutes later, Tom shouted, "Here comes one! I returned to Tom's computer and eagerly watched his screen as sixteen more student responses came across his e-mail list. Our bodies took up every inch of Tom's small office for a self-indulgent, foot stomping happy dance.

The moment offered the sort of energy we hoped would propel us effortlessly through the recruiting process. A really good push was needed to get beyond some of the roadblocks in our way. Not only had we started too late to plug into the campus's orientation schedule for incoming students, but also the College of Liberal Arts and Sciences had already had its major meeting to tell the advisors about programs such as ours. We kept asking ourselves, how hard can this be? Our next steps would be to hold two evening information meetings for students and parents and prepare an application for students to fill out. Unlike the 172 e-mail responses that rushed back to say "I'm interested," gathering the students and their parents in person during the middle of proms and graduations proved much more difficult. The RSVPs trickled in at an agonizingly slow pace. Calling each of the students' homes sometimes allowed us to speak to the student or parent, but more frequently, there was no answer at all to our many phone calls. More important, though, we learned from the few students we were able to contact that many students had only looked quickly at the brightly colored web page and had not taken the next step of clicking on the "How does it work?" link that displayed a detailed time line for the five-course program. Students had responded eagerly to the general notion of leadership, civic engagement, writing, and community-based experiences without learning much about the program as a whole.

About two weeks after sending out the invitations for our information sessions, we found ourselves enthusiastically shaking the hands of parents and students. We had clearly tapped a vein of student interest: those students who had been involved in service activities during high school were eager to continue in their new college setting. Students recognized that leadership and writing and other communication skills would be important components of their professional profile. But our biggest surprise was the enthusiasm of the parents for this program. They saw, much more than their young students, that our program would provide a "lived experience" that could connect academic work to the sort of lifelong skills students would need to negotiate the complexities of living in the rapidly changing economy of metropolitan Chicago. The students who attended our information sessions were clearly high achievers and practiced at handling many activities at once. When they asked questions about the courses required in the certificate program, we knew they were marking a mental tally sheet that listed activities on one side and available hours in the day on the other.

Only forty-eight students had attended the information sessions and only about half of that group applied to the program. The most serious drawback seemed to be the two-and-a-half year commitment to the program, which worried these students who weren't at all sure what they would major in or what new interests they would discover. We would have been pleased to accept almost any of the students who came to the information sessions; they were talented, articulate, and enthusiastic and had already been involved in substantial civic activity. The information sessions showed us what questions students would ask about the program, and we felt ready to broaden our reach. Our next recruitment strategy—which we wish we'd thought of sooner—was to include the application form that we had been mailing or handing out to students on the Web site. Once students had applied, we interviewed them in person or over the phone and gave them registration instructions. By the Friday before classes began, we had a group of thirty-seven students from several colleges with a variety of interests who had committed to the program; they appeared in our basement classroom in Burnham Hall the following Monday. But recruiting interested students was only the beginning.

Developing Community-Based Partnerships

Developing working partnerships with local not-for-profits would define the infrastructure for CCLCP and would also create the backbone for our students' community-based writing projects. More important, we hoped that these core partnerships would develop as reciprocal relationships that offered benefit to both students and agencies. Launched from our English department's first-year writing program's pedagogical base, we aimed to build on our commitment to rhetorically motivated writing and situated learning. While this theoretical commitment does not, in principle, require that students leave the classroom to discover the rhetorical underpinning of any given writing situation, CCLCP offered an opportunity for students to work with leaders at community-based organizations to develop writing projects. This new community partner-student-teacher triumvirate created a learning opportunity focused on the value of reciprocity among partners for learning to write.

Our agency partners were most familiar with two models of university-community interaction. Either undergraduate students visited agencies to provide direct service like helping youngsters with homework, or, graduate students from the College of Urban Policy and Public Affairs worked at agencies as interns, applying the lessons of their graduate classes. CCLCP offered something different: first-year students would work with agency development officers or leaders to produce communication documents needed by the agency. The community partner would now become a co-teacher and together we would learn how to integrate our academic language with the agency's vernacular, project-oriented shop talk.

Reciprocity, which is at the heart of this knowledge-making endeavor, could only emerge as we worked together on projects that would not only benefit student learning, but also could build community capacity. At the start we didn't know if the student projects would be usable by the agencies, but at the very least, our agency partners felt that educating students through CCLCP could broaden students' understanding of not-for-profits and even influence their future career choices. In addition, they told us, communication projects, such as the ones we had built into the first-year writing class curriculum were always the last projects to be undertaken and the first to be scuttled under the pressure of more immediate needs.

To identify and partner with appropriate not-for-profits, we developed a formal RFP, or "request for proposal," process, through which agencies could apply. For the past decade, as part of UIC's Great Cities Commitment, UIC Neighborhoods Initiative (UICNI) had been developing working partnerships in two neighborhoods immediately adjacent to the campus—the largely African-American neighborhood to the west and Pilsen, a Mexican-American community to the southwest. What is meant by partnership has been a key topic throughout our planning process. Our goal was to work closely with partners to determine and meet mutual needs as the planning process went forward. CCLCP community partners would play an important role in co-developing the community-based writing projects, in assessing student work, and in mentoring students as they learned about the agency's mission and culture.

With the UIC Neighborhoods Initiative's help, RFPs were sent to about twenty community agencies within a reasonable transportation distance from UIC. The letter explained the project, directed the agency to the Web site flyer, and invited representatives to a meeting to talk about the grant project. The application, itself, posed questions for the agencies to address concerning their communication needs and how they might benefit from partnering with CCLCP. The RFP also asked about a recent agency initiative to learn how the agencies approached specific projects.

Several weeks later we sat around a conference table in the rehabilitated loft space of the Great Cities Institute opening large brown envelopes that contained the agencies' applications. Several agencies had been able to articulate a very clear sense of their communication needs and offered a good fit for CCLCP. Figure 4.1 describes each of the five agencies and the communication needs they identified in their application to work with the Chicago Civic Leadership Certificate Program.

Developing partnerships requires time to get to know one another, to develop trust, and to include partners in the planning stages of CCLCP. Once we had identified the five agencies, we met with the representatives who would be working with us on two Tuesday evenings at the Great Cities Institute over a light dinner. We were particularly glad for this opportunity to break the ice and connect with each because we were well aware that UIC has had a complex and sometimes contentious historical relationship with its surrounding neighborhoods (see Luiton 1998; Rosen 1980; Eastwood 2002). At the first meeting, each agency representative or director spoke of his or her agency's history, goals, and challenges. I spoke briefly about the history of the grant project and what we hoped to accomplish. The first dinner meeting was devoted to getting to know each other's agencies and institutions, which made it easier, at the next dinner meeting, to launch the more challenging conversation about what the curriculum would look like and what problems we might face. Candice Rai and Megan Marie had sketched the broad outlines of a year-long syllabus and had settled on writing projects based on needs that all the agencies had identified.

During the week before the start of school we visited each agency to work out the details of the first semester's work. More important, working with our agency partners, we finalized detailed descriptions of the community-based writing projects that students would undertake during their first semester. Agency representatives planned visits to the classroom to meet students and introduce the work they would do at their agencies. We designed processes for

Figure 4.1. Chicago Civic Leadership Community Partners for Year One, 2004–2005

Changing Worlds

Changing worlds is a nonprofit organization dedicated to building respect for, understanding of, and appreciation for human diversity. It serves students, teachers, and families through programs emphasizing oral history, writing, and art. Founded in 1996 and incorporated in December 1999, Changing Worlds is a valuable cultural and social resource for more than 7,000 Chicago area residents who participate in in-school partnerships and professional development opportunities for teachers. Changing Worlds also provides a variety of ready-to-use curriculum materials and sponsors traveling exhibits.

Communication needs: Production of an annual report; development of an organizational newsletter; development of an organizational public relations packet or brochure; marketing and outreach materials for traveling exhibits

Gad's Hill

Gad's Hill is a family resource center established in 1898, in an era when hundreds of thousands of immigrants turned for advice and aid to Chicago's world famous system of "settlement houses." Today, in collaboration with individuals and organizations in the Chicago community, Gad's Hill Center develops and supports programs to empower the economically and educationally disadvantaged residents of the Pilsen, Little Village, and North Lawndale neighborhoods. Gad's Hill's broad goal is to develop human capital—children, youth, adults, and families—in these neighborhoods.

Communication needs: Comprehensive press kit; expand donor communications through electronic media such as Web site or e-newsletter.

Illinois Institute for Entrepreneurship Education (IIEE)

IIEE aims to foster the growth of entrepreneurship among citizens of Illinois by forging links between education and business communities. IIEE believes that entrepreneurship is an answer to job loss caused by rapidly changing economic forces, to the school drop-out rate among disaffected and/or uninterested students, and to tough problems of community economic development or redevelopment.

Communication needs: Brochure revision, press releases for ongoing projects, overall communications campaign specifically targeted to the North Lawndale community, newsletter, Web-site enhancement.

Latinos United

Latinos United is a nonprofit advocacy organization serving Latinos/as throughout the Chicago area; it is particularly active in city neighborhoods with significant Latino/a populations, such as Pilsen and Little Village.

(continued)

Figure 4.1. (*continued*)

A major aspect of Latinos United's mission is the struggle to ensure that Latinos/as have equal access to public housing. The agency, which has been working for Latinos/as for nearly 15 years is poised to launch new public policy initiatives in the areas of immigration, education, employment, and health care.

Communication needs: Press releases, brochures, annual reports, newsletters, articles, policy briefs.

The Resurrection Project

The Resurrection Project is a neighborhood organization founded in 1990 by a coalition of six Roman Catholic parishes that serve mainly Latino/a congregations. Its mission is not only to build relationships within the community, but also to challenge people to act on their faith and values to create healthy communities through education, organizing, and community development. A major focus is providing new and rehabbed housing in decaying areas within a neighborhood and to offer alternatives and solutions to lifestyles that lead young people to become involved with gangs.

Communication needs: Inventory and evaluate current marketing materials such as brochures, fact sheets, publications; develop a brand to market and communicate campaign goals; public relations kit.

Source: Chicago Civic Leadership Certificate Program (CCLCP).

communicating about students who were having difficulties attending meetings with the agencies or with their writing. And, we talked about how agency representatives could take on the role of mentor. We could have used an extra month or two for our planning process, but on the day before classes started, we felt we were as ready as we could be.

Designing a First-Year Curriculum for CCLCP

The summer, at least according to an academic's schedule, was now over. The Chicago Civic Leadership Certificate Program was to start in three days. It was the Friday before the start of the fall semester at UIC and our team had returned to the Rebecca Port Coffee Shop to conclude our curriculum design. In only one short weekend the tunnel vision devoted to planning would be transformed into the teaching we had so anticipated. On Monday, we would meet our new students face-to-face and begin teaching writing in the context of this new program.

But sitting against a concrete wall in an orange Naugahyde fifties-style booth in the Rebecca Port Coffee Shop, our computers plugged in for a long afternoon of work, we still looked at each other as if to say, "Here we are again!" Papers littered the table: syllabi, letters to community partners, schedules, and letters of application for the position of project coordinator we had not yet filled. The first-year curriculum for the Chicago Civic Leadership Certificate Program was based, in part, on the writing needs of the community partners with whom we had agreed to work. The group of incoming students in the program would take CCLCP versions of the required first-year writing courses, English 160 and English 161, as a year-long pair. Work conducted in these courses would prepare students for the program's second year, comprised of two general education courses in urban planning.[4] During the third year students took a capstone course in which they developed a community-based partnership and writing project on their own. With their certificate, the students who wished to continue their community-based work could continue as interns to work with community partners on writing and research projects for a semester at a time.

The curriculum for English 160 asked students to produce writing for their agency partners and for their classroom teachers. Both sorts of writing entail a strong focus on genre, which requires that we see writing as a performance in a rhetorical situation. Figure 4.2 illustrates the key course activities. This plan for teaching neither separates the community-based experience from classroom writing, nor does it treat writing exclusively as a learning device. Instead, this curriculum design aims to put in place the components of a community of practice in which groups of students and community partners work strategically on writing projects to fulfill mutually recognized needs. Whereas reflection has been frequently positioned as a commentary on experience, this curricular effort focused on shaping writing as a rhetorically motivated action within a particular situation.

The term, a "community of practice," refers to a group of people who come together to solve a problem or accomplish an important task; they interact in order to learn how to do it better (Wenger 1998; see chapter 2 as well). Students, teachers, and community partners all participated to some extent in forming flexible but focused groups aimed at producing important pieces of writing. At its center, figure 4.2 displays four terms that contributed to students' understanding of the rhetorically infused writing situations they found themselves in. Developed initially by Ellen McManus, these concepts have been incorporated into a textbook used throughout first-year writing courses at UIC (McManus 2002; Feldman, Downs, and McManus 2005). The four rhetorical terms I refer to—Situation, Genre, Language, and Consequences— travel flexibly between community and classroom because they are both user-friendly yet they consolidate important rhetorical concepts. Thus, students could use these terms in conversations with community partners as

Figure 4.2. Chicago Civic Leadership Certificate Program Curriculum for English 160

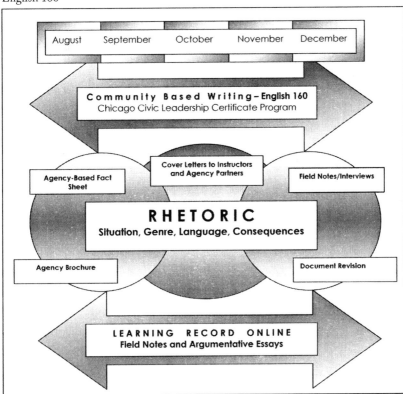

Source: Graphic by Megan Marie.

well as with each other as they planned and executed writing projects. Figure 4.3 defines each of these terms and suggests how they help to support our approach to community-based writing.

During classroom sessions, students analyzed the rhetorical features of agency documents and learned this new language for participating in the communities of practice they found themselves in. The four key terms—Situation, Genre, Language, and Consequences—became tools for unraveling the documents they read and wrote. They also learned, for the first time, what the term discourse community meant and saw how different situations gave rise to different possibilities for writing. Students read about the history of the UIC campus and how the arguments for campus expansion into existing neighborhoods had shaped the contentious debates attending UIC's birth and growth.

Students also explored the notions of service that they brought with them to CCLCP. For the most part, student applications to the CCLCP program

Figure 4.3. Rhetorical Framework for Writing

Rhetorical Framework	
Situation	How histories, cultures, communities, and individual experiences influence the writing and reading of texts. This concept helps students consider the complex contexts from which a piece of writing emerges.
Genre	The forms—in writing, speech, or any other medium—that have evolved in response to repeated situations, needs, or desires. As readers, students learn to think about what genre a piece of writing belongs to and how that has shaped its way of representing the world. As writers, they understand that they choose and modify a genre in response to a specific situation.
Language	The words, sentences, organization, and design of a text. Often the language of a text is considered only in terms of correctness on the one hand or as a matter of individual voice on the other hand. Our approach is to help students as they read and write, to see language issues in light of both genre and situation.
Consequences	The effects of writing in the world. Especially when writing in a classroom, it is easy to forget that writing has consequences, that this is why we write, and that these projected consequences guide our writing.

Source: A. M. Feldman, N. Downs and E. McManus, *In Context: Reading and Writing in Cultural Conversations*, 2d ed. (New York: Addison, Wesley, Longman, 2005), p. xxvii.

portrayed service as a way of "doing for" others. Students offered these reasons for joining the program: "I want to help people and I want to help make Chicago an even better city." Or, ". . . the opportunity to volunteer and serve the community excites me the most." And, "I have volunteered at soup kitchens and hospitals. I have also tutored young kids in math, coached youth soccer teams, and given French lessons." CCLCP's academic agenda asked these students to rethink the meaning of service. Rather than seeing service as noblesse oblige, they saw their community-based work as a way to participate in a consequential context where writing could possibly make a difference.

The CCLCP section of English 160 was designed not only to build connections between academic and community-based writing and research, but also to consider how both kinds of work are connected to even broader public contexts. The design of this year-long curriculum builds on Joseph Petraglia's argument that in a rhetorical education, knowledge and meaning emerge from an interaction between an individual's prior experiences, perceptions, and social circumstances and the various social contexts that the individual encounters. Although rhetorical education may be seen as simply "the study of argument and persuasion," Petraglia asserts that "we now appreciate that education is equally rooted in social interaction and the individual's capacity for drawing on evidence to impose coherence on a jumble of perceptions that have no direct relationship to the external world" (2000, 85). Petraglia captures here what we have called a "communities of practice" approach in which learning emerges through participation. Figure 4.4 lists the various writing projects students produced during the first semester, many of which built on heightened participation.

In addition to writing interviews, fact sheets, and brochures students in English 160 wrote cover letters for their teachers, elaborating the rhetorical choices they had made on each of their writing projects. Students also used an electronic learning portfolio called "Learning Record Online," or "LRO."[5] This Web-based tool asked students to report on reading assignments and to enter field notes about agency visits. From these observations or data, students develop, at the midterm and end of semester, an argumentative essay that crafts a representation of the learning they accomplish in the course. This classroom-based writing, I contend, is also writing that matters; it functions overtly as a petition for a grade, consequential indeed, by asking students to craft an argument persuading the teacher of what the student has learned. The LRO documents, however, must be handled with caution, lest we fall into the trap of assuming that students are pouring out literal reports of their experience. These texts, too, are written within the classroom's community of practice and elements of the classroom situation have an impact on how the writing is shaped. Just as Vivian Gornick urged us to read her memoir as a performance, not as fact, we must approach these LRO documents as performances for the teacher. Our instructional approach, then, asked students to develop an argument that could persuade the teacher of what the student claimed that he or she learned.

The Web-based version of Learning Record Online was designed by Margaret Syverson as an extension of a paper and pencil, K–12 classroom assessment tool, originally developed in England and influenced by Vygotskian approaches to learning (Syverson 1999). Although we did not utilize all the features of Learning Record Online, we signed on to Syverson's core value that an assessment of learning should be integrated into the ecology of the classroom. Unlike many current Web-based portfolios that function as a scrapbook for student work, Learning Record Online provides a structure that combines a list of generic dimensions of learning with a short list of specific goals for the particular class.[6] The four learning outcomes for English 160 and 161 are rhetoric,

Figure 4.4. First-Semester Writing Projects for CCLCP

First Semester CCLCP Writing Projects	
Interview	Students learn qualitative research methods; learn to synthesize primary and secondary sources; begin participating in agency practices and work; and gather agency and community contexts from which their writing emerges.
Fact Sheet	Students build on the contextual foundation gathered during the interview by applying basic design and copy guidelines for public relations writing. Students learn and apply rhetorical principles by justifying every choice as a rhetorical one.
Brochure	Students continue participating in agency work and learning about agency specific contexts while producing a more complicated project that requires sophisticated understanding of applied rhetoric within concrete circumstances.
Revision of Brochure/ Fact Sheet	Students begin to act as consultants and work closely with their agencies to produce professional writing projects that integrate their academic and community-based knowledge and experiences. Students are encouraged to take responsibility and ownership for their writing while increasing their reliance on collaborating with peers, agency supervisors, and instructors for feedback and guidance.
Learning Record Online	Students learn to record fieldnotes, responses to readings, progress reports, preparatory notes and draft material for mid-semester and final argumentative essays.
Mid-Semester and Final Argumentative Essay	Students take a position and craft an argument for the teacher that documents what they have learned based on the course goals. These goals include: rhetoric and academics, community-based writing and research, civic engagement, and leadership. Completed at midterm and final.
Cover Letters	Students write detailed cover letters to their instructors that articulate the rhetorical situation from which they write, and which justify all writing choices as rhetorical. These letters, particularly in the second semester are the primary means through which students communicate to instructors the situation, genre, language, and consequences of their writing projects.

Source: Chicago Civic Leadership Certificate Program (CCLCP).

community-based writing and research, civic engagement, and leadership (see chapter 5 on the development of an assessment matrix). Students in the CCLCP program began to use Learning Record Online first as a way to collect data about their work in the course. All of this work built on the course's core learning concepts and what students perceived they were learning. Candice Rai and Megan Marie commented at various intervals, guiding the students' work and asking questions where appropriate. These observations, which students contributed to several times a week, provided the basis for argumentative essays completed at the midterm and at the end of the semester.

During the second semester, the program continued to help students make meaningful connections between their academic and community-based learning through the issues they addressed at their agencies and through classroom-based discussions of broader public contexts and inquiries. (See figure 4.5). This second course, English 161, required of every student at UIC, focuses

Figure 4.5. Chicago Civic Leadership Certificate Program Curriculum for English 161

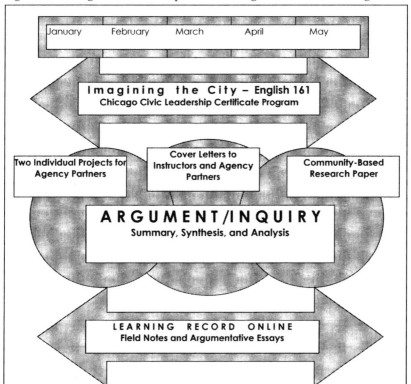

Source: Graphic by Megan Marie.

on instruction in argument and inquiry. Students learn how disciplinary inquiry proceeds and how arguments are developed to support those inquiries. In English 161 students negotiated specific projects with their agencies, and they planned and wrote a research-based paper on either a topic of interest to their agencies or on undergraduate service-learning experiences. Many of the readings assigned during this semester focused on the ways in which arguments are employed to shape reality. Students examined specific cases of argument that continued the course's emphasis on local university history and development. During the second semester, students continued working with the same agencies. This year-long affiliation was intended to increase students' familiarity with their agencies and thereby facilitate their participation. The schedule of agency visits for the second semester depended on the particular projects that the agencies wanted the students to work on.

A particular discussion on the rhetoric of Chicago public housing in civic discourse that took place during the second semester helps illuminate one way students were invited to view argument as negotiated rhetorical constructions (Petraglia 2000).[7] Students read composition scholar David Fleming's article, "Subjects of the Inner City: Writing the People of Cabrini-Green" in which he argues that various representations in civic discourse draw on and perpetuate a warehouse of *topoi* about public housing that influence public opinion, work in the interests of certain stakeholders, and further disenfranchise public housing residents by "depriving them of their rhetorical and political agency" (2003, 210). After examining hundreds of primary documents, and by participating in discussions on the future of residents to be moved from the Cabrini-Green complex, which was slated for demolition, Fleming argues that public discourse denies residents political agency in ways that parallel their material deprivation and perpetuates the cultural stigmas attached to public housing residents.

Before discussing Fleming's article, students watched a short documentary, *Voices of Cabrini*, which covered town hall meetings in which the Chicago Housing Authority (CHA) rolled out its *Plan for Transformation* to the Cabrini-Green residents (2000). The Plan for Transformation is an ambitious ten-year plan to reform and revitalize Chicago public housing. Core features include demolition of all high-rise complexes, reconstruction of mixed-income communities to house some displaced residents, and an extensive section-8 voucher component that, in theory, enables displaced residents to relocate to any apartment, anywhere, that falls within a given price range. The film includes conversations with residents and city officials, and footage on early phases of demolition and evidence of controversial community impact.

The class discussion of Fleming's essay was intended not only to help students see how arguments couched in the rhetoric of public discourse function with force in the world, but also to acquire a sense of how academic work can be applied in public contexts, particularly those related to the CCLCP agencies. Fleming, for example, conducts an in-depth analysis of primary documents and draws from disciplinary knowledge. The complexity of Fleming's project illustrates ways that academic, community, and civic contexts can mingle and merge in reciprocal inquires and that such reciprocity is one of the aims of knowledge production in an engaged university.

The class discussion of Fleming's research was neither simplistic, one-dimensional sympathy for public housing residents, nor wholesale condemnation of the policies and practices of the Chicago Housing Authority. The conversation, instead, gave rise to a more nuanced understanding of language use and how issues of poverty and patterns of disinvestment and renewal are connected to larger social, cultural, and economic forces that lie beyond the ability of any one agency to address. One student asked, "Why couldn't the city simply ask the people in the community what was best for them? Why couldn't more people be more involved?" Another student chimed in, "Yes, by the time the CHA rolled out the plan to public housing residents, many of the major parts of the plan had been decided. The town hall meetings seemed purely symbolic." A third student added, "I think it's a great idea to ask everyone in the community for their opinions of the plan, but think about the amount of money that is going into this transformation: $1.5 billion is going to be spent on this demolition before reconstruction can take place. Talking to people takes a long time. Things have to get done. Besides, how much expertise do ordinary people have to offer urban planners?" Another student asked, "Since only 30 percent of the new construction at Cabrini-Green will be for the public housing residents who lived there, what criteria will be used to select people?"

There aren't any easy answers to such difficult questions; especially ones that can be discovered in a class period, or even in a semester. Instead, the course activities pushed students to consider how rhetorical and writing practices are integral to the Cabrini-Green situation specifically, and, more generally, to working on any social problem. Students were encouraged to consider how the CHA's *Plan for Transformation* is articulated and implemented in public discourse through CHA publicity and documents. In turn, students began to extend these considerations to the work that takes place at their own partner agencies. Students wondered: What larger forces contribute to the social issues that my agency addresses? How are these issues and how are my agency's constituents represented in public discourse? What are the consequences of these representations? What ideological and material challenges does my agency face? What action is possible given these challenges? How does writing contribute to accomplishing my agency's overall mission? Answers to questions like these led students to produce research papers that tackled core agency concerns through academic inquiry and documents that supported the agency's mission and activities.

Recapping the Argument

Remember, if you will, how Vivian Gornick's memoir was assumed by her critics to be a factual account of her life. And, based on this assumption, members of the audience at Goucher College were outraged when they learned that Gornick had "manipulated" the facts. What Gornick argued—and what I believe to be the case—was that these critics did not understand the genre of memoir. From Gornick's perspective, her task was not to tell a true story, rather it was to perform in writing; that is, she used language to shape the reality— obligated, as she was, to a particular situation. She wanted to present to her readers her fierce attachment to her mother. When we read, we rely on our beliefs or expectations about what the writer of that text intended. These beliefs are constituted in forms called "genres" that shape how and under what circumstances language can be called into service.

Historically, the seventeenth-century legacy of René Descartes who's "I think, therefore I am" has evolved into our image of the solitary self. This solitary, private self could ignore the rhetorical aspects of language and claim to represent experience neutrally. This "self," as J. S. Nelson, A. Megill, and D. McCloskey aver, "could see directly the results of their experiments and feel directly the experiences of their souls, letting the wordiness of discourse take care of itself" (1987, 6). Nelson, Megill, and McCloskey trace the historical path of Cartesian philosophy to reconsider the idea of the scientific method, or as they say, "Method" with a capital M. Method, they argue, drives the idea that scientific study can uncover truth. Method often masks the situatedness and the interestedness of scientific or disciplinary work. This masking process works in much the same way as certain reified genres that function to portray reality as though natural and unquestionable (7). This vision of the solitary self who can report factually on his or her experience "haunts us still" (11). We find vestiges of this philosophical legacy in the literacy narrative and in service-learning's reflective essays, which invite the writer to look inside and record what the writer has learned.

The myth of the solitary self continues to inform the idea of written reflection as a genre. When we hear students telling us—in class discussion or in writing—what they experienced at their service-learning site, we want to hear it as a naturalistic or factual rendering of the experience. What is much harder to remember is that all language activity is situated and thus responds to the immediate context. These two views of language are in constant conflict. This chapter relies on Vivian Gornick's story to argue against reflection when used as a genre in community-based writing. Plans for student writing in CCLCP aimed to engage students in writing as a rhetorical activity, not as a way to record the experiences of a Cartesian self. With this understanding of writing, we could not, we felt, send students out to the community to use writing as a member of a community of practice, but bring them back to the classroom to report on the experience of an essential self.

Chapter 5

⬛━━➤◦◀━━⬛

Assessing Writing and Learning in Community-Based Courses
(with Candice Rai and Megan Marie)

Entering a New Situation

Imagine that you are a college freshman arriving at a large urban campus from a city neighborhood or from an outlying suburb. If you're from a suburb, the city may seem exciting and foreign to you, but even if you're from the city, you'll be working with a community agency with which you probably aren't familiar. You applied to the Chicago Civic Leadership Certificate Program (CCLCP)[1] because you thought that getting involved with a community-based program would allow you to help those less fortunate. You hope to make a difference and want to be part of something larger than yourself.

So, you ride the elevated train into a warren of unfamiliar city streets that run through a working-class ethnic neighborhood which at first seems unwelcoming. You are concerned about getting lost and hesitant to cross the threshold on your first agency visit. You have never thought much about the issues that drive your agency. You neither can imagine yourself as part of this community, nor are you sure that you have anything useful to contribute.

You have had no previous experience with public relations writing, yet within two weeks of your introduction to your agency, you struggle to create a fact sheet that your instructors tell you must "take into account the rhetorical situation of your partner organization." You have just begun to understand what rhetoric means, and you are not sure what it has to do with leadership or with working in a local community. Before you begin to design or write the copy for your second project, the brochure, you must wade through folders

135

packed with agency documents and interview the staff. You have never worked in an office, conducted interviews, or analyzed primary sources.

Soon, you become frustrated with the complications of working with peers and community members; you are overwhelmed by the contradictions between your instructors' expectations and those of your agency. Collaboration is difficult and communication is slippery, flawed, and sometimes unproductive. Leadership is no longer about taking charge and solving problems to get immediate results. You're not sure how you might help people change their life situations or even what "helping" might mean. Your understanding of service shifts along with your notion of what action is possible in the real world. The social problems that your agency addresses are complicated and seemingly irresolvable; they are connected to other larger and infinitely more complex issues. There are too many contingencies; there is no clear path. Leadership for change, you begin to see, involves working from and through this complicated situation by connecting to others, building relationships, and engaging with social issues. You begin to see that writing is not ancillary, but central to such an endeavor.

We begin this chapter by describing CCLCP's newness for students to provide some background for the assessment activities we eventually undertook. Everything about CCLCP brings students into new environments: What was service in high school is now something different and what was writing in high school is even more different. In the next section, "Situated Writing and Learning," we explore the ways that situation influences writing. We offer examples of the writing students did for community partners as well as for teachers. Our argument for situated writing and the description of CCLCP student work helps lay the groundwork for our discussion of assessment. However, before we illustrate a slice of our program's initial assessment activities, we offer a note of caution. The section, "Complicating Assessment," points out that because assessment is often conducted through writing, it is, itself, a rhetorically motivated activity. In the next section, "Developing an Assessment Matrix," we describe what we wanted to know about student writing and learning. The final section of the chapter, "Conducting Assessment," describes our approach to assessment as academic research.

Situated Writing and Learning

The impetus to consider how writing functions as rhetorical action in historical, contextually bound space and time is a core goal of civic education in the engaged university. As teachers in a community-based writing course, we are deeply concerned with the ways that language can be used to facilitate social change in concrete situations. Situated writing and learning, then, involves the recognition that one's actions have ramifications beyond personal inquiry; learning is not a solipsistic activity. Students must see themselves as agents whose actions are contingent upon and responsible to already-established communities of practice. Situated writing occurs when students, as members of a community of practice, learn over time to understand how rhetoric shapes the realities that, in turn, shape individuals (Wenger 1998). As Joseph Petraglia argues, learning is "an essentially rhetorical enterprise, for rhetoric is, in its deepest and most fundamental sense, the advocacy of realities" (2000, 83). Emphasizing the ways that learning develops from experience, helps connect learning with rhetoric, and more important, for our purposes, with writing instruction.

When learning to write entails "the advocacy of realities," issues of situatedness have enormous consequences. The criticism leveled at the Sophists centuries ago—that a rhetorical education was only available to those who could pay for the service—must be evaluated in contemporary community-based writing programs where distinctions are frequently made between the server and the served (Mailloux 1995). Conducting community-based learning with a group of students who have, despite their avocation for service and volunteerism, experienced a different quality of life than the constituents at their agencies presents a challenge. Some have argued that service-learning's emphasis on educating citizens could backfire if the only students who enroll in service-learning courses are the ones who can afford the luxury of an elite postsecondary education (Butin 2006).

Situated writing and learning, then, should provide opportunities for a wide variety of writing projects that engage students in meaningful communities of practice. In what follows, we examine writing projects from CCLCP students' first-year classes to exemplify how such work demonstrates learning about writing, about rhetoric, about leadership, and about civic engagement. The first-year writing program at UIC stipulates that students learn to write the argumentative essay, a staple genre in academia. Such essays, in which students take a position on a particular issue, are characterized by a thesis supported by data. In conventional writing classes, students might read a case study on a particular topic, which, for instance, tells what happened when author Sandra Cisneros used non-code paints in a historic suburb of San Antonio to paint her house a bright shade of purple. Students might write an argumentative essay taking a position about some related issue that had occurred in their own neighborhood. Chapter 2 illustrates an editorial produced by a student from a related assignment, in which a student argued that neighborhood pushcart vendors were being treated unfairly.

In CCLCP classes, students wrote argumentative essays addressed to the teacher that argued for what they had learned in the course. Like the conventional classroom essays described above, CCLCP essays depend on evidence to develop an argument. In this community-based setting students relied on field notes drawn from readings, from classroom discussion, and from community-based experiences. A Web-based tool called Learning Record On-Line (LRO), introduced in the previous chapter, allowed students to catalog their field notes and responses to readings. The student field entries appear to constitute reflection; as we read them we can almost hear the student thinking aloud, musing, consolidating knowledge. Yet, as you will recall, in chapter 4 we caution against assuming that such ersatz reflections are neutral transcriptions of experience. Instead, we must assume that these reflective comments are rhetorically motivated and that students are considering how their experiences might be cast in an argument for what they have learned in the course. Here is an excerpt from the beginning of Caitlyn Costello's midterm argumentative essay which argues for what she has learned in the program.[2]

> My definition of service has changed from the most basic idea of helping others to a more complex idea of working with a community, rather than for one. I have most definitely become more involved in civic affairs and become a more well-informed citizen. I have learned that rhetoric is a facet of everyday life, whether it is word choice in creating a document or forming a respectful, yet effective argument. Finally, I feel that I have grown in leadership skills, in doing everything from projects for Latinos United to learning how to disagree without being disagreeable. (Midterm essay, Spring, 2005)

Caitlyn made several claims and developed each more fully as the argumentative essay proceeded. The language she uses responds directly to the learning goals articulated vigorously in class discussion and promoted through the course syllabus. In the example below, Caitlyn crafts an argument for what she learned about civic engagement through her work at Latinos United, a housing advocacy organization,

> I knew in basic terms that gentrification was occurring and longtime residents were being forced out of their homes. However, it wasn't until working with Latinos United that I discovered how serious a problem it was. For example, according to the information given to me from Latinos United, in 1994 the average resident of Pilsen was spending 64 percent of his or her income on rent. National standards for affordable housing put affordable housing at a unit that costs 30 percent or less of the person's income. Getting informed about issues such as these that are everyday problems in the city make me feel like a much better citizen. (Midterm essay, Spring 2005)

Writings such as these, both from LRO notes and argumentative essays are frequently examined by service-learning scholars for evidence of changes in attitude. Caitlyn writes that learning about gentrification makes her feel like a better citizen. Her attitudes may have changed, but we, her teachers, are looking for her argument. We ask: can she marshal evidence that supports her claim that she has learned much about gentrification and what might be done about it? CCLCP's curriculum seeks to emphasize the ways in which students such as Caitlyn have shaped an analysis of their learning as part of an academic endeavor. Teachers are the audience for this endeavor and as such, they have expectations for whether or not the course curriculum has succeeded and whether or not students are able to demonstrate what they have learned. Caitlyn's task is to persuade the teacher of what she has learned. Frequently community-based writing is undervalued as vocational learning and classroom writing is overvalued as practice in academic skills. CCLCP asks students to understand that each of these writing contexts ask students to advocate for a reality suited to the particular context.

As we explained, community-based writing projects in CCLCP were designed in collaboration with community partners. Students began their first project by writing interviews to learn how primary sources contribute to crafting and asking questions. Further, the interview introduced students to the people they would be working with, as well as to the interpersonal dynamics, mission, and core practices of their agency. This initial participation is central to the aims of situated learning. The process of becoming a member of a community of practice, according to Etienne Wenger, means entering a "living context that can give newcomers access to competence and also invite a personal experience of engagement by which to incorporate that competence into an identity of participation" (1998, 214). Students used the information gained through their interviews to produce a fact sheet for their agencies.

The fact sheet below was developed by Tiffany France for Gad's Hill (see figure 4.1 in chapter 4 for a description of the agencies we worked with). Tiffany interviewed Gads Hill's Chief Development Officer, Janet Beals, and the Club Learn Project Coordinator, Jose Gonzalez. In addition, she studied all of the available agency documents, including annual reports. She constructed an early draft of the two-sided document you see below. She turned the fact sheet in as a class assignment to her instructors; she also received feedback from her agency mentors. Each audience had somewhat different comments and suggestions. Later, when students were asked to choose a project for revision, Tiffany chose to continue working on the fact sheet and consulted closely with Gads Hill's grant writer.

In her cover letter, Tiffany acknowledged the document's audience as potential funders, partners, and parents. Documents like Tiffany's and those produced by other students are indeed impressive, given that these students are

Figure 5.1. Fact Sheet for Gad's Hill Center

Gads Hill Center
Where a Vital Community Comes Together
Founded 1898

GADS HILLS CLUB LEARN

HISTORY OF GADS HILL CENTER

- Gads Hill Social Settlement was founded on April 18, 1898 by Leila Moss Martin and Hettie Perry.

- Gads Hill began the first nursery school in the district in 1908.

- Gads Hill established a library consisting of 25 children's books. In 1928 this library was made a sub-branch and staffed by the Chicago Public Library.

- In 2002 Gads Hill opened a Child Development Center in collaboration with the Sinai Community Institute.

MISSION & PURPOSE

- Gads Hill, a family resource center established in 1898, partners with our community to develop the assets of children, youth, adults, and families.

- Gads Hill Center is a community-based, family resource organization serving the low income population of Chicago's Pilsen, North Lawndale and Little Village neighborhoods.

- Gads Hill provides comprehensive programs for children, youth, adults and families which promote positive personal growth, strengthen the family unit and develop a strong sense of community.

AWARDS

- 2001: *BP Leader Award* for work in collaboration with the Chicago Department of Environment to provide environmental education and a "green" setting for the Gads Hill community.

- 2003: *United Way of Chicago's Youth Impact Venture Grant* for Gads Hill's science program Primero La Ciencia.

- 2004: Mujeres Latinas en Acción's *Maria 'Maruca' Martinez Community Service Award* and the North Lawndale Employment Network's *Creating a Community That Works Award* to Chief Executive Officer Barbara Castellán for her work in the community and at Gads Hill Center.

GADS HILL FUNDING

- Gads Hill Center is 70% government funded, with 20-25% from private foundations and roughly 5% coming from private funds such as parent fees, United Way and endowments.

STATISTICS

- Gads Hill Center works with three low-income communities in Chicago: Pilsen, North Lawndale, and Little Village.

- 93.5% of the population in Pilsen and 83% of the population in Little Village are Latino. 73% of the population in North Lawndale are African-American.

- 94.5% of families in Gads Hill are low income with an average income per family $12,014 compared to Chicago's median family income of $51,504.

- A single female care provider (mother, aunt, grandmother) heads 85% of the families Gads Hill serves.

MATH & READING SCORES FOR THE 2002-2003 SCHOOL YEAR

Many of the students that Gads Hill Center serves attend schools that are struggling to keep students up to grade level in reading and math, such as Whittier Elementary School in Pilsen and Chalmers Elementary School in North Lawndale.

% OF STUDENTS UP TO GRADE LEVEL

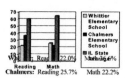

Reading   Math
Chalmers: Reading 25.7%   Math 22.2%

IL State Average: Reading 60.4%   Math 64.8%

1919 W. Cullerton St   Chicago, IL 60608   2653 W. Ogden Avenue   Chicago, IL 60608
Phone: (312) 226-0963   Fax: (312) 226-2248   Phone: (773) 521-1196   Fax: (773) 521-4793
www.gadshillcenter.org

(continued)

Figure 5.1. (continued)

HISTORY OF CLUB LEARN

☐ Club Learn comes out of a rich tradition based on the early settlement house programs, which were designed to promote love of learning and model democracy in action.

☐ Club Learn has doubled in size and has achieved measurable success since its inception in 1997.

CLUB LEARN

☐ Club Learn is a comprehensive, strength-based, child and youth development program that provides an increasing array of services for children ages 6-13.

☐ Club Learn serves 130 children: 105 children attend the Cullerton site in Pilsen and the remaining 25 attend the Ogden site in North Lawndale.

☐ Club Learn provides a safe and caring setting for children to be creative, do their homework, make friends, and grow.

☐ Besides enrichment clubs, the program's core components include:
   *Academic Assistance   *Positive Adult Mentors
   *Parental Involvement   *Technology Skills
   *Community Service   *Recreation & Sports
   *Cultural & Artistic Activities

☐ Club Learn's goals for the year are for all the students to excel in school, to complete all of their homework, to have their parents involved in their learning and to have excellent school attendance.

☐ Club Learn has many outstanding and long-term partnerships with the various communities and organizations of Chicago, including:
   *Chicago Public Library
   *Chicago Park District's Harrison & Douglas Park
   *Chicago Fire Department
   *12th District Police Department
   *Mexican Fine Arts Center Museum   *Union
   Boys & Girls Club of Chicago

PARENT COUNCIL MEETINGS

☐ Parental involvement is a critical piece of the program.

☐ Monthly parent council meetings are held with training on parent-selected topics, such as child safety, and crime prevention.

☐ With parents as partners, Gads Hill is able to reinforce the assets developed at the Center in the home.

EDUCATIONAL ENRICHMENT CLUBS

☐ At the heart of Club Learn are educational enrichment clubs designed around themes.

☐ The clubs meet five days per week for 30-90 minutes each day, are divided by age group and change themes every 14 weeks.

☐ The projects are determined by the group worker to provide hands-on experiential learning.

☐ The children engage in interactive learning through different mediums such as reading, writing, computers, and the Internet, arts and crafts, oral presentations, guest speakers/storytellers, and sharing through one on one relationships with peers and caring adults.

CLUB LEARN EXPO

☐ At the end of the 14 weeks in the educational enrichment program, each club presents their work at an exposition for parents, families and community members.

☐ The kids create interactive presentations that appeal to the other kids in Club Learn as well as regular displays of information.

CLUB LEARN BUDGET $427,997

☐ Club Learn is budgeting for roughly a $26,000 surplus. This money will be used for extra expenses.

Group Workers & Staff Salary $206,000
Food Cost $36,000
Field Trips & Supplies $27,000
Supporting Services $158,000

For more information on these or other programs contact Gads Hill Center

1919 W. Cullerton St   Chicago, IL 60608
Phone: (312) 226-0963   Fax: (312) 226-2248

2653 W. Ogden Avenue   Chicago, IL 60608
Phone: (773) 521-1196   Fax: (773) 521-4793

www.gadshillcenter.org

Source: Graphic by Tiffany France.

first-semester freshmen. However, analyzed from the perspective of situated learning, Tiffany's fact sheet might still be considered an individual project; it could have been produced, we argue, from a group of materials assembled in a textbook case study. While opportunities to produce fact sheets from data may take students beyond the basic composition pedagogy of writing essays about other essays, CCLCP aims to add the consequential element of participation that is frequently undervalued or missing from the conventional composition classroom. What we're after in CCLCP, is more than community-based writing; rather, we want students to ask how their writing might be of use in this new community of practice.

The curriculum for CCLCP's second course, English 161, created greater opportunities for students to become participants in communities of practice, both within their agencies and within the writing classroom. Through active participation, students learned how writing links, shapes, and limits action in a community of practice. If CCLCP students can produce various genres, they can, perhaps, more easily navigate the activity systems that circumscribe those genres. Students might even come to see the ways that genres represent a constituent structure of society, thus increasing their capacity for reproducing and challenging institutional power structures (Miller 1994). Genres are more than containers for information; they act as a nexus between the creator of text and the context in which the text will exist. CCLCP writing courses position students to witness firsthand how genre-based writing practices function as part of a larger social activity system. To see genres in this way—as a midpoint, but also as a catalyst—between individual and society suggests that rhetoric has a pivotal role in the engaged university. As Carolyn Miller suggests, genres support, "the practical need to marshal linguistic resources for the sake of social action" (1994, 71). This view of language and genre focuses on possibilities for creating knowledge rather than on definitions of service that depend on an unequal definition of helping others.

During the second semester, based on the partner's communication needs, students developed site-specific projects so that each student worked on a different project. Some students worked on feature stories; others worked on Web content; and still others created biographies of board members or profiles of community members. In addition, students planned and wrote a research paper based on the needs of their particular agency. Unlike the first semester, in which CCLCP teachers and community partners identified and designed two standard projects for the students before the semester began, all of the projects during CCLCP's second semester were designed specifically to fill an agency need.

Figure 5.2 is the feature story written by CCLCP student Jee Eun Nam for a newsletter published by The Resurrection Project (see agency descriptions in chapter 4, figure 4.1). Writing effectively requires intimate and ongoing

Figure 5.2. Feature Story for The Resurrection Project Newsletter.

Casa Puebla Homework Club: The Fruit Tree of the Community
By Jee Eun Nam

One afternoon last summer, the Rojas family visited their local library to get help with some schoolwork. Upon leaving, Ms. Rojas heard gunshots and she screamed to her children, "Get back inside!" Immediately Ms. Rojas's motherly instincts kicked in as she grabbed hold of her children and brought them to safety. Unfortunately, this traumatic experience has marked the local library as an unsafe place for the Rojas family.

Ms. Rojas is more than willing to be there for her kids and has been acting on the recommendation from her children's teachers to be actively involved in her children's schoolwork. However, Ms. Rojas, like many other parents in The Resurrection Project's (TRP) target communities face challenges that limit this participation. Ms. Rojas's knowledge of the English language is limited. Not only do parents in TRP's target communities face linguistic barriers, but they also face safety issues that, unfortunately, limit a child's access to resources such as public libraries and tutoring services.

Although these barriers existed, Ms. Rojas was creative and began a discussion with TRP about the possibility of creating a homework club in one of its recent residential development projects, Casa Puebla. Ms. Rojas, a tenant of Casa Puebla, began speaking with other parents at Casa Puebla about her idea and mobilized them to reach out to TRP to help create a solution to their issue.

The parents, with the help of Maria Arciniega, TRP's Property Manager, and Sergio Perez, a TRP staff member passionate about children, quickly rounded up resources and support to make the homework club happen.

Today, Sergio is the program coordinator and a tutor. He says that he couldn't have done it alone without the dedicated tutors. The homework club is supported by TRP, the parents of Casa Puebla, from a generous individual donor, and through a partnership with DePaul University's Steins Center. Cecilia Romero, a sophomore at DePaul and a community resident, explained that the most important attribute of this program is that it is focused on children and their academics. For Cecilia, her involvement is aligned with her personal goals. As an elementary education major, the program excites Cecilia. Cecilia appreciates the flexibility of this program because it challenges Cecilia to be a leader and learn about working with children. She says, "Every student is different, and needs a different approach to solving a problem."

Although the community has not been able to witness the long-term outcomes of this program, the initial success has been uplifting. The club has a dual purpose of helping children finish their homework and providing a safe after school environment. As an added bonus, the students are having

(continued)

Figure 5.2. (*continued*)

a good time, doing their homework of all things! The parents are thrilled that their children are in a healthy and safe environment. Ms. Rojas, one of the earliest and most passionate supporters of the club, has been able to personally witness the change this program has stirred in her son Ricardo. Ricardo is a bright first-grader who needed guidance and a little support. After joining the Casa Puebla Homework Club, his school grades have improved and his teacher is ecstatic with the results he has shown. Ricardo is also proud of his schoolwork and improvement.

People from different parts of the community are also noticing the positive change the club is instilling in the area. "This program is high in demand," praises Sergio and due to the popularity, an expansion of the program is currently being discussed. But three limiting factors are impeding the expansion; these include the amount of space, the number of volunteers and the need for additional funding. In total there are about 152 apartments in Casa Pueblo and this club is serving roughly one-third of the units. Because the club only began this January and is just a seedling, some components have not been established. The program still needs future partners and resources to stabilize a foundation. Committed tutors and volunteers are needed.

Various people are responding to the need. One of the first donors was an anonymous donor who donated over $1,000 in incentives for the students and tutors. They donated Bulls tickets to recognize the great job being done. Sergio says that the students "became so excited and energized" about the tickets. "That's all they've been talking about for a month," revealed Sergio.

It's has only been four months since the initiation of the Casa Puebla Homework Club and already the tree is bearing fruit. It is exciting to share the story of the families who are enjoying the sweet reward of their hard work and dedication.

participation within communities of practice, which implies active engagement in the everyday activities, processes, and undertakings of a particular agency (Wenger 1998). In her midterm essay written in March 2005, Jee Eun traced her increasing sense of participation. Just as Jee Eun had used a pivotal moment—Mrs. Rojas' experience with gunshots at the library—to construct the *Casa Puebla Homework Club* feature story, she used the same rhetorical strategy to argue for what she had learned thus far in CCLCP. Jee Eun wrote about a pivotal moment traveling alone to a café in Pilsen to conduct an interview. She characterized her short trip as a benchmark experience against which she could compare experiences from her first semester in the program. She explains:

"... walking toward The Jumping Bean, a café in Pilsen, at 8:45 PM, I was amazed at my bravery and solitude. Most people might think that this short walk from the Blue Line to The Jumping Bean is not a big enough experience to build leadership skills. . . . But after examining the process leading up to this experience, the development of leadership skills is evident. Stepping-stones in this process were my personal effort to gain familiarity with the neighborhood, actively reaching out and working with other community members . . . and having a keen sense of working with rhetoric and always asking who my audience is." (Midterm Essay, Spring, 2005)

Achieving the quality of participation Jee Eun desired depended on more than the ability to gather adequate amounts of information; it also depended on understanding what walking in the Pilsen neighborhood meant. Traveling to The Jumping Bean Café alone was particularly important to Jee Eun, because she felt a certain hypocrisy in working for The Resurrection Project, "yet feel[ing] unsafe in the very areas they're trying to promote." Jee Eun understands very well that this level of participation—becoming comfortable in a social context—contributes to her ability to write for her agency. Our point here is that experiences like Jee Eun's travels in Pilsen—experiences that depend on participation in everyday activities—are often discounted or undervalued as contributions to learning, while learning portable skills, like the parts of an argument, are overvalued (see the discussion of transferability in chapter 6).

Jee Eun reports that during her early days in CCLCP she saw writing skills as portable: give her a template and she will fill it in. "All I previously wanted and thought I needed was a model of a "good brochure." And then I would make a replica of it." Jee Eun described a process of increasing participation that led to an understanding of how the structure of a particular genre such as a brochure or feature story could be brought to life by her engagement with her partners at The Resurrection Project. What Jee Eun learned, we would say, is that genre can function as a mediating tool between structure and agency. In the classroom, students learn general design, formatting, and guidelines for various reified genres that included fact sheets, brochures, press releases, media kits, newsletters, and annual reports. However, to understand how genre contributes to social action, students must participate in the lived realities of their agencies. This sense of participation is crucial to learning; as argued in chapter 1, writing practices, when undertaken in particular situations, allow students to take hold of a sense of purpose that propels the writing forward.

Throughout the year, Jee Eun worked closely with Julio Guerrero, then at The Resurrection Project, who assigned Jee Eun the feature story assignment. She remembered an early interview with Julio about which she commented, "I didn't know how to initiate the conversation; I didn't even have the presence of mind to ask good follow-up questions." Returning to the story of her solo trip to The Jumping Bean Café, Jee Eun reported that when she left her interview she felt that she had grown and changed, "I know that I achieved the well-rounded experience I hoped to reach through interviewing several different people on *Casa Pueblo* Homework Club." When examined as a rhetorical construction, we see that Jee Eun has adopted a growth metaphor—"I used to be, but now I am"—to characterize her learning. She has used a rhetorical strategy to argue how she has changed over time and how different her abilities are now than they were before. For instance, she explained: "I thought rhetoric was the inborn skill of an eloquent person. . . . Now that I look back at it, I was so naïve to think that rhetoric was some abstract idea that I couldn't grasp." What might look like a thoughtful insight, a reflection, drawn directly from a person's experience is now seen as a carefully crafted rhetorical argument.

The "rhetorical process," Jee Eun Nam says, "is like a domino effect." No longer an abstract idea, the rhetorical process requires, as Jee Eun says, "a situational threshold." For her feature story, the situational threshold is, "the ongoing struggle for the parents of the Pilsen community to find a safe place where their kids will be able to get help with homework and hang out in a positive environment." Jee Eun's ability to connect a consequential situation with a writing project helps her to see genres as structures that enable action. Carolyn Miller argues that "rhetorical communities," or what Etienne Wenger calls "communities of practice" operate in part through genre "as the operational site of joint, reproducible social action, the nexus between private and public, singular and recurrent, micro and macro" (1994, 74). Jee Eun now sees her use of powerful words, her use of material from interviews, and her core focus for the feature story as a way, as we have argued, to advocate for a specific reality. Jee Eun's feature story, a genre designed to make a point through a personal story, aims to educate the community about the *Casa Pueblo* Homework Club. The CCLCP community-based writing projects, like the ones we illustrate here, were designed not only to encourage students to use genre to move back and forth between the classroom and the community, but also to move between lived participation and the portability of reified knowledge of writing.

We offer a caveat here that appears elsewhere in this book: it is not the physical movement to a community outside the university that creates a lived experience for students in CCLCP, but the rhetorical activity of advocating for a specific reality. The Chicago Civic Leadership Certificate Program has allowed us to make genre function the subject of study in our classroom along with topics such as rhetoric, civic engagement, and leadership. These samples of student writing provide a core product of the program, but, as you will see, they were not the only sources of data for our ongoing assessment activities.

The rest of the chapter focuses on assessment, initially through a cautionary note, followed by a report of our first foray into the deep waters of assessment.

Complicating Assessment

The Oxford English Dictionary defines the verb "assess" as follows: "to evaluate (a person or thing); to estimate (the quality, value, or extent of), to gauge or judge." But this definition is, according to the OED, a "transferred sense," taken from earlier uses of the word, when in the fifteenth century, it meant to evaluate the value of property in order to determine the amount of taxes to be paid by a person or by a community. This historical note offers a cautionary sidebar, suggesting that assessment can be used by others as an external tool to determine a program's value. Such a definition suggests, then, that assessment should provide a straightforward and objective analysis of whether CCLCP's goals were achieved. However, understanding the rhetorical nature of knowledge-making serves as a reminder that what might be portrayed as an objective analysis always involves rhetorical decisions. This lesson—that the making of knowledge is always a collaborative and constructivist activity—is the very same lesson that CCLCP is designed to teach students.

Chapter 1 introduced Keith W. Hoskin's study of writing and its role in the genesis of disciplinarity. Hoskin's examination of teaching and learning focused on a pivotal moment in the latter half of the eighteenth century when European universities moved from oral examination to the wide use of writing. Hoskin argued that writing played a dual role. The emerging focus on writing not only created new situations for learning, but it also created a way to evaluate and assess learning.

In this chapter, we return to Hoskin and to his article with Richard H. Macve on the history of accounting as a discipline (Hoskin 1993; Hoskin and Macve 1993). This brief, but important, detour explores the possible dangers of assessment if it is seen, not as a rhetorically driven activity, but as an objective add-on intended to determine CCLCP's learning outcomes according to the terms of others. Hoskin and Macve argue that accounting emerged as a discipline that depended on an increased use of writing. Accounting, they say, which in the mid-1800s provided a low-level system for bookkeeping, was seen as a supplement to daily business practices; it entered the mid-nineteenth century as a discipline that would exhibit a "shift in power-knowledge relations" (1993, 46). Through an historical analysis of accounting in the context of the growth of disciplines, Hoskin and Macve offer a way to understand the possible relationships between assessment and writing instruction. Can assessment function as an objective analysis of value? Or, is it as rhetorically charged as the student writing projects we reviewed earlier. We review Hoskin and Macve's argument in some detail to consider the role assessment will play in the Chicago Civic Leadership Certificate Program.

A major transformation in accounting occurred between the mid-1800s, when accounting was seen as "menial bookkeeping" and the mid-1900s, when it took on a critical role in a newly evolving business architecture, the hierarchically segmented corporation. In this new business context, managers of smaller units reported up the line to other managers who had greater responsibility for overseeing a larger group of units. Each of these smaller units used accounting to, as they say, "keep their books." The supervisory managers perched higher up the ladder were responsible for coordinating the information that flowed to their offices from the separate units below. The modern manager's capacity for coordinating this upward movement of information resulted in greater profits through higher productivity combined with lower costs. This transformation, Hoskin and Macve argue, illuminates the growth of the modern corporation. During this growth process management accounting moved from a mechanism for internal coordination of information to a mechanism for overseeing the massive growth that occurs in complex organizations that employ many thousands of individuals. These organizations must respond to equally large numbers of shareholders while sustaining their increasingly global reach. This rapid growth, occurring over a hundred year period, spurred the development of increasingly sophisticated accounting systems aimed at obtaining the "twin ideals of efficiency and effectiveness" (1993, 27).

The increasing acceleration and sophistication of financial accounting practices have, as Hoskins and Macve put it, "begun to penetrate the public sector, into the large-scale health, education, and government systems that are the hallmarks of all modernized states" (27). As such, accounting impacts assessment. Assessment in recent years has taken on the character of an educational audit—with the threat of punitive taxes—in national attempts to improve education through George Bush's highly controversial "No Child Left Behind" initiative. Universities and colleges undertake massive efforts to sustain their accreditation, which is monitored by agencies, who themselves, attempt to define appropriate ways to track learning and improvement. Standardized tests for college admission now require a writing sample, which redirects high school pedagogy. Federal grant agencies as well as private foundations struggle with how to ascertain that the funds they have distributed have had the promised impact. To understand these contemporary challenges, Hoskin and Macve look to historical precedents of accounting practices to consider how assessment came to be seen as an external add-on to educational practices.

One reading of the brief history above suggests that the changes in accounting were generated as a response to changing business practices. Hoskin and Macve propose a different explanation. What underlies these changes, they argue, can be attributed to a "disciplinary breakthrough" in the use of writing (28). We must, they argue, look beyond the apparent answers offered by technological change, at least as it is typically used to refer to simple improvements in the efficiency of machines used for data processing. What interests Hoskin and Macve are what they call "invisible technologies." Such human technologies include the ability to act on expert knowledge by culling objective measures that can be used, in turn, to articulate goals and standards, which can then be used as a predictive device to forecast future directions (28). Such practices are disciplinary practices.

Building on Michel Foucault's *Discipline and Punish*, Hoskin and Macve point out how such expert knowledge has a disciplinary function that "regulates and shapes" corporate strategy. Thus, disciplinary practices enact both power and knowledge. Going further, however, they locate the emergence of these disciplinary ways of knowing, not in the halls of modern businesses, but earlier, in the late-1700s when German, French, and Scottish research universities shifted from a dependence on oral examination to the use of writing. Writing became not only simultaneously regulative—through examination and through ranking—but also innovative as students used language in new ways to contribute to the growth of disciplinary knowledge (Hoskin 1993). We now see that the underlying force in the rise of accounting is not a technological advance in "keeping the books." Rather, the invisible advance is found in the higher-level activity of coordinating the multiple offices that contributed numerical representations of its work.

Through a fascinating genealogy, Hoskin and Macve track the educational experiences of those in the nineteenth century who had a key role in reshaping modern business (see Chandler 1977). Advances in hierarchical management and accounting had occurred in both manufacturing and the railroad. In a factory setting, Daniel Tyler, an army lieutenant with no business training, used a time and motion study to calculate the performance of workers to establish an appropriate salary. This time and motion study, Hoskin and Macve point out, predates, by fifty years, F. W. Taylor's better-known time and motion study (Hoskin and Macve 30). And, in a railroad setting, another Army officer, George Whistler, developed a line and staff system in which lower-level divisions, such as the transportation and machinery divisions, reported to a central manager. Neither Whistler nor Tyler had run businesses; what they had in common was the U.S. Military Academy at West Point, which they attended together in 1819. They were both students of Sylvanus Thayer, who had been sent to the École Polytechnique in France to research its new curriculum based on "writing, examination, and grading" (31). And, when Thayer returned, he enacted reforms at West Point that prefigured the management practices of coordinating the flow of information through the constant production of written reports.

Thus, Hoskin and Macve conclude that this disciplinary transformation can be characterized as grammocentric, by which they mean the knowledge and power relationships they studied depended on writing. Further, these relationships depended on calculability, which does more than "put a number on a performance; it puts a value on you" (32). Writing, and not numbers, then, is what lies behind accounting's regulative practices. The consequences of Hoskin and Macve's scholarship, however, quickly moves beyond the borders of possible subject matter for business school classes. The same invisible technology that lies behind accounting drives the broader activity of assessment with which we are concerned here.

Assessment, like accounting, depends on the two key features that emerge as modern disciplines develop in the research university: grammocentrism and calculability. On the one hand, assessment depends on the rhetorical construction of reality through language: surveys, essays, and tests; on the other hand, these language-based items are the key to a calculability that ascribes a particular value to them. But there's more. Assessment, like accounting, can be seen as a supplement, a dangerous supplement, to the core activity it aims to evaluate. The supplement is dangerous because it suggests that language is not a representation but rather a transparent window on reality; it "freezes meaning, it stops the flow of dialogue, it replaces living thought with dead ideas" (34). The calculability of assessment, that is, its ability to ascribe value, now takes on a greater role as a supplement. It now becomes central and its power to ascribe value makes enormous differences in the lives of children and college students, for whom grades and scores create or diminish opportunities.[3]

Hoskin and Macve point out how writing can be seen as "freezing" a more authentic speech, but here, in this project, we contrast the writing of assessment, so easily seen as a transparent supplement, with the community-based writing that offers a neo-sophistic rendering of public spaces. Once speech in ancient times, the writing now conducted in community-based settings offers a pragmatic response in these settings. The challenge for us, in assessing the Chicago Civic Leadership Program is to keep in mind how the largely invisible power-knowledge double bind described here can turn assessment from making knowledge to levying a tax. In other words, if others use externally generated, inappropriate calculations to evaluate CCLCP, perhaps through a decontextualized, skill-based test of CCLCP students' knowledge of grammar, we risk losing the opportunity of assessing the kind of learning and writing skills the program was designed to foster. The next section of the chapter outlines our strategy for program assessment, which began with the very challenging activity of articulating—in writing—what students would learn and developing a process for measuring that learning. This project is already in Hoskin and Macve's double bind—its work is both grammocentric and calculable. We use writing to construct our reality, and we are also responsible for calculating the results of our assessment activity.

Developing an Assessment Matrix

The assessment plan for the Chicago Civic Leadership Certificate Program came together at the same time as the curriculum for the first year's writing classes. The five-semester program focused on three areas: student learning, faculty development, and community partnership. This chapter focuses on assessment of student learning during the first year of the program. Evaluation of the two other very important aspects of the overall plan will be carried out as the project goes forward. Four broad purposes guided the assessment activity: First, we aimed to develop tools that could help us assess what students had learned in the CCLCP program. Second, we required a method for measuring student learning that could justify broader institutional support. Third, and perhaps more important, this assessment activity could be helpful in opening a space for conversation among our faculty, our community partners, university administrators, and potential funders. Finally, throughout the project, we considered assessment as research—that is, a way to make knowledge about how students learn to write and what students learn about civic engagement in the context of the CCLCP program. And as such, this assessment activity, itself, must be recognized as rhetorically situated writing.

The first task was to develop an assessment matrix that could identify what students would learn and how we would know if they had learned it. Higher education scholar, Barbara Holland, joined the CCLCP team as an assessment consultant. Her published guide, *Assessing Service-Learning and Civic Engagement: Principles and Techniques*, illustrated matrices that served as useful models (Gelmon, Holland, et al. 2001). Early in the planning process, Holland encouraged the difficult task of articulating learning outcomes. "Above and beyond the valuable assessment tool you will create," Holland wisely told us, "the collaborative process of producing nuanced criteria for measuring student learning will help you crystallize as a group the core mission, goals, and tensions of the program you are assessing." And she was right; our conversations about assessment were transformative. The design for teaching shaped assessment, but the reverse was also true. Working together to design the matrix (see figure 5.3) challenged our team's usual ability to work out differences and come to agreement. The following basic questions guided us as we proceeded to develop the matrices: "What is the aim of the assessment? Who wants or needs the assessment information? What resources are available to support the assessment? Who will conduct the assessment? How can one ensure that results are used?" (Gelmon, Holland et al. 2001, 5).

Figure 5.3. Assessment Matrix for Student Core Concepts

Chicago Civic Leadership Certificate Program
Student Assessment Matrix
English 160/161 Year 1

	We want to know . . . (Core Concepts)	And we will know by . . . (Key Indicators)	Method
Rhetoric and Academics	How do students apply the rhetorical dimensions of situation, genre, language, and consequences in the context of their work with community agencies?	Articulation and application of rhetoric to specific situations.	Analysis of cover letters, field notes, other writing samples, student focus groups.
	How does writing and learning in this program facilitate writing and learning in other university classes?	Articulation of how students' understanding of rhetoric has facilitated writing and learning in other university classes.	Course surveys; student focus group, field notes, and other student writing.
Community-Based Writing and Research	How effective are the documents created for the community partners?	Feedback from community partners. Feedback from faculty. Student self-evaluation of changes in writing skills.	Community partner focus group; faculty interviews; analysis of field notes and student surveys
	How do students apply communication methods and skills to conduct research within various discourse communities?	Feedback from community partners. Feedback from faculty. Student self-evaluation of changes in research skills.	Student focus group, analysis of field notes, and student surveys.

(continued)

	We want to know . . . (Core Concepts)	And we will know by . . . (Key Indicators)	Method
Community-Based Writing and Research (*continued*)	How do students adjust their communication styles to enable them to function optimally in both complex community-based and university-based situations?	Perceived change in ability to identify communication problems. Feedback from faculty. Feedback from community partners.	Student focus group, analysis of field notes, faculty interviews, community partner focus group
Civic Engagement	How do students value civic engagement for its impact on society at large?	Articulation of knowledge about community and public issues. Recognition of changes or possibilities for change in public life as a result of their actions. Understanding of community strengths, problems, resources. Identification of community assets and needs.	Analysis of research papers, student focus group
	How do students integrate their civic engagement activities with their academic, career, and personal goals?	Choice of a major that allows students to pursue civic engagement activities. Career decisions that allow students to pursue civic engagement activities. Extracurricular activities that allow students to pursue civic engagement activities.	Student surveys; student focus group
Leadership	How does participation in this program shape students' understanding of leadership	Articulation of a dynamic definition of leadership that includes examples. Articulation of how leadership skills have been demonstrated by community partners.	Student focus group, community partner focus group
	How does participation in this program shape students' ability to lead?	Sense of responsibility for solving problems and taking ownership of projects. Ability to collaborate with others and facilitate teamwork.	Faculty interviews, community partner focus groups, student focus groups

After exploring these questions in the specific context of CCLCP, a set of "core concepts" emerged to describe what students would learn: "key indicators" articulated measurable evidence of student impact and "methods" were identified that could be used to gather this evidence. The greatest challenge was in agreeing on the core concepts and determining how we would know that student learning had occurred. Once we settled on concepts and indicators, it was not difficult to identify the method by which information could be gathered about that concept.[4]

Let's take a close look at the first core concept in the matrix, "civic engagement," which, in the context of the engaged university, refers to the collaborative making of knowledge with those outside the university. Further, civic engagement focuses on partnership and on building reciprocal partner-university relationships. Considering what students might learn about "civic engagement" opened up a variety of questions that clarified this core concept. As the second column of the matrix indicates, we formulated two questions that would allow us to explore civic engagement. We asked: "How do students value civic engagement for its impact on society at large?" And, we asked: "How do students integrate their civic engagement activities with their academic, career, and personal goals?" These questions grew directly out of the program's commitment to situated writing and learning. The first question considers how students understand the impact of civic engagement on society, and the second question asks whether students' sense of civic engagement had had an impact on their academic or career goals. The next step was to complete the sentence, "We will know by . . ." As displayed in the matrix, we will know that students have come to value civic engagement for its impact on society at large if students can, for instance, articulate what they know about community and public issues. We would also know that students value civic engagement's public impact if they see possibilities for change that might result from their work with community agencies.

Once the core concepts were articulated and key indicators for them identified, it was easier to decide what methods might help identify student learning. These methods for identifying what students learn about each of the four core concepts would come from several sources, as figure 5.3 suggests. The most obvious source was writing produced by the students. In addition to the written documents produced for community partners, students had written cover letters to their teachers that analyzed their decisions about key rhetorical issues. As discussed earlier in this chapter, and in chapter 4 as well, students used Learning Record Online (LRO) to produce field notes that would contribute to argumentative essays, in which students formulated what they had learned during the semester. In an example below, the material included in LRO provides data for a pilot discourse analysis that allows the CCLCP team to pose questions about particular aspects of the core concepts. The assessment plan also included focus groups with both students and community partners, which Barbara Holland conducted. She planned to ask a series of questions based on the assessment matrix that would give participants a chance to speak honestly about the program in a confidential setting. Holland also interviewed the instructors in the program during her site visits. Surveys that had been used for years in the composition program were adapted, by adding a few additional questions, for use with the CCLCP students. This allowed for broad comparisons with students in other UIC writing classes. In addition, a survey was designed exclusively for use in the CCLCP program that would allow students to comment confidentially on their experience in the program. Finally, a comparative study of research papers written by CCLCP and mainstream students was carried out (Feldman et al. 2006).

Conducting Assessment

The usefulness of the matrix became obvious as we looked over the work of the students at various points in the semester. Its broad scope helped see beyond our usual focus on student products and allowed us to choose the specific features of our program that should be evaluated. In the sections that follow, we explore two questions drawn from the core concepts in our student learning matrix:

Question 1: How does participation in the Chicago Civic Leadership Certificate Program shape the students' understanding of writing in community-based settings?

Question 2: How does participation in the Chicago Civic Leadership Certificate Program shape students' understanding of leadership?

Writing in community-based settings. All writing classes in the First-Year Writing Program at UIC are designed to support situated writing. However, the CCLCP classes have the marked advantage of real-time participation in communities of practice with agency partners, whereas students in conventional writing classes use case-study materials. These differences prompted us to revise a survey first developed for use in all the First-Year Writing Program courses. This portion of the evaluation focused on whether CCLCP students' perceptions of what they had learned by writing for community agencies differed from the students whose regular writing classes had focused on case studies. The survey asks questions about demographics, classroom activities, and perceived improvement. The results reported below focus on perceived improvement. Early in the survey, students answer a set of questions that asks them to indicate on a scale of one to five how easy or how difficult they perceived specific activities were before taking English 160. Near the end of the survey, students are asked how easy or difficult the same set of activities seemed after taking English 160. The results from these two sets of responses are compared for the percent of change in students who perceived that a particular activity was "not difficult" after taking English 160. Figure 5.4 summarizes the results for students in regular UIC classes ("reg") and students in the CCLCP class.[5]

Figure 5.4. English 160 Survey—Percent Change in "Not Difficult" Responses

Percent Change in "Not Difficult" Responses Before and After Taking English 160 at UIC	REG (%)	CCLCP (%)
Writing in a variety of genres	17%	20%
Imagining various situations in which writing might take place	12%	23%
Reading texts in various genres	12%	17%
Recognizing that writing has consequences beyond receiving a grade	15%	37%
Discussing an important academic or social issue with others outside of class	7%	20%
Discussing an important academic or social issue in other classes	9%	13%
Improving grammar	19%	13%
Working together in small groups	8%	3%
Responding to another student's writing	18%	27%
Learning to read carefully	15%	17%
Getting involved in a community or neighborhood and connecting that experience to academic goals	14%	37%
Writing in a setting outside of school, such as a community agency or a workplace	18%	50%
Using writing skills in a leadership role outside an academic situation	16%	43%
Number of students enrolled in English 160	1780	37
Number of students who took the survey	1275	30

Source: First-Year Writing Program, University of Illinois at Chicago.

While these results are not statistically significant and can only be discussed as trends, they suggest that students in the regular and CCLCP classes share similar perceptions about some activities, however, other activities produced divergent perceptions of learning. If we compare the responses from both groups—Reg versus CCLCP—with a difference of 10 percentage points or less (an arbitrary choice that merely helps to illuminate the trends), we see that students in both groups reported the following activities less difficult after taking English 161: writing in a variety of genres, reading texts in a variety of genres, improving grammar, working together in small groups, and learning to read carefully. As we explained above, writing in a variety of genres was not unique to the CCLCP classes; rather, this activity reflects the conceptual framework that drives all first-year writing classes at UIC.

The activities students perceived to be less difficult at the end of the semester in the CCLCP classes (with a difference of greater than 10 percentage points) seemed to emerge from the unique experiences offered through their community-based writing experiences. These activities included:

- imagining various situations in which writing might take place;
- recognizing that writing has consequences beyond receiving a grade;
- discussing important academic or social issues with others outside of class or in other classes;
- responding to another student's writing;
- getting involved in a community or neighborhood and connecting that experience to academic goals;
- writing in a setting outside of school, such as a community agency or a workplace; using writing skills in a leadership role outside an academic situation.

Although we must be cautious about the strength of these findings, the activities listed above that CCLCP students reported "less difficult" suggest that the students, themselves, perceive some important changes in their understanding of the rhetorical features of community-based writing situations. We are aware, of course, that this is one narrow set of data from a single semester's work. Ideally, subsequent assessment activities over several years that draw on other sources of data, perhaps from student focus groups or from student presentations, writing samples, and from Learning Record Online, will contribute to a richer picture of CCLCP student learning outcomes.

Understanding leadership. This section reports on preliminary attempts to assess what CCLCP students learned about leadership. Our approach, which focuses on what students say they learned about leadership, is tentative and preliminary. First, we should explain that we designed the Chicago Civic Leadership Certificate Program with a somewhat unique understanding of leadership. Leadership, in this program, is conceptualized as rhetorically infused action in the lived reality of a particular situation. Leadership neither consists solely of transactions or exchanges, nor does it require a top-down mode of activity; instead leadership involves the negotiation of meaning. Meaning must be negotiated not in isolation but as a part of "being together, living meaningfully, developing a satisfying identity, and altogether being human" (Wenger 1998). This dynamic vision of leadership asks students to identify examples of leadership around them, particularly among their community partners. Leadership also contributes to a sense of teamwork and of responsibility for solving problems in complex contexts. More important, it asks students to recognize that it is possible to affect others and be affected (Wenger 53). The core concept of leadership described in the assessment matrix (see figure 5.3), offers a somewhat simplified version of this very complicated human activity.

An initial reading of midterm and final argumentative essays suggested that students were developing interesting but distinctive views of leadership. We undertook an exploratory analysis aided by a computer-based discourse analysis tool to produce a fine-grained analysis of specific written comments made by the students. The initial corpus for this pilot project included LRO midterm and final essays for eight students, which were read and reread in order to establish an initial coding scheme. This scheme was further refined and narrowed to those categories that seemed to be coded reliably.[6] Figure 5.5 illustrates the seven indicators for leadership used in the analysis with an explanation of the indicator and an example.

The corpus of data was then narrowed to essays written by three students. Three essays from each student were read: an LRO midterm essay from fall 2004, an LRO final essay from fall 2004; and a midterm essay from spring 2005. The unit for coding was a coherent, self-contained claim or anecdote, but occasionally a particularly rich passage was given two different codes. To organize the coded units of discourse, we used TAMs Analyzer, an open source software package available for Macintosh computers. This discourse analysis program facilitated downloading the units of discourse into Excel spreadsheets for further analysis. It is critical to remember that qualitative software does not analyze data; it simply manages information and helps researchers make connections across large amounts of written or transcribed materials.

It is also important to remember Keith W. Hoskin and Richard H. Macve's cautions about assessment, which suggest that the analysis conducted here is also a rhetorical construction. As we said earlier, assessment, like any rendering of reality through language, traps us in the double bind of grammocentrism and calculability. Grammocentrism reminds us that the leadership analyses of student writing are themselves constructed in writing. Calculability reminds us that data on student perceptions of leadership might, in the end, become objectified "truths" about this data. With these cautions in mind, the analysis constituted a preliminary foray into discourse analysis that could suggest further research on student perceptions of leadership.

Based on the units of coded discourse, leadership profiles were developed for each student. Preliminary data suggests that the three students, Meera, Pam, and Toni (all pseudonyms) view leadership quite differently. The most striking difference exists between Meera and Toni. Meera sees leadership in terms of "negotiating complexity," in which, according to the leadership indicators, the student "accounts for the complex processes and ideologies of various communities of practice that both constrain and enable action." Toni, on the other had, sees leadership as a set of "individually derived skills and personal characteristics."

Figure 5.5. Content Analysis Codes for Leadership

Indicators of Leadership Capacity	Explanation of Indicator	Example
Negotiating Complexity	Student demonstrates understanding of leadership that accounts for the complex processes and ideologies of various communities of practice that both constrain and enable action.	Student explicitly talks about the challenges of learning to juggle the writing expectations for the academy and for their agency.
Engaging Social Issues	Student demonstrates engagement with social issues and arguments within public discourse. Engagement includes the intellectual work of thinking through "problems" and physical work (lobbying, passing out flyers, writing proposals, etc.).	Student discusses reading the newspaper or visiting a local art installation to learn more about policy changes to Chicago public housing.
Problem Solving	Student demonstrates the application of classroom and community-based learning to social issues and problems. And, student demonstrates the ability to contend with personal and interpersonal challenges, conflicts, and problems.	Student discusses various ways that their agency attempts to address an issue and the effectiveness and the problems with their agency's work.
Collaboration/ Teamwork	Students demonstrate a capacity for collaborating with peers, instructors, agency supervisors, and others.	Student discusses working closely with a peer to complete a collaborative project for their agency, detailing challenges, procedures, and lessons learned.
Social Definition of Leadership	Students define leadership as situational, contextual, and social.	Student discusses agency leadership in terms of their effective collaboration with constituents and institutions to better connect individuals with resources.
Individual Definition of Leadership	Students define leadership as individually derived skills and personal characteristics.	Student identifies themselves as a leader based on increased confidence and ability to speak in front of groups about a civic issue.
Project Ownership	Students articulate increased ownership of projects and learning experiences.	Student discusses an instance in which they take responsibility over completing their agency or school projects.

Source: Candice Rai and Megan Marie.

For Meera, leadership means being able to account for the complexities she finds at her partner agencies. Most of her comments fall into the "negotiating complexity" category and illustrate situations in which action is both enabled and constrained. She wrote:

> As I became more aware of problems with public housing, I seemed to see them everywhere. The most obvious example is UIC itself. UIC's position in Chicago is one of contradiction. Its placement in the city was a major disruption in the community it now serves. How can we reconcile this idea of service with the destruction the campus caused?

Meera also suggests that leadership requires engaging with social issues by thinking through problems. In response to the crisis of public housing in Chicago, Meera comments:

> It is not enough to simply help feed people or find better housing. There must be deep change to the underlying social structure of a society that allows its citizens to go without food and shelter. Only by dealing with public housing on several levels is recovery possible.

Project ownership was a feature of leadership that each of the three students argued for in multiple comments. Meera wrote about her organizational skills:

> Not until the end of the semester did I feel that I had a system. . . . Knowing I would generally have to write up an observation or cover letter, I began to take mental notes about what I was doing. At home I kept track of all the e-mails and phone calls I was making. . . . Keeping track of not only what I was learning, but how, has helped me stay focused and in control.

Project ownership, however, meant more to Meera than being organized. She began to feel a sense of involvement in her work for Latinos United, "When creating documents for my agency, I used my previous knowledge to decide what information deserved priority. It helped me to understand what the public needs to know about Latinos United, because just a few short weeks ago, I knew nothing about them."

A major theme throughout Pam's essays centered on her personal growth throughout the program. She saw project ownership as the ability to connect to the work of the CCLCP program,

> Last semester, I did not completely understand the work CCLCP wanted me to complete. . . . However, soon after my LRO midterm, I began working more closely with the CCLCP program and Latinos

United. I also began taking an interest in the work of other not-for-profit agencies. I suddenly realized that CCLCP covers topics that are very relevant in my life and interesting at the same time.

Pam's interest in negotiating complexity grew out of class readings and the work she conducted with her agency,

The readings fascinated me. . . . I have become very interested in rhetoric, (logical) arguments, and especially in the people affected by both community discourse and the new urbanism. I now feel comfortable with conducting my very own arguments on such matters, for . . . . I have contemplated both sides of such issues.

Although Pam does not define leadership as an individual activity, we can see from her comments that she organizes her thoughts about negotiating practices and project ownership through a lens of personal growth.

Toni, like Pam and Meera, comments frequently on project ownership, but for Toni project ownership is closely tied to a highly individual definition of leadership. "A leader," Toni explains, "is someone who excels in particular subjects in school, rallies the team and encourages teammates to do better, and to lead the way in ideas or fashion, not caring what everybody else thinks." While she discusses the importance of collaborating with others frequently, she often sees team-oriented experiences through the lens of her own leadership abilities.

I have learned how to stand up for myself through the difficulties of working with my agency. I had to negotiate meeting times, make a clear point while still being respectful. . . . I believe that during times of challenge and hardship people who are leaders step up and take action.

Toni articulates a strong sense of ownership for her projects.

I learned that working and writing for my agency was not as easy as it sounded. I always knew I was a good writer; it just takes me many drafts and a lot of editing to make my papers sound the way I want them. I sit at my computer for hours at a time, because I know I am doing something this agency needs and they are relying on me to get their message out into the community.

Toni also explains how decisions must take into account her position in a particular community. For instance, "I had to develop a balance between writing for the UIC academic community versus writing for an agency in Pilsen." Toni remembered making a change in a document to remove material that reflected negatively on the Pilsen community. She commented: "If the brochure had solely been for a grade, I could have incorporated those negative statistics and it wouldn't have mattered. Because this was a document created for our agency, we had to be careful in our choice of words." Toni's writing project, in this case, helped her to see the complexities of writing in a community-based setting.

One begins to see that important questions about leadership emerge, even in this small sample and preliminary analysis. Why, for instance, did all three students say so little in their LRO essays about collaboration when students often worked in teams on writing projects at their community agencies? Or, would Pam's highly individual view of leadership shift toward a more social definition of leadership after more time in the program? We'd like to know whether a larger group of students could tell us more about the relationship between collaboration and leadership. How do students' understanding of leadership grow over the two-and-a-half years, or through the five courses that comprise this certificate program? What sorts of projects will students undertake as part of their capstone course or as part of their work as interns? How will these projects signal new understandings about leadership?

The two assessment activities we discuss here represent the start of a long and complex process of exploring both learning outcomes and the viability of the Chicago Civic Leadership Certificate Program. Continued analysis of a wide range of data will provide feedback about how instruction can be improved, how support can be provided for future groups of students, and how the tools of assessment, themselves, can be improved. In the context of a research university, such analysis demonstrates the close connections between making knowledge and teaching. Further, the lessons learned about the importance of situated writing help argue against assessment tools that are "added on" to instruction as a "tax" on learning.

Perhaps the most important outcome of assessment has to do with its impact on the institution in which it is situated. CCLCP offered an opportunity to redesign first-year classes to demonstrate a richer version of situated writing than was possible in conventional classrooms. In addition, this program helped illustrate a unique way to connect the work of first-year writing courses with general education courses, in this case, courses in urban planning. Finally, this assessment project illustrates a certain kind of engaged scholarship. Although this chapter did not focus on the collaborative work conducted between the community partners and the first-year writing instructors, this area, too, offers an important opportunity for assessment research on teaching and learning in community-based settings. Most important, such research identifies student writing as an important site in the engaged university.

Chapter 6

———⟫•⟪———

Teaching the Teachers

"What is so wrong," Patrick Shannon cried out in frustration, "with asking students to read essays and write about them?" Patrick, who had just begun his studies as a PhD student in the English department, found himself in a course, English 555, for new teaching assistants.[1] It seemed to him appropriate, even compelling, to provide for his students the very same opportunities he longed for as a graduate student. He would approach teaching in the way he had been taught: students would read important works and write essays in response to them. What could possibly be wrong with that?

In this chapter, I examine how the training of graduate student teaching assistants changes when a first-year writing program adopts a pedagogy based on engaged scholarship and situated writing. We begin, in English 555, by examining how the first-year writing syllabus constitutes a genre. Like all situated social practices, we examine the context in which the syllabus is written and anticipate the consequences of particular textual choices. However, one cannot propose change for writing instruction without responding to the ongoing debate among composition and rhetoric faculty who argue for abolishing the freshman writing requirement and offering these courses as electives. The purpose of this book, as I have said throughout, is to create instructional contexts that make writing matter. In the next section of this chapter, I describe writing projects designed by two graduate students that build on plausible, if imaginary, situations in which students feel that they are embedded in consequential situations. I conclude with a manifesto written by Jennifer Bryant as a graduate student in English 555 that articulates the swirl of complex issues she felt as she participated in the seminar and prepared to teach writing at UIC. Teaching new graduate students—especially those who hope to join the professoriate— to design writing instruction becomes a critical institutional activity that has an

163

enormous impact on English studies as a discipline, on PhD programs, on undergraduate education, and on the shape of the engaged university.

Patrick Shannon—along with fifteen other graduate students with a wide array of expectations for the first-year writing classroom—was enrolled in English 555: Teaching College Writing. Participants in this semester-long course will prepare for teaching by planning detailed syllabi, tracing the recent history of first-year writing instruction, learning about contemporary trends in rhetorical theory, tutoring in the Writing Center, and teaching for several weeks in a mentor's class. Sometimes these newcomers arrive at graduate school having taught literature in high school, or they may have already taught first-year writing classes at another college or university. They typically report having had little preparation for their teaching. Some worked from model syllabi that focused on writing processes; others came from programs that focused on teaching particular modes as students wrote essays in response to other essays. Several graduate students had never taken first-year writing classes, having been exempted from them as a reward for their success at academic writing.

The group's experience as writers varied widely: some reported a relatively narrow profile of academic and personal writing—papers, letters to friends and family, and personal journals; others had extensive experience with workplace writing—employee reviews, computer documentation, and newsletters. One student was excited about a piece to be published in the "Chicken Soup for the Soul" books. Others had published a smattering of poems and short stories. A few of these graduate students had returned to school after working as journalists or freelance writers and had produced feature stories, opinion pieces and various articles, or had edited books. One graduate student had founded a local 'zine for mothers and another had worked in marketing, writing press releases. When, during a "round the room" set of introductions, a student reported that she had been writing summaries of architectural and engineering projects, another student shouted out across the room: "That'll send you right back to graduate school!" She responded definitively, "Yup, that'll do it."

Writing About Essays

Even with these diverse experiences, students arrive at the first class session of English 555 with an intuitive sense that the writing of essays will be the unquestioned genre of the first-year writing class. When I ask the graduate students to imagine a plan for the first writing course they will teach at UIC they begin, typically, by compiling a list of readings around a particular theme. For instance, a graduate student who wants to design a course around the theme of social justice might begin by identifying readings such as Plato's *Republic*, Nietzsche's *Beyond Good and Evil*, Mary Wollstonecraft's *A Vindication of the Rights of Women*, and Richard Wright's *Native Son*. Here's what a portion of such a syllabus might look like.

Figure 6.1. Readings-Based Syllabus

Class 1: Introduction: What is Justice?
Class 2: *Republic*, Discuss Book 1
Class 3: *Republic*, Discuss Books II and III
Class 4: *Republic*, Discuss Books VIII, IX, and X
Class 5: *Beyond Good and Evil*, Discuss 1–76
Class 6: *Beyond Good and Evil*, Discuss 77–170
Class 7: *Beyond Good and Evil*, Discuss 171–246
Class 8: Writing Workshop: Plato and Nietzche Draft Due
Class 9: Paper #1: Plato and Nietzsche

   Such a readings-based syllabus is seen by these students as shorthand for the way classes should be conducted; it lists the readings for each class meeting indicating when papers are due and provides a workshop to go over drafts. Each class focuses on the reading of a particular text and the day's activity is listed simply as class discussion. Other dates indicate when drafts for essays based on the reading are due and when the final essay must be turned in. This syllabus articulates a comfortable approach to writing instruction that validates and complements these graduate students' work in English studies. New graduate students, embedded as they are in a disciplinary context that drives their own desire to read and write specific sorts of texts, transfer those expectations to their future writing classroom. Student writing will emerge effortlessly, they imagine, from classroom discussions; writing will be learned largely through reading and discussion, just as they learned to write, or at least just as they *remember* learning to write.
   Designing a syllabus that makes writing matter in a public or broader academic context turns this sort of readings-based syllabus on its head. It begins not by responding to texts but by examining a plausible situation that calls for writing. In the syllabus above, the ideas in the readings drive the writing. The genre of the source texts is unquestioned, leaving the content for the class's primary focus. Rather, the writing classes I ask graduate students to design focus extensively on genre, not as a rigid form but as a link to a particular situation.

Thus, the writer's embeddedness in a specific situation—not the ideas contained in the readings—drives the writing.

My argument for making writing matter, however, should not be mistaken for an argument against reading important texts central to humanistic thought. Nor should it be taken as an argument that students must leave the classroom as they do in the Chicago Civic Leadership Certificate Program (see chapters 4 and 5). Some of the most exciting learning takes place when student imagine themselves in a liminal space defined by a rich set of case materials. We can imagine a classroom project using the same texts in the readings-based syllabus above, in which students select a text for Chicago's "One Book, One Chicago" reading initiative. Let's consider the improbable choice of Nietzsche's *Beyond Good and Evil*. Even if we have trouble imagining that Chicagoans would read portions of this challenging philosophical work, the enthusiastic student who wants to argue for Nietzsche will think differently about the project when seeing him or herself embedded in a particular situation. Instead of explicating Nietzsche to the teacher-audience, the student will write a proposal to the panel of judges who will choose the book that all Chicagoans will read. Nietzsche's arguments about how we should live our lives and how we become who we are must now be cast in the context of issues Chicagoans think about daily. Perhaps this student will connect Nietzsche's work to recent debates about smoking bans in public spaces. Or, perhaps the writer will examine an individual's personal decision to smoke and one's responsibility for others' health and safety. Situating writing projects in specific, local contexts changes how students see writing. For this student, in this context, writing becomes a way to "participate in" a situation rather than "write about" a text, thus, teaching the larger lesson that all texts—even classroom assignments are situated and shaped in specific contexts.

The genre of the readings-based syllabus provides an emblem for the pedagogy of the privatized, teacher-centered classroom. When graduate students imagine this readings-based writing course, they are functioning, as James Crosswhite suggests, as "literaturized selves" who participate in a rhetorical community in which one studies texts, often canonical fiction and criticism, and writes about them as a way to explore the values or meanings suggested by the texts (1996). Graduate students who enter English 555 as Crosswhite's literaturized selves frequently ponder whether or not writing can, in fact, be taught. They imagine that writing is a talent: either you have it or you don't. Such assumptions support a classroom context in which the teacher functions as a brilliant muse who inspires successful writing through the discussion of important texts and the ideas they contain. If participants of English 555, as students with a long record of successful scholarship in the humanities, regard their own writing ability as a talent, and if they imagine that their own writing emerges from the humanistic Zeitgeist of the essential creative self, then being a teacher would mean reproducing that mysterious energy at the front of the classroom—largely through the discussion of important texts and the ideas they convey. Further, these same graduate students walk from English 555 to graduate seminars on critical theory where faculty members teach as muses, yet, at the same time, through discussions of critical theory, deny the essential self while promoting the contingency of language. Woven through the fabric of the English department, these contradictory messages coexist, challenging future writing teachers to examine their own assumptions and practices as they join a discourse community that asks them to become both teachers and scholars.

The Syllabus as Genre

What happens when graduate students begin to consider the role of genre in their own writing and in the writing projects they design for their first-year students? In response to an early assignment, participants in English 555 had posted electronic responses to Anis Bawarshi's *College English* article, "The Genre Function," which reevaluates Foucault's author function and promotes genre as a way to function as part of a social sphere (2000). Writers position themselves within genres to "negotiate . . . and articulate . . . desires as recognizable, meaningful, consequential actions" (2003, 145). Peter Koval, poet and PhD student responds to Bawarshi's claim as a poet who is unwilling, as he sees it, to immediately and irrevocably dispense with notions of voice and style in favor of Barwarshi's argument for the dominance of genre. Koval, immersed in the disciplinary work of poetry, can easily see how an oversimplified view of genre would squash important differences in the two poems he reproduces for English 555's consideration (see figure 6.2).

Koval knows, as a poet, that an oversimplified genre classification of both of these poems will land them in one container, that of the lyric poem. The more interesting subtlety, for him, is found in what he calls "voice" or "style." While focused intently on *interpretation*, that is, on a close reading of the two poems, Koval wonders how one could teach a student to "use the lyric poem as a means of communication." And, even though he creates an opposition between a too-literal definition of genre on the one hand and, on the other, an author-centered view of voice and style, we can find a hint in his "means of communication" question at the social motive that Bawarshi is after.

In a response the next day, Jack Arquette picks up on the notion of function, cautioning Peter that it's not the core identity of the poet that seems important but the "author's voice function" (see figure 6.3). Arquette's meta-analytic comment also recognizes a commitment to a literary frame of reference and that the work of English 555 might mean progressing to "the mind of the writer," and not that of the critic. This pair of e-mail responses, Arquette hints, does just what literature graduate students are expected to do: respond to

Figure 6.2. Blackboard Response to Reading on Genre

Date: Fri Aug 27, 2004 3:14 am
Author: Peter Koval <pkoval3@uic.edu>
Subject: Re: Genre Function in Bawarshi

While I think that genre theory has good practical applications for helping students understand effective rhetorical strategies for work in their own disciplines, I still feel that the theory may be a bit reductive. Let me give an example. Below I will reproduce Jean Valentine's poem "Mare and Newborn Foal" and a portion from section XII of Yannis Ritsos's poem "Carnal Word":

Mare and Newborn Foal
When you die
there are bales of hay
heaped high in space
mean while
with my tongue
I draw the black straw
out of you
mean while
with your tongue
you draw the black straw out of me.

From "Carnal Word"
. . . But in your dancing, you do not hear me. Well then, duration,
is a whirlwind, life is cyclical, it has no ending. Last night
the horsemen passed by. Naked girls on the horses' rumps;
    perhaps this is why the wild geese were screaming in the bell tower. We did not hear them
as the horses' hoofs sank in our sleep. Today before your door
you found a silver horseshoe. You hung it above the lintel. My luck—you shout—
my luck—you shout, and dance. . . .

I use these as examples because they fit into the same genre: lyric poem, or much more specifically contemporary free verse lyric poem involving strong horse imagery. Suppose, however, that one wants to teach a student how to effectively use the lyric poem as a means of communication. Both of these fit the bill; however, they are entirely different. Both are effective, but in entirely different ways. It would seem that the "author-function" cannot be ignored. "Jean Valentine poem" is different from "Yannis Ritsos poem" even if the genres are the same. Rather than constructing an assignment that asks the student to examine the rhetoric of the lyric poem, wouldn't it be more effective to ask the student how Valentine and Ritsos specifically differ stylistically and in voice? Any thoughts? (Reply) important texts from a critical perspective. Yet these graduate students will not only function in the realm of ideas. They know, at some level, that these ideas will be put into action designing syllabi for a writing class.

What Bawarshi brings to the challenge of refiguring writing instruction is a way to recalibrate our commitment to Foucault's author function. The genre function, Bawarshi claims, offers a broader and more useful discursive construct that can be applied to contexts for student writing. In the author function, as Foucault explains, ". . . the essential basis of this writing is not the exalted emotions related to the act of composition, or the insertion of a subject into language. Rather, it is primarily concerned with creating an opening where the

Figure 6.3. Blackboard Response to Reading on Genre

Current Forum: Week 2 Posting

Read 49 times

Date: Sat Aug 28, 2004 11:56 am

Author: Jack Arquette <jarquett2@uic.edu>

Subject: Re: Genre Function in Bawarshi

Interesting that you should bring into focus two fictional genres in the effort to understand more completely Bawarshi's assertion. I think, however, that the question doesn't lie in the "Jean Valentine"-ness of the poem, but rather in the author's voice function. (By this I mean that the "Jean Valentine"-ness is a secondary composite identity, not particularly the "author-voice" functional identity.)

In the context of the genre argument, I think it's still most important to assert their "lyrical poem"-ness, but more individually, to recognize the author-voice function. So it seems you would have a point : that it *is* important to stress their differences stylistically in an effort to locate the author-voice. I think this has a place in Bawarshi's schema, but I also agree with you that it can become too easily obscured in this effort to "genre-ize" pieces of writing.

I guess that's my biggest complaint, too. The emphasis is on identification of genre, use of genre, and adaptation of genre, but for us literature folks, that seems counterintuitive. From the literature standpoint, it seems easiest for us to categorize per genre (this is an epistolary novel, *that* is a one-act play) and then, secondarily identify difference and analyze. But maybe that's what this 555 is about, eh? Learning to drop the shackles of our traditional literary selves and progress to the mind of the writer—not critic.

(Reply)

writing subject endlessly disappears" (Foucault 1993, 116). As the process and momentary excitement of writing disappears, we are left not with the writer but with an "author." The status of the work "and its manner of reception are regulated by the culture in which it circulates" (1993, 123). The author occupies a subject position that stands apart from the usual spaces in which literary works are valued as a commodity. In the genre function, Bawarshi pleads, we can be "all 'authors' and 'writers' alike." Our focus should concern how texts emerge from social situations and how they have effects on those situations. Beyond this social function in which genres help us know how to behave and write in particular situations, genres have an epistemological function that helps us shape and thereby represent our worlds (Bawarshi 2003).

Let's return to the English 555 classroom: I had handed out an example of the sort of syllabi produced in English 555 and watched while the graduate students leafed through the document. Patrick leaned forward, hunched over his desk, rapidly paging through the document, shaking his head from side to side. I asked, "What's wrong, Patrick?"

His voice quivered as he tried to disguise his anger and anxiety, "Do our syllabi really have to be fifteen-page tomes like these? I want my students to see me as creative and spontaneous, not a drudge following pages and pages of specifications." Patrick's plea locates him in the cultural space of a readings-based, essayistic pedagogy, which I argue against in English 555. The syllabus illustrated above with its list of readings on social justice provides a textual and generic analog for the pedagogy that Patrick desires to enact (see figure 6.1). The social justice, reading-centered syllabus that typifies Patrick's wished-for pedagogical approach, functions as what Carolyn R. Miller calls a "cultural artifact." In her 1984 landmark article, "Genre as Social Action," she noted that for students, "genres serve as keys to understanding how to participate in the actions of a community" (1984, 165). And, she noted, "the failure to understand genre as social action afflicts the typical first-year college writing program" by teaching students to create texts that "fit certain formal requirements (67). The course syllabus is also a text produced by first-year writing programs, and it illustrates how a writing class's goals are social actions.

The first-year writing syllabus, as a genre, functions at a midlevel between a cultural construction on the one hand and a set of regulative rules on the other. As Miller suggests, it embodies a "system of actions and interactions" that function in specific social contexts but that also function to reproduce recurrent or repeated functions (1984, 70). The most prominent activity in the readings-based syllabus is the discussion of particular readings. The sparse, readings-based syllabus assumes that the connection between the reading of essays and the writing of essays will be transmitted by the teacher, through discussion. The classroom designed around a deeply contextual view of writing in which students see themselves embedded in a social situation, will require a syllabus constructed specifically to carry out this social function. Students in the writing-centered, activity-based classroom will complete several writing projects that depend on a particular rhetorical problem presented by a particular situation. These projects, emerging as they do out of social situations, will require analysis of the genre requirements of that particular situation (Bawarshi 2003; Feldman, Downs and McManus 2005).

If writing requires a context, then much of the first-year writing classroom's work depends on activity aimed at building that context. This dynamic view of writing instruction requires a very different sort of preparation than the readings-based classroom. I have asked my English 555 graduate students to think of writing their syllabi as if preparing a treatment for a screenplay. This genre, the treatment, offers a scene by scene synopsis used to plan the structure of the final screenplay. As such, the treatment anticipates but does not provide the moment by moment dialogue of the completed screenplay.[2] Similarly, the activity-based course syllabus anticipates each class session as the students build toward completion of their writing project. The syllabus charts a carefully orchestrated sequence of participatory student activity that builds toward each writing project. The teacher anticipates what needs to happen during each class period so that students can complete the project. The syllabus is designed with a specific trajectory in mind; one may not have the precise details worked out but the basic activities to achieve the goals of the scene or the class are in place. Each scene lays the groundwork for the next one, so it's crucial for the integrity of the syllabus/screenplay that each scene builds in the proper way. Understanding the syllabus as a genre makes it possible to use it as an epistemological tool to learn how genre goes beyond shaping knowledge to generating it. I am eager to demonstrate how we craft syllabi in the graduate seminar I teach, but first I must respond to an issue, the proverbial elephant in the room, that overshadows whatever innovative pedagogical work we might undertake. This shadow is cast by the continuing questions about whether first-year writing, given its political, economic, and intellectual challenges, should be a required course in the university.

Against First-Year Writing

In this book, I ask how writing instruction can contribute to a rich and rewarding institutional vision for student learning. Writing instruction should, I claim, provide for students an opportunity to participate actively in the very same engaged scholarship that also drives faculty research. I have outlined elsewhere (see chapter 1) the rhetorical turn that encouraged scholars to look closely at how they have constructed the knowledge developed in their specific fields. Scholars of history, economics, and political science all have come to realize the extent to which their claims are articulated through rhetorical strategies (Nelson, Megill, and McCloskey 1987). When faculty members examine their role as practitioners, that is, as builders of knowledge and as writers who represent that knowledge for others, they look at the context of their work in new ways. Michel de Certeau encouraged us to "inquire into the 'underside' of scientific activity" (1984, xxiii), as a way to critique the relationship between disciplinary practices and the products that emerge from those practices. This reexamination rarely makes its way into the writing classroom. The wished-for link between the situated writing classroom and rhetorically driven faculty research can best be made if faculty members teach first-year writing and are able to communicate to students the discursive nature of their research. Only rarely, if ever, does this connection occur in the contemporary university because faculty members, with a few exceptions, do not teach first-year writing.

If university faculty do not participate in shaping writing instruction, then graduate students may be the only teachers who can jump-start this institutional agenda. As we all know, the vast majority of first-year writing students are taught by graduate students and adjunct lecturers. Conducting rhetorically informed, engaged research, and teaching writing to first-year students turns out to be two completely different things, for scholars, who value the rhetorical aspects of meaning-making in their specific disciplines, do not typically communicate this important perspective to first-year writing students. The challenge of designing writing instruction that focuses on the relationship between meaning-making practices in specific contexts—academic or public—rests on the ability of the institution to create a space and an economy in which to train graduate students to teach writing from this perspective. In institutions where graduate programs don't exist and first-year writing is taught by a staff of part-time lecturers, this intractable problem has contributed to calls from within the profession to dissolve the composition requirement.

Talk about eliminating the composition requirement had begun in hallway conversations at professional meetings and conferences, but the argument was galvanized in an essay published by Sharon Crowley in 1991 in the journal *Pre/Text* and presented again, revised to include a personal history of the responses to her proposal, in her 1998 book, *Composition in the University*. Crowley launched two major arguments for eliminating first-year writing as a required course and offering it instead as an elective. The first argument has to do with the overwhelming administrative structure of the course, "Its very size subjects its administrators, teachers, and students to unprofessional and unethical working practices on a scale that is replicated nowhere else in the academy" (1998, 229). Our own graduate student union organizing committee's buttons say, "UIC works because we do" and there is truth to that statement.

The combined teaching force provided by adjunct faculty hired to teach individual courses at exceptionally low pay and graduate students who trade teaching for a minimal salary and a tuition waiver have created situations like those I portrayed in chapter 3 in which educational practices hinge on budget decisions. This is not what Crowley wishes for composition programs, but it is what often happens. Her suggestion, that the course become an elective, is in fact, quite reasonable. However, this change cannot be carried out without a comprehensive analysis of how these writing electives will fit into the broader undergraduate general education programs that support students' movement through the first two years of college until they choose and enter their major. Some universities have done this, but too often this conversation about eliminating the first-year writing requirement is self-contained, considered only among composition and rhetoric faculty and not across disciplines and colleges.

Crowley's second complaint about first-year writing concerns the content of the course: its emphasis on correctness, she argues, creates a border checkpoint for students entering the university and its focus on the specious genre of the academic essay limits what might be learned in the course. This narrowly defined content separates the course from the rest of the curriculum and helps to maintain an academic hierarchy in which disciplines and epistemology reign above basic skills (235). Her lament is a familiar one: Current instruction in composition offers only a pale shadow of the rich rhetorical possibilities modeled by the Quintilian rhetor who dwells in a specific time and place (1998, 264). These two concerns—the administrative dimensions of first-year writing programs and the quality of writing instruction—are intimately related.

Crowley laments that composition's pedagogy emphasizes correctness and serves as a gatekeeping mechanism; but most composition and rhetoric faculty don't see instruction in correctness as the problem. More commonly, composition scholars describe as the problem a pedagogy they refer to as General Writing Skills Instruction or GWSI. GWSI encompasses a wide range of curricula common to first-year writing programs and offers a pedagogy that "sets for itself the objective of teaching students 'to write,' which means to give them skills that transcend any particular content and context" (Petraglia 1995, xii). This pedagogical approach, Petraglia claims, is supported by the textbook industry and contributes to the perennially low status of composition courses. I include the readings-based pedagogy discussed above within the broad framework of GWSI for the high level of generality with which it approaches writing instruction. Essays in such courses are produced along standardized lines: a thesis is supported by evidence from the text, or alternatively from personal experience.

In the first chapter of *Reconceiving Writing*, the late Robert Connors offers a historical review of the debate about freshman composition that goes back to its inception at Harvard in the late nineteenth century (Connors 1995). He traces the swing of the pendulum from arguments for reform of the course, on the one hand, to arguments for abolishing the course on the other. Connors, who clearly sides with those who want to eliminate the course, adopts a most unfortunate term— abolitionism—that achieved some currency in the ongoing debate. Linking this term that is so intimately tied to the antislavery movement of colonial America confuses the issue. As language scholars surely we must recognize that some words can never shed their contextual connotations; that faculty members who want to eliminate either the course or the university-wide requirement call themselves "abolitionists" cannot not help their cause. Yet the issues surrounding the first-year course are real and must be dealt with. Composition insiders—now senior faculty and administrators themselves—are fed up with this first-year albatross.

The efforts of the composition-abolitionists is further complicated by the fact that it is "their own" course that they wish to free from the shackles campus-wide requirements. I put scare quotes around "their own" and, indeed, I could have said, "my own" because while I am responsible for the course, it has become an institutional fixture and has taken on a life of its own. I am told to hire, or to fire, but in any case to provide a seat for every student. The unfortunate use of the word abolition notwithstanding, this course and its massive presence in the first-year curriculum makes me and other composition specialists feel enslaved by administrative shackles that keep composition scholars from pursuing any scholarly work at all. Composition specialists have been tied to these devalued and deformed courses, which are seen as teaching basic skills, and tied as well to an ugly and intolerable labor situation, while the discipline itself has extended its work into new domains and fascinating studies of literate practices and rhetorical theory in a variety of contexts. When composition directors are forced to hire large number of adjuncts on a course by course basis, they acquire with them a hodgepodge of teaching approaches. This untenable labor situation poses more of a threat than any particular skill-based pedagogy because the labor market for composition instructors pulls the instructional wagon. Training or orientation is rarely provided and the best laid plans for a coherent program will quickly be destroyed by the enormous numbers of students and the sheer number of instructors needed to staff classes.

In any conversation about the viability of the freshman writing course the large number of adjunct lecturers who staff our writing programs becomes the elephant in the room. When part-time staff teach one course here and another there and when composition directors are told to hire as many staff as they need to provide a seat for each first-year student, a tower of babble results. This situation sickens us when we think of our hard-won disciplinary stature that allows for wide-ranging research studies in disciplinary rhetorics, technical writing, writing across the curriculum, visual rhetorics, community-based writing, genre theory, public sphere and democratic theory, and many other areas. The uncompromising administrative space that houses first-year writing courses does not allow us to activate the best theoretical knowledge the field has to offer. The first-year writing course becomes the repository for other agendas: prepare students for upper-level classes; use writing to show what students have learned; teach students critical thinking; develop basic grammatical knowledge; or, familiarize students with academic research and methods (Bazerman 1995).

Typically, I spend time each summer interviewing and hiring adjunct lecturers. As part of the interview process, I examine the syllabi that the applicants had used at previous institutions. Most of the syllabi I examined taught some version of the modes—narration, description, exposition, and persuasion. Some claimed to teach critical thinking. Typically, the syllabi were readings-based or as James Crosswhite puts it, "literaturized writing courses" in which students wrote about humanistic essays grouped according to a common idea, such as authenticity or identity (1996, 199). Most paid attention to the composing process. But, what characterized them as a whole was an emphasis on decontextualized skills—skills that seemed to promote something called "good writing." If I hired these lecturers and invited them to bring their current approaches with them, the composition program would dissolve into a jumble of best intentions with one instructor teaching a composing process course based on workshopping, another teaching a modes course characterized by comparison-contrast or persuasive essays, and another teaching a readings-based course, for example, through literary essays on the natural world.

Most of the adjunct lecturers I hire are either freelance writers, trained in some fashion to teach writing while they obtained an MFA in creative writing, or recent PhDs in literature, who also had been trained to teach writing during their graduate work and now wanted this adjunct position to solidify their vita and pursue tenure track jobs. To fight the chaos of hiring adjuncts with such a wild array of approaches, I required these new employees to attend a summer syllabus workshop and develop new syllabi that articulated UIC's approach to first-year writing. I hoped that I could build on the pedagogical strength already provided by the large numbers of graduate students who had spent their first semester learning about composition and rhetoric and designing syllabi that articulated UIC's approach to teaching writing to balance the influx of new lecturers. But this chapter is not primarily about the large numbers of lecturers we must hire to sustain the first-year courses. Alas, I cannot solve that problem here.

The Paradox of Transferability

Traditional educational theory depends on decontextualized instruction to produce a learning attribute called transferability. This means that writing skills learned in one context can be transferred, with some amount of efficiency, to another context. For administrators who see writing courses as an educational precursor to subsequent, more demanding undergraduate courses, transferability seems like a way to tie first-year courses to those taught later in the curriculum. Will this happen? Transferability depends on understanding knowledge and skills as independent of any particular context. The impetus that drives writing instruction as a set of abstract, decontextualized skills requires that those same skills be put to work in another class, perhaps a history class or a psychology class. Isolating or decontextualizing writing skills in the context of one college class for the use of those same skills in another college class creates a paradox because each of these classes, in fact, has its own context; the institutional and social arrangement of each college class makes a unique use of the skills which were purported to be generalizable.[3]

Learning to write should always be tied to local practices and the aims and desires of people who work together in socially and historically defined contexts. Recall my point in chapter 1 based on Stanley Fish's argument for embeddedness as critical for disciplinary work. Embeddedness is necessary for writing projects in the first-year classroom. Perhaps if writing projects can be tied to a situation rather than a decontextualized learning strategy, students will see how writing can be the product of lived experience. One way to understand this more complex and contextualized view of writing is to examine how David Russell (1995) uses activity theory to draw attention to the contextual underpinnings of writing activity.[4] For instance, when narrative is stripped of its generic underpinnings and seen as a discrete skill, it becomes a form of writing that, in fact, does *not* transfer to other contexts. With tongue in cheek, Russell likens this sort of writing instruction to learning ball handling as a generalizable skill. Each game that uses a ball has a different objective—baseball aims for home runs while basketball aims at shooting baskets. These different games—for which the ball is a key tool—can each be seen as part of a particular activity system that has developed historically with a unique set of rules and behaviors. Russell asks whether learning to use the ball for one game will generalize to using the ball for another game. Can learning to use a ball to play jacks, for instance, enhance your swing at the driving range? Of course not. Perhaps there are some very general skills that transfer like keeping your eye on the ball, but teaching ball-using skills alone will not offer much help (Russell 1995, 57–58).

You begin to see, I'm sure, where Russell is heading. It is true that balls are indispensable to a wide variety of games. When one learns to play a particular game, one is participating in the deep complexity and contextuality of an activity system. The GSWI course that teaches writing as discrete skills is teaching students the equivalent of ballhandling. Russell suggests that we teach writing as an activity system by paying close attention to the way that writing is used in particular activity systems. He explains that many sorts of activity systems are conducted through writing and writing is as vital to them as balls are to a variety of games (58). The context for the activity, with its historical legacy and through its habitual use, becomes associated with a particular genre. Writing, seen as a tool in an activity system, changes with each new context and so does the syntax, organization, level of detail, expression of coherence as well as other particular features of writing (58). If students see writing as part of a rich, ongoing context for making meaning and, particularly, if students desire to participate in that context, writing can become a meaningful activity, and students will come to see how they might want or need to apply this new understanding in a different context.

When students write a comparison-contrast paper that analyzes the differences between two essays about, say, authenticity, this skill—comparing and contrasting—is claimed to be transferable. Those university administrators who see the first-year writing course as providing basic skills that prepare students for upper-level work depend on transferability. However, when students are asked to apply this skill in a criminal justice class, an earth science class, or even a literary criticism class, the skill dissolves, leaving university faculty outraged at students who arrive at their door seemingly unable to write. The rhetorical turn that has informed the knowledge-making activity of faculty members about the epistemology of their particular disciplines has not informed first-year writing instruction, which remains mired in a basic skills approach. The student becomes a vessel for knowledge and not a participant in an ongoing inquiry or conversation. The skills that had been isolated specifically for the purposes of transfer to another classroom go nowhere and die on the floor of that first-year writing classroom.

Designing Situated Writing Projects

As we have seen, some argue that the space of the first-year writing classroom is a rigid, limiting space. What is learned there, in this view, has little application to other spaces: it is not malleable and its inability to be transferred is echoed in the oft-heard faculty member's claim that students cannot put two sentences together. Even as Sharon Crowley mourns the disintegration of freshman writing, she recalls how the classical rhetorician's sense of place offers possibilities for learning in the writing classroom:

> Quintilian's rhetor is located in time and space; she inhabits a community where public opinion influences the course of events; where discourse itself is acknowledged to bring about change; where emotions influence behavior, and where people express their "deprecation or desire" when the course of events requires them to make and state moral judgments. (1998, 264)

Crowley challenges us to restore the central energy of Quintilian's rhetor who senses that participation in a public situation, the impulse to step in and intervene, derives, at least in part, from the immediacy of location.

Planning instruction that makes writing matter must take space or location into account. Indeed most of the examples of student writing and writing projects in this book emerge from local situations. In one of the two writing projects below designed by participants in English 555, graduate student Kristen Schaffenberger develops a case study that offers students an imaginary, yet plausible, local situation within which students will develop a proposal. The idea of location is dangerously seductive; it deceives us into thinking that by moving our writing activity from one place to another we can recast our knowledge-making practices and breathe life into our writing. Rather than depending on the idea of being physically present in a particular location or even imagining one's self as present in a particular location, writing depends on a rhetorical construction of that reality.

Understanding that language provides a rhetorical tool for constructing reality helps us to think critically about location. We usually understand location as a physical reality where data might be collected and analyzed. I made the point in chapter 1 that this traditional understanding of space represents what postmodern geographer, Edward Soja, calls firstspace. As I explained in a bit more detail, firstspace is the calculable environment that traditional urban planners, for instance, rely on to map neighborhoods or count populations in census tracts. Moving into Soja's secondspace offers a "storehouse" of epistemological power," which allows us to conceive of space in Utopian terms. Secondspace is the "primary space of Utopian thought and vision" where academics conceptualize how public spaces might be made better (1996, 67). The imagination of the literature scholar is at work here, as is the social scientist who wants to improve the lives of residents. Soja's unique contribution to a new understanding of location comes with thirdspace, which moves us into lived space and the "limited knowability" of a social space that is filled not only with the "real and the imagined," but also that which encompasses the political choices that must take place in spaces and "counterspaces" (1996, 68). Thirdspace is defined by a deep contextuality characterized by activist motives. Such a complex notion of space creates the possibility that students, embedded in situations, can see themselves writing in a radical present and taking action through a geo-rhetorical stance. As difficult as it is to capture it in syllabi, in student writing, or in scholarly publications, this complex notion of thirdspace as a geo-rhetorical construction suggests possibilities for seeing student writing as engaged learning.

Writing produced through performance in a space, perhaps in thirdspace, takes into account its rhetorical gaze. The inquiries conducted as engaged scholarship emerge from an agenda that values participation as a way to shape and represent reality. This turn to engaged scholarship by scholars at urban research universities certainly takes location into account, perhaps, at times, as Soja's thirdspace does. A researcher's intent to contribute to the public good, depends to some extent, of course, on a sense of "being there," of being present in our particular locations, just as Sharon Crowley suggests for Quintilian's rhetor. But it is more complicated than that; it takes more than a sense of being present and speaking to others from a particular location, in part because Quintilian's culture, with its male rhetors and homogenous classes, no longer exists.

The public university's recasting of scholarship rides a deep change in intellectual perspective that transforms a writer from an enlightenment subject to a strategically defined subject.[5] Professors in the humanities and the human sciences have increasingly questioned the separation of producing knowledge from the social uses of that knowledge. Along the same lines, the vision of the lone scholar who observes phenomena as a spectator has shifted to a vision of a scholar who participates in investigations with others outside the academy and who deliberates together with others about the value and usefulness of their findings. We have become increasingly comfortable with the notion that producing knowledge means advocating for change. This shift has been motivated, in part, by increasing attention to genres that have emerged through historical practices such as the academic research report, the ways arguments are carried out, patterns of persuasion, and what counts as facts in particular contexts. The engaged scholar now approaches her research with a clearer sense of how the making of knowledge depends on a rhetorically informed awareness of the structuring of contexts, of genres, and of texts. This new awareness makes it possible to envision research not only in collaboration with partners outside the university, but also to envision research that aims to create change in those social contexts as an integral part of the knowledge-making agenda of urban universities.

This developing epistemological agenda, that insists on the contextualization of knowledge, has important implications for designing instruction in first-year writing classes. It complicates the ways we understand writing: a writer—student or teacher—is always embedded in consequential contexts that animate the rhetorical complexity of experiences in any space or location. This is the lost connection that must be reestablished in order to design opportunities for learning to write in first-year classes. Exigency, that is, a desire for specific consequences, must be learned (Miller 1984, cited in Bawarshi, 2003 41). Rather than see first-year writing as a way to develop isolated skills in students such as critical thinking that will purportedly move up the undergraduate ladder with them, or seeing first-year writing as a version of literary study in which students are asked to participate in a disciplinary context that is not theirs, my approach to writing offers students an opportunity to consider themselves participants in a particular context and write from their interest in that context.

You might argue that school-based writing projects, often crafted as case studies, are imaginary, unreal and thus useless for learning to write. From this perspective, every piece of writing produced in the classroom becomes a rhetorical response called "doing school" (Petraglia 1995, 89). While some argue that what is needed is an authentic situation for writing, which can only occur outside of the first-year writing classroom, I argue that whenever we write we are writing out of a particular subject position, driven by our desires, and compelled to locate this particular self at the intersection of our desire and the structures of institutions and genres. This rhetorical space constitutes what might be called the "liminal classroom," in which students are freed from "doing school" to see how writing is always a communicative act that evokes the possibilities of genre within existing social structures (Carnes 2004, 4). The question is not whether students are in an authentic situation or a real location; this is, itself, a fiction. What matters for the first-year writing classroom is whether or not the students see themselves as constructing a rhetorically driven representation of that real or imagined situation. As students write in these embedded or liminal spaces, they come to terms with exigence and consequences. The challenge for first-year writing is to train new graduate students to design instruction that can bring students into such liminal spaces where student's rhetorical imaginations take hold.

Let's take a look at two writing projects designed by graduate students who were enrolled in English 555. In the first project, students produce a proposal that argues for a particular use of a vacant building. Students will read sample proposals; they will read several interviews with architects; they will read from a case study, comprised of a variety of genres, in which Sandra Cisneros' argues to the local landmark housing board in her suburb of San Antonio that painting her house purple should be acceptable (from Feldman, Downs, and McManus 2005). Kristen had also invited Carol Ross Barney, a nationally known architect, who designs schools and other public-use buildings, to speak to the class. Figure 6.4 shows a portion of the task that Kristen designed for her class.

Figure 6.4. Writing Project Designed by Kristen Schaffenberger

---

The Situation:

The (fictional) City of Ovaltine, Illinois, was once an industrial suburb of Chicago. In the last thirty years, most of its original factories have been demolished to make way for single and multifamily residential developments, "big box" retail stores, and chain restaurants. While this city once relied on factories like its namesake, the original Ovaltine factory, for its infrastructure, Ovaltine has now become a hot spot for young families who commute in and out of Chicago. Ovaltine is proud of its heritage as one of the first major industrial towns outside of Chicago and does not want to lose its identity to new development.

About ten years ago, the Ovaltine Corporation moved its turn-of-the-century headquarters and manufacturing division to a previously undeveloped part of town. When the Ovaltine Corporation moved, it sold its 100-year old factory building to the City of Ovaltine. The city talked to several architects and developers, who suggested using the building for retail space, an entertainment complex, or high-end loft residences.

Many citizens have expressed concern over these potential uses. While the factory is large enough to hold nearly ten "big box" stores, the city is already home to Wal-Mart, Target, Best Buy, Sam's Club, Linens-n-Things and several other large retail stores. Area parents have been alarmed by plans to turn the building into an evening entertainment complex, complete with several nightclubs and bars. These parents argue that the building's size would make it difficult to supervise, which might make it a hot spot for underage drinking or gang activity. Finally, all of the city's residents seem to agree that the Ovaltine building represents something unique to the city and

---

(continued)

Figure 6.4. (*continued*)

---

its heritage. Area citizens believe that using the building as a high-end residential complex would benefit a residential developer, but would not maintain the building's symbolic meaning as a public landmark.

The Task:

Exasperated by opposition to most development schemes for the Ovaltine building, members of the city's development council have decided to ask members of the public for their recommendations for the building. The city has developed a Request for Proposals (RFP) for the residents of Ovaltine and its surrounding areas. The five best proposals will be presented to the citizens of Ovaltine, who will vote for the final development scheme.

As a Chicago-area resident, your job is to respond to the RFP (attached) with a creative proposal that identifies a way to develop the Ovaltine building with historical sensitivity and an eye toward Ovaltine's future.

Your proposal will respond to the questions in the RFP, and it will include visual elements that support your ideas. I have posted several photos on Blackboard. You may use these to represent your ideas about the Ovaltine building, or you may find your own.

Evaluation Criteria:

Does the piece fulfill the requirements of the RFP? Does it support or modify the features of the genre in appropriate ways? Does it make use of creative visual elements, including appropriate font, white space and mages, to support the proposal? Does it demonstrate a creative, thoughtful solution for the residents of Ovaltine? Is it free of grammatical or mechanical errors that might confuse or distract the reader? Does it use evidence to support claims and legitimize the author's proposed development scheme? Does it use appropriate language and style for the intended audience?

In addition to the actual project description that constitutes the "assignment," Kristen Schaffenberger developed an RFP, or Request for Proposal (see figure 6.5) that provided students the initiating document that their proposals would respond to. To do this, Kristen relied on writing experience that she had gained in a large architectural firm where she worked after completing a master's degree in twentieth-century literature at the University of London. As one of only two individuals who comprised the marketing department, Kristen responded to proposal requests, wrote and designed marketing materials, did media relations work, and booked photography for the firm's finished projects.

Figure 6.5. Request for Proposal Designed by Kristen Schaffenberger

Request for Proposal:

Ovaltine Factory Building
Redevelopment

Photo by Stephen Mifsud © www. Maltawildplants.com

The City of Ovaltine, Illinois, hereby requests proposals from interested parties for a redevelopment of the historic Ovaltine headquarters and factory building.

The Ovaltine Headquarters Building was built in 1903 and has long been a symbol of our community. Although Ovaltine was originally developed as an industrial city, the Ovaltine factory building is the only standing reminder of our industrial heritage.

Ovaltine seeks a development proposal that will preserve our city's heritage, yet anticipate our future as a growing town of successful, diverse individuals. While our city has experienced unprecedented growth and development over the last several years, our citizens feel that the Ovaltine building should be used for a purpose other than luxury housing, big box retail stores and chain restaurants. Our city wishes to encourage local business, community activities and an interest in local heritage. We also feel it is important to take our residents' interests into account when planning the redevelopment of the Ovaltine building.

(continued)

Figure 6.5. (*continued*)

Earlier this year, we surveyed our residents to determine their interests and goals. We have provided some of this data in the hope that it generates thoughtful, creative proposals for our redevelopment project (please see charts).

How do Ovaltine residents like to spend their free time?

Fitness/Sports – 17%
Movies/Theatre – 14%
Museums/Galleries – 11%
Family Activities – 19%
Cooking/Restaurants – 16%
Learning New Skills – 11%
Arts and Crafts – 12%

What do Ovaltine residents value in their community?

Family-Friendly Environment – 22%
Town Heritage – 21%
Safety/Security – 15%
Modern Conveniences – 20%
Local Educational System – 22%

All proposals must include: A cover sheet that includes your name and contact details; letter of transmittal; a summary of your understanding of the City of Ovaltine's values or ideas; and, a summary of your proposed redevelopment plan for the Ovaltine building. At this point, we are most interested in hearing what area residents believe should be incorporated into the building's redevelopment and why. Specifics such as construction and timelines should not be included at this time.

While Kristen Schaffenberger's writing project and the one shown in figure 6.6 frame an assignment for students, I don't want to ignore daily instruction, which must rewrite the "read and discuss" model of essay-based writing courses. The section from Kristen Schaffenberger's syllabus below reveals a critical feature of designing situated writing instruction. If you recall in chapter 2, I refer to Ira Shor's democratized classroom in which students write proposals to change something about their campus. The problem with carrying out his admirable plan is that students read novels to learn about Utopias and about social change, but they don't have much to do with proposals, as a genre, until they must sit down to design their own. Kristen has included some focused instruction on the writing of proposals, which students need as a starting point for their own projects. Here's one class session's plan for tying a relatively standard genre to the specific features of the situation students are working with.

Having examined the features of several proposals and imagined the contexts in which they were written, students can view their own projects as rhetorical constructions and can draw on specific features of the proposals the students

Figure 6.6. Classroom Activity for Evaluating Proposals

Wednesday, September 28: The Look and Feel of a Proposal

Group Activity: Work in small groups to review the sample proposals I provide. Consider such elements as font, white space and use of images, as well as
language choice, style, and other elements. More important, examine the
rhetorical elements of these proposals. What characteristics define this genre?
How do these proposals change or shift the usual genre? What context were
they deployed in? How are they using language to shape a reality for their readers? What might be the consequences of such proposals?

As a group, determine which proposals you believe are most successful.
Please prepare and present a list of the key features of successful proposals.
How does language use contribute to that success? We will summarize
your groups' work and consider how you might use these features in your
final drafts.

Grammar Activity: How verbs add to a proposal's effectiveness.

---

examined. The transferable skills learned here are not basic, generalized skills,
but an understanding of how to move back and forth, flexibly and strategically between the contingencies of a particular situation and the possibilities of
particular genres.

Let's take a look at a project that is not so dependent on an imagined location. This project, designed collaboratively by Mary Hibbeler and Nicole Russo,
counters the literacy narrative assignment. Here, Mary and Nicole try to move
students away from such attempts at identity writing by focusing students on the
way that structure and agency interact in a specific discursive context. (See my argument against the literacy narrative in chapter 4.) As you will see in figure 6.7,
students write letters to the editor in response to two situations in which identity
plays an important, but contrasting role. In one situation young people proudly
claim a Latino identity by shifting their style to reflect current urban trends; in
the other situation an author hides his Caucasian identity in order to publish an
authentic Latino identity narrative. By asking students to write letters to the editor in response to both situations, the instructors press students to notice what
sorts of arguments might be made about claiming and representing identity. By
asking students to follow up with a cover letter to the teacher, the instructors ask
students to examine how participating in a public conversation through the genre
of the cover letter influenced their textual choices. Included below are the situation, task, and evaluation criteria.

Mary Hibbeler and Nicole Russo have attempted, in designing this writing project, to nudge their students away from writing literacy narrative. More

Figure 6.7. Writing Project Designed by Mary Hibbeler and Nicole Russo

Situation 1. While visiting a friend in San Jose, you flip through the Sunday paper and find Nell Bernstein's "Goin' Gansta, Choosin' Cholita." After reading it, you feel so strongly about the issues she addresses about claiming an identity that you simply must share your opinion with other readers of the *San Jose Mercury News.* Maybe you support a certain aspect of Bernstein's article and want to add supporting information, or maybe you strongly disagree with something in her piece and want to correct what you consider a gross misrepresentation.

Situation 2. Almost a year after reading Danny Santiago's widely acclaimed coming-of-age Chicano novel *Famous All Over Town* (or even just an excerpt, as you have) and David Quammen's review of the novel, you run across Edwin McDowell's article in the *New York Times* online. You are shocked, confused, and uncomfortable; or, maybe you think the author's pseudonym choice was necessary, even funny, given that he was a seventy-year Caucasian male. Again, you either support or question an aspect of McDowell's article so much that you are driven to develop a letter to the editor that adds to the ongoing conversation.

Task. Join the conversation! Write one letter to the editor of the *San Jose Mercury News* in response to Bernstein's article and another letter to the editor of the *New York Times* in response to McDowell's piece. Although a letter to the editor is an opportunity for you to express strong opinions, it is not a rant. Your letters should be based on well thought-out and organized arguments, and your opinions should be based on supporting examples. Also, you should include a one-page cover letter addressed to me elucidating your participation in this type of "public" conversation.

Evaluation Criteria for Letters to the Editor:
- Your letter expresses a *decided* stance within or against the conversation at-large.
- Your letters are based on a *well-developed* argument that is supported by exemplary material/individual experiences.
- Your letters use appropriate language and take into consideration the audience for which they are written.
- Each of your letters is a potentially publishable contribution to the (written) conversation. That is, they address issues appropriate/relevant to the discussion and are (relatively) free of grammatical errors.

Evaluation Criteria for Cover Letter:
- You explain how the readings have shaped the choices made in your letters.
- You explain what you have learned about the letter to the editor as a genre (that is, in terms of its situation, language, and consequences).
- You address how you have attempted to participate in this written conversation or discourse.
- You explain how the key notions of situation, genre, language, and consequences have motivated particular revisions

than anything else, Mary and Nicole are attempting to teach exigence or
motive by designing situations that can, potentially, drive students out of the
comfort zone of the school-based essay with its dependence on a learned but
tacit formula of personal disclosure. By asking students to consider their position in two distinct situations, the designers of this project hope to pull that
predictable school-based rug out from under these first-year students. On the
one hand, students read Bernstein's news article reporting on young people who
feel authorized to adopt an identity largely through fashion. On the other
hand, students read a chapter from Danny Santiago's coming-of-age novel and
later learn that the author, who was not Latino, had falsely claimed a Latino
identity. Students not only might argue that it's acceptable for a youth to claim
an identity, but also might argue that it's unethical for a seventy-year-old, Caucasian male to pass as a Latino youth.

Much of the writing that first-year students typically read in composition
anthologies are not upended in surprise reversals like the Danny Santiago authorship dilemma. Instead, first-year anthologies largely represent writers op-
erating in what Michel Foucault has characterized as the author function.
Foucault identifies three features of the author-function: first, the work of an
author is a commodity, a form of property; second, this property is typically
seen as a literary work; and third, the author function doesn't represent an individual, but rather a "rational entity," composed from authenticating features of
the text (Foucault 1993). Students cannot imagine the essay's author in the
context that gave rise to the essay. The author is situated for the student only in
an opening note, if at all. Thus, both the author and the text occupy an identity,
or "mode of existence" that is lost to students who are given the impossible task
of writing an essay in response to a literary work or a critical essay.

Literary works, produced and included in a composition anthology for students to respond to, offer only a reified experience of a once lively moment of
textual production. Etienne Wenger, whose work on communities of practice
focuses on the relationships between learning, meaning, and identity asks us to
think about the contrast between participation and reification (see chapter 2).
Individuals, who feel a sense of agency when they write, can point to the sense
of engagement and participation in the process itself. But this sense of engagement, Wenger tells us, goes beyond the straightforward practice of writing. It
is, he tells us, "a constituent of our identities. As such, participation is not something we turn on and off" (Wenger 1998, 57). Wenger characterizes the difference between these two concepts as follows:

> Whereas in participation we recognize ourselves in each other, in
> reification we project ourselves onto the world, and not having to rec-
> ognize ourselves in those projections, we attribute to our meanings an
> independent existence. (Wenger 1998, 58)

In learning to write, both participation and reification cooperate to set the backdrop for the practices we teach our students. Foucault's author-function emerges directly from disciplinary formations in which discursive constructs give the author privileged status. Students, whose writing only focuses on responses to great authors, can never achieve the status of author as Foucault has framed it (Stygall 1994). In the writing project above, students to do more than write, in an abstract way, about the topic of identity. The student sees him or herself as a producer and a participant rather than a responder or a spectator.

A Manifesto for First-Year Writing

This chapter began with a graduate student who cried out for writing courses that would support his disciplinary interest in literary studies. Next, two graduate students wondered how the notion of genre, which they had, until now, relied upon as a tool for analyzing aesthetic texts, could be put to use in a first-year writing course. During the subsequent weeks and months, these students and all the others who would teach in the first-year writing program, learned how to envision writing as embedded in both situation and location. Near the end of the semester, graduate students in English 555 produce a project like the situation-based writing assignments they designed for their students. We hold a "Genre Gala" and invite 555 students to choose a genre that will allow a critique, comment, or roast of the instructor and/or the course. The manifesto shown in figure 6.8 was written by Jennifer Bryant, a poet, who received her master's degree at the University of Illinois at Chicago and who is currently in the PhD program in English Literature at the University of Washington at Seattle; she teaches in the university's expository writing program.

Thoroughly exhausted with the demands of her first-year in graduate school, Jennifer Bryant decided to articulate her frustrations through a manifesto. To plan this piece, she began thinking about discourse in her academic field— British and American modernism, poetry, and the relationship between warfare and the arts. She wondered how writing in those contexts had been situated historically. She thought, in particular, of author and painter Wyndham Lewis who had produced a highly visual journal called "Blast," which was initially published in 1914 in England in the weeks leading up to the Great War. This journal launched the Vorticists, an avant-garde arts movement that built on the example of Futurists, whose members produced graphic manifestos, which, they hoped, would create a swirling vortex at the center of London's urban arts community. Jennifer Bryant built on this historical context to produce a manifesto that sorted out her ambivalence to the approach taken by UIC's first-year writing program. She told me, "the resulting piece, I think, was a way for me to bring into some sort of conversation my own individual interests and expectations as a student with what was being asked and expected of me as an instructor, and to try to find a place for them to meet." With this manifesto, Jennifer Bryant articulates her wish that her students ride "the wild mountain railway from idea to action," recognizing the dangers of failure and the possibilities of impotence. This piece of writing offered Jennifer Bryant, too, a way to shout out, to claim a seat for herself on a railway of words and in doing so to make writing matter.

Figure 6.8. Manifesto for Composition

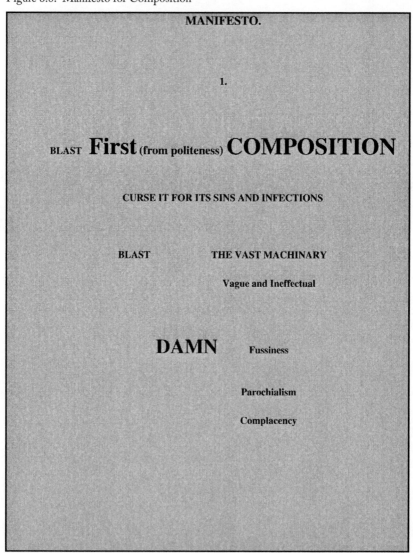

MANIFESTO.

1.

BLAST First (from politeness) COMPOSITION

CURSE IT FOR ITS SINS AND INFECTIONS

BLAST　　　　　**THE VAST MACHINARY**

Vague and Ineffectual

DAMN　　Fussiness

Parochialism

Complacency

(continued)

Figure 6.8. (*continued*)

2.

OH BLAST FRANCE

that is to say

BLAST FOUCAULT

dark piggish privileging

Author-Function

CREAM OF THE SNOBBISH CLASSROOM

3.

BLAST

FAULTY COMPOSITION THEORY

years 1966 to Present

CURSE abysmal inexcusable **ERROR**

BLAST

pasty shadow cast by gigantic PROCESS

(*continued*)

Figure 6.8. (*continued*)

> **4.**
>
> **CURSE**
>
> **WITH EXPLETIVE OF WHIRLWIND**
>
> misuse of Pronouns!
>
> misplaced Modifiers!
>
> poor Coordination!
>
> **SINS** and **PLAGUES** of this (not nearly finished) vegetable
>
> # GRAMMAR

(*continued*)

Figure 6.8. (*continued*)

1.

BLESS COMPOSITION

BLESS COMPOSITION

FOR ARGUMENT.

Claims

Warrant

Evidence

but also Situation!

BLESS ENGLISH 161

BLESS

the GRAMMAR STRAND

BLESS the vast planetary abstraction of THEORY

(*continued*)

Figure 6.8. (*continued*)

2.

BLESS ORDINARY WRITING

It is the great barbarous weapon of

the genius among students

BLESS SOCIALLY CONSCIOUS WRITING,

The wild MOUNTAIN RAILWAY from IDEA

to ACTION, or else from idea to sensation of impotence.

3.

BLESS VOICE

BLESS FOUCAULT for DISCOURSE,

the better to control the use of Voice

(*continued*)

Figure 6.8. (*continued*)

4.

BLESS GENRE

editorials

political cartoons

debates and interviews

opinion pieces

letters to the edititor

just not in **THIS CLASS**

BLESS

Context   Language   Consequences

Kolln   Bean   Harris

engaged pedagogy   the genre function

adverbials   adjectivals   the known-new contract

etc etc etc

Source: Signature for Manifesto: Jennifer Bryant.

Notes

Chapter 1: Engaged Scholarship at the University

1. There is another side to Stanley Fish's discussion of disciplinarity and his engagement with composition and rhetoric. In two recent volumes—a book-length treatment of Fish's work, *Justifying Belief* (Olson 2002) and an edited volume, *Postmodern Sophistry* (Olson and Worsham 2004)—scholars remind Fish that composition continues to be fact-on-the-ground in English departments. As Evan Watkins points out, Fish's discussion of the distinctiveness of literary work ignores the "material resources required to sustain the "intelligibility" of a distinct disciplinary set of practices and the "wayfaring pilgrims" who wish to inhabit the discipline (2004, 239–240). In the case of composition and rhetoric, discussions about material resources—the hiring and firing of adjunct staff, for instance—often subsume and subvert discussions about the epistemological aims of the discipline. Entrenched in the institutional structure of universities as it is, writing instruction frequently generates more talk about its administrative management than about its disciplinary practices. Often seen as a support for other, more important academic endeavors, the contributions that first-year writing can make to student learning in the early years of an undergraduate program are ignored. As I argue in this book, the way to extricate first-year writing classes from their entrenched function in the university is to highlight the ways that writing is embedded in social situations.

2. Defining engagement has, of course, been a key activity in the Kellogg Commission's work as well as in numerous public and academic contexts. Public institutions are, for the most part, attempting to redefine engagement in contrast to earlier approaches which characterized the relationship of universities to their surrounding communities as one of noblesse oblige, charity, or outreach. Most who struggle with this definition are also aware of too-easy conceptions of community as sites of connection and agreement. The Kellogg Commission's evolving definition of engagement illustrates their struggle. In the 1999 report, engagement was defined as follows: "institutions that have redesigned their teaching, research, and extension and service functions to become even more

sympathetically and productively involved with their communities, however communities may be defined" (20). By the next year's report, the word sympathetic has disappeared from the definition for engagement and disciplines were described as permeable rather than as silos.

3. Whether or not these investigations are "political" is simply beside the point. Students will develop their own moral capacities and political agendas outside of the instructor's pedagogical agenda. And here I grudgingly agree with Stanley Fish. Students will, on their own, become advocates for change based on their educational experiences; teachers do not need to plan for such change.

4. This quote and subsequent ones as well were transcribed by the author from a videotape of the public square event, "Women Activists: The Path to Freedom" that took place on January 16, 2004. The event was aired on CANTV's channel 19 on February 1, 2004. The Public Square is currently sponsored by the Illinois Humanities Council (IHC). To learn more about The Public Square, go to the IHC Web site http://www.prairie.org and click on Educational Programs and Grants.

5. Barbara A. Holland. "Building and Sustaining Community-Campus Partnerships." Keynote address to Ohio Campus Compact/Wright State Conference on Civic Engagement. Dayton, September 2004.

6. http://www.princeton.edu/pr/pwb/98/1207/singer.htm. *Princeton Weekly Bulletin* December 7, 1998. The President's Page. The Appointment of Professor Peter Singer. Harold Shapiro.

7. Sponsored by the University of Pennsylvania, the Penn National Commission on Society, Culture and Community invited leading scholars and public thinkers to study the increasing levels of incivility in public discourse and find solutions that could help communities engage in robust conversation and create models of effective deliberative discourse. The archives of the commissions work are posted on a Web site (http://www.upenn.edu/pnc). An edited volume offers essays that develop aspects of the commissions' work (Rodin and Steinberg 2003). The commission met from November 1996 through December 1999.

8. See P. Harkin (1991) for a discussion of lore as a way to understand pedagogical practices.

Chapter 2: Writing as Participation

1. Excerpted from the following portion of a conversion narrative from Caldwell, *The Puritan Conversion* (1983, 28). Cited from Shepard, "Confessions" (1981, 99–101).

And thought here the Lord might be found, and doubtful whether I had a call to come because I was to leave my friends. Hence I remembered that Scripture—I'll be with thee in the first waters*—and I knew I should be armed like Jacob in all straits to have a promise. And in our way when ready to be cast away, stand still and see salvation of God,[†] and them heard Lord is my portion.[‡] So I came hither. (100–1)

*Isa. 43:2; [†]Exod. 14:13; 2 Chron. 20:17;
[‡]Ps. 73:26; 119:57; 142:5; Lam. 3:24; Ps. 16.5

2. Miller, *Assuming the Positions* (1998), draws this case from Buckley, "Placed in the Power of Violence" (1992).

3. Ellen McManus, Nancy Downs and I used the Chiem article "Taggers spray over" (1996), to introduce the idea of context and situation in our textbook (Feldman, et al. 2005).

4. T. O. Beebee asserts that "our practice of speaking of it [genre] as a "thing" rather than as a relationship between a user and a text" creates a "veil of an aesthetic ideology that continues to posit genre as universal" (1994, 18–19). Thinking of genre as use-value, that is, as a relationship, rather than a category or type, helps to pierce the "veil of . . . ideology" that sustains the notion of genre as universal.

5. See also Appleby, "Building Community" (2003), who argues that museums, in particular, are reaching out as community-builders through a variety of civic-minded activities.

6. It's important to note, though, that the exhibition did not engage in radical change by moving its art into the city as Richard Serra's *Tilted Arc* did in 1981 when he installed a curving steel wall that divided New York City's Federal Plaza, nor did it break new ground by inviting the public to redo their own versions of the old masters, as other museums have done. In addition, the exhibit was justly criticized for not including enough women (McQueen 2001).

7. My thanks to Leslie Walowitz for calling my attention to this article and to Tom Moss, Jerry Graff, Nadya Pittendrigh, Glenda Jones, Matt Pavesich, and Tracey Layng-Awasthi who discussed the article with me.

8. Fletcher's guide, available at the Whitney, introduced each artist, described each installation and its location, and mentioned the student who had identified the location.

9. E-mail correspondence with Harrell Fletcher, 2/28/2005.

10. This student essay was edited to correct surface-level errors in a conference with the student on October 24, 2003. Other material is

drawn from a personal interview, July 7, 2003 with permission. Approved by UIC's Institutional Review Board project # 2000–0057.

11. The university is simultaneously many things, some of which contradict its efforts at engagement. Two recent discussions of these issues may be found in Readings, *University in Ruins* (1997), and Downing and others, *Beyond English* (2002).

Chapter 3: Telling Tales Out of School

1. All graduate students' names have been changed and represent composite portrayals of more than one person. Similarly, administrators are portrayed as composite characters. The only individuals whose names have not been changed are Sylvia Manning, Michael Tanner, Betsy Hoffman, Stanley Fish, Walter Benn Michaels, Gerry Graff, David Perry, and Tom Moss.

2. With posthumous apologies to the legacy of Bill Readings (1996) whose "university in ruins" refers to the modern university's hopeless search for excellence, which is based on, Readings argues, an empty concept. The university that protected and defended culture is now gone, and the current status of the university is dependent on a postmodern world in ruins.

3. In previous years, students with an ACT score in language of 29 or higher were offered a waiver of English 160. By lowering the cut-off to 26, we could reduce the size of the program by exempting more students from the course.

4. I develop this argument more fully in chapter 4 of this book.

Chapter 4: Rethinking Reflection in Community-Based Writing

1. Williams offers the term mediation as a materialist counter to the basic dualism suggested by reflection. Mediation, describes a more active process, ". . . all active relations between different kinds of being and consciousness are inevitably mediated, and this process is not a separable agency . . ." (98). In the next section, I use the term participation rather than mediation for its connection to contemporary social learning theory.

2. See also J. Comas, T. B. Hiller, and J. Miller for an example of a civic engagement program conducted through an introductory business course that adopts a communities of practice perspective (2005).

3. See my extended discussion of genre in the first part of chapter 2 and for examples of student writing from classroom and community-based contexts in a variety of genres see chapter 5.

4. For the next cohort of CCLCP students, we streamlined the program to include only one general education course instead of two. With this change the program now included four courses and students could complete the program during their first two years of college before they began study in their major.

5. See http://www.cwrl.utexas.edu/~syverson/olr/. Learning Record Online was developed by Margaret (Peg) Syverson at the University at Texas at Austin's Computer Writing and Research Lab.

6. The dimensions of learning that underlie Learning Record Online are as follows: confidence and independence, skills and strategies, knowledge and understanding, the use of prior and emerging experience, and reflectiveness. It is important to note that Peg Syverson names reflectiveness as one of her learning dimensions; by this she means a metacognitive ability to analyze one's own learning. While this ability does not necessarily mean the same thing as the now standardized written genre called "the reflection essay," reflectiveness is still troubled by the critque I present in this chapter.

7. This discussion was contributed by Candice Rai and draws on her dissertation project, "Rhetorics of Democracy in Contested Urban Space," which is currently underway at the University of Illinois at Chicago.

Chapter 5: Assessing Writing and Learning in Community-Based Courses

1. The Chicago Civic Leadership Certificate Program began as a three-year pilot program funded by a *Learn and Serve America* matching grant from the federal *Corporation for National and Community Service*. The pilot version of CCLCP, which was launched in August 2004 and ended in May 2007, included five classes, one each semester. The Chicago Civic Leadership Certificate Program began with thirty-seven students and seventeen students received their certificates. Candice Rai and Megan Marie designed the syllabi for the first-year courses.

2. Caitlyn Costello's writing and the writing of all other CCLCP students included in this chapter is used with the students permission granted through informed consent obtained under the auspices of IRB protocol # 2004 0361 for research conducted at the University of Illinois at Chicago.

3. Keith W. Hoskin and Richard H. Macve depend for this portion of their argument on Jacques Derrida's notion of "the supplement." Citing *Of Grammatology* (1976), they recount the way in which writing has been seen as a supplement to speech that refigures what might be taken as authentic speech.

4. Developed by: Ann Feldman, Tom Moss, Megan Marie, Candice Rai, and Diane Chin November 10, 2004. Revised with Barbara Holland on February 21, 2005.

5. Tom Moss, the CCLCP assessment liaison, analyzed the data reported here. To determine the percent of change, scores #1 and #2 were combined to determine a score for "not difficult." UIC's Survey Research Lab reviewed the respondent's sample size and calculated the following margins of error: CCLCP: 8 percent; Reg: 1.4 percent. For this reason we see the results as suggestive trends rather than as statistically significant differences.

6. Candice Rai and Megan Marie developed the coding scheme and conducted the analysis described in this chapter.

Chapter 6: Teaching the Teachers

1. Patrick Shannon is a composite character drawn from several graduate students over a period of time.

2. The way in which our program's syllabi functioned as a treatment for a screenplay became clear to me during a discussion with John Chapin, a freelance writer who taught in our first-year writing program. When I explained how our syllabi articulated, in detail, plans for completing specific writing projects, Chapin immediately saw a connection between writing such a syllabus and writing the treatment that he develops prior to writing a screenplay (e-mail conversation on October 11, 2004).

3. Jean Lave makes this point in the introduction to *Understanding Practice: Perspectives on Activity and Context* in an attempt to clarify the typical formalist duality posited between context and decontextualized learning (Lave & Chaiklin 1993). She contrasts this duality with the deep contextuality that defines activity theory in which the production of knowledge (and I would say, writing) is an improvisational process of interacting with the world through local practice.

4. David Russell's application of activity theory to the teaching of writing invites us to take advantage of a rich resource for understanding writing as a deeply contextual activity. Closely related is Jean Lave and Etienne Wenger's (1991) work on learning as participation and Yrvö Engeström's (1990) study

of expertise as activity immersed in institutions, developed collaboratively, and drawn from historical contexts. This approach is rooted in Soviet advances in sociocultural understandings of learning and development (Wertsch 1981).

5. Several books and edited volumes have charted the evolution from the Cartesian subject to Homo Rhetoricus. See Lanham, *Motives of Eloquence*, 1976; Bernard-Donals and Glejzer, "Introduction," 1998; Nelson, Megill, and McCloskey, *Rhetoric of Human Sciences*, 1987; Mansfield, *Subjectivity*, 2000; Taylor, *Souces of the Self*, 1989; and Goodman and Fisher, *Rethinking Knowledge*, 1995.

Works Cited

Adler-Kassner, Linda, R. Crooks, and A. Watters, eds. 1997. *Writing the Community: Concepts and Models for Service-Learning in Composition*. Urbana, Illinois: NCTE published in cooperation with AAHE (American Association for Higher Education).

Anson, Chris. 1997. "On Reflection: The Role of Logs and Journals in Service-Learning Courses." In *Writing the Community: Concepts and Models for Service-Learning in Composition*. Edited by L. Adler-Kassner, R. Crooks and A. Watters, 167–180. Urbana, IL: NCTE.

Anzaldúa, Gloria. 1993. "Chicana Artists: Exploring Nepantla, el Lugar de la Frontera." NACLA Report, 27, no. 1 (July–August). Reprinted in A. Feldman, N. Downs, and E. McManus. *In Context: Participating in Cultural Conversations*. First edition. (New York: Addison, Wesley, Longman, 2002) 96–104.

Appleby, Joyce. 2003. "Building Community in the Twenty-First Century." In *Public Discourse in America: Conversation and Community in the Twenty-first Century*. Edited by J. Rodin and S. P. Steinberg, 213–226. Philadelphia: University of Pennsylvania Press.

Bacon, Nora. 2002. "Differences in Faculty and Community Partners' Theories of Learning." *Michigan Journal of Community Service Learning* 9, 1: 34–44.

Bacon, Nora, T. Deans, J. Dubinsky, B. Roswell, and A. Wurr. 2005. "Community-Based and Service-Learning Writing Initiatives: A Survey of Scholarship and Agenda for Research." CCCC research report prepared for the National Council of Teachers of English.

Bakhtin, Mikhail M. 1993. *Toward a Philosophy of the Act*. Translation and Notes by V. Liapunov. Edited by V. Liapunov and M. Holquist. Austin: University of Texas Press Slavic Series, University of Texas.

Bartholomae, David. 1985. "Inventing the University." In *When a Writer Can't Write: Studies in Writer's Block and Other Composing-Process Problems*. Edited by M. Rose, 134–165. New York: Guilford, Perspectives in Writing Research.

———. 1996. "What Is Composition and (if you know what it is) Why Do We Teach It?" In *Composition in the Twenty-first Century: Crisis and Change.* Edited by Lynn Z. Bloom, A. Daiker and E. M. White, 11–28. Carbondale: Southern Illinois University Press.

Bawarshi, Anis 2000. "The Genre Function." *College English* 62, 3: 335–60.

———. 2003. *Genre and the Invention of the Writer: Reconsidering the Place of Invention in Composition.* Logan: Utah State University Press.

Bazerman, Charles. 1995. "Response: Curricular responsibilities and professional definition." In *Reconceiving Writing, Rethinking Writing Instruction.* Edited by Joseph Petraglia, 249–259. Mahwah, NJ: Lawrence Erlbaum Associates.

———. 1997. "The Life of Genre, the Life in the Classroom." In *Genre and Writing: Issues, Arguments, Alternatives.* Edited by Wendy Bishop and Hans Ostrom, 19–26. Portsmouth, NH: Boytnon/Cook Heinemann.

———. 1999. *The Languages of Edison's Light.* Cambridge, MA: MIT Press.

Beauregard, Robert A. 1995. "If Only the City Could Speak: The Politics of Representation." In *Spatial Practices: Critical Explorations in Social/Spatial Theory.* Edited by H. Liggett and D. Perry, 59–80. Thousand Oaks, CA: Sage Publications.

———, ed. 1999. *The Urban Moment: Cosmopolitan Essays on the Late-20th Century City.* Thousand Oaks, CA: Sage Publications.

Becker, R. 2003. "Illinois Governor Urges State Colleges to Think Lean. *Chicago Tribune,* February 14, 2003.

Beebee, Thomas O. 1994. *The Ideology of Genre: A Comparative Study of Generic Instability.* University Park: Pennsylvania State University Press.

Belsey, Catherine. 1980. *Critical Practice.* New York: Methuen.

Bender, Thomas. 1988. "Afterword." In *The University and the City: From Medieval Origins to the Present.* Edited by T. Bender, 290–297. New York: Oxford University Press.

———. 1998. "Scholarship, Local Life, and the Necessity of Worldiness." In *The Urban University and Its Identity: Roots, Locations, Roles.* Edited by H. van der Wusten, 17–28. Boston: Kluwer Academic Publishers.

Bernard-Donals, Michael, and R. R. Glejzer. 1998. "Introduction." In *Rhetoric in an Antifoundational World: Language, Culture, and Pedagogy.* Edited by M. Bernard-Donals, and R. R. Glejzer, 1–30. New Haven, CT: Yale University Press.

Bishop, Wendy and H. Ostrom, eds. 1997. *Genre and Writing: Issues, Arguments, Alternatives.* Portsmouth, NH: Boynton/Cook Heinemann.

Bizzell, Patricia and B. Herzberg. 1990. *The Rhetorical Tradition: Readings from Classical Times to the Present*. Boston, MA: Bedford Books of St. Martin's Press.

Bloom, Lynn Z., D. A. Daiker, and E. M. White, eds. 1996. *Composition in the Twenty-First Century: Crisis and Change*. Carbondale: Southern Illinois University Press.

Boggs, Grace L. 1998. *Living for Change: An Autobiography*. Minneapolis: University of Minnesota Press.

Bowden, Darcie. 1999. *The Mythology of Voice*. Portsmouth, NH: Boyton/ Cook Heinemann.

Boyd, Richard. 1991. "Imitate Me; Don't Imitate me: Mimeticism in David Bartholomae's 'Inventing the University.'" *Journal of Advanced Composition* 112: 335–345.

Boyer, Ernest. 1990. *Scholarship Reconsidered: Priorities of the Professoriate*. Princeton, NJ: The Carnegie Foundation for the Advancement of Teaching.

Boyte, Harry C. and N. N. Kari. 1996. *Building America: The Democratic Promise of Public Work*. Philadelphia, PA: Temple University Press.

Bringle, Robert G. and J. A. Hatcher. 1995. "A Service-Learning Curriculum for Faculty." *Michigan Journal of Community Service Learning* 2: 112–122.

———. 1999. "Reflection in Service Learning: Making Meaning of Experience." *Educational Horizons* (Summer): 179–185.

———. 2003. "Reflection in Service Learning: Making Meaning of Experience." In *Campus Compact. Introduction to Service-Learning Toolkit: Readings and Resources for Faculty*, 2nd ed. 83–89. Providence, RI: Brown University.

Bringle, Robert G., R. Games, and E. A. Malloy, eds. 1999. *Colleges and Universities as Citizens*. Boston, MA: Allyn and Bacon.

Brukardt, M. J., B. Holland, S. Percy, and N. Zimpher. 2004. *Calling the Question: Is Higher Education Ready to Commit to Community Engagement? A Wingspread Statement*. Report published by the Milwaukee Idea Office, Milwaukee: University of Wisconsin-Milwaukee, P.O. Box 413, Milwaukee, WI 53201, (414) 229 2585.

Buckley, T. 1992. "Placed in the Power of Violence: The Divorce Petition of Evelina Gregory Roane, 1824." *Virginia Magazine of History and Biography* 100: 20–78.

Burke, Kenneth. 1962a. *A Rhetoric of Motives*. Berkeley, CA: University of California Press. (Orig. pub. 1950.)

———. 1962b. *A Grammar of Motives*. Berkeley, CA: University of California Press. (Orig. pub. 1945.)

Butin, Dan, ed. 2005. *Service-Learning in Higher Education: Critical Issues and Directions.* New York: Palgrave Macmillan.

———. 2005. "Service-Learning as Postmodern Pedagogy." In *Service-Learning in Higher Education: Critical issues and directions.* Edited by D. Butin, 89–104. New York: Palgrave Macmillan.

———. 2006. "The Limits of Service-Learning in Higher Education." *The Review of Higher Education* 29, 4 (Summer 2006): 473–498.

Caldwell, Patricia. 1983. *The Puritan Conversion Narrative: The Beginnings of American Expression.* Cambridge: Cambridge University Press.

Callenbach, Ernest. 1975. *Ecotopia: The Notebooks and Reports of William Weston.* Berkeley, CA: Banyon Tree Books (distributed by Bookpeople).

Campus Compact Service-Learning Toolkit. 2003. *Introduction to Service-Learning Toolkit: Readings and Resources for Faculty,* 2d ed. Providence, RI: Brown University, Box 1975, Providence RI 02912; www.compact.org.

Carnes, Mark C. 2004. "The Liminal Classroom." *The Chronicle of Higher Education: The Chronicle Review.*http/chronical.com/weekly/v5/i07/07b00601. htm. From the issue dated October 8, 2004.

Chandler, A. 1977. *The Visible Hand: The Managerial Revolution in American Business.* Cambridge, MA: Harvard University Press.

Chicago Housing Authority. 2000. "The CHA's Plan for Transformation." <http://thecha.org/transformplan/plan_summary.html>.

Chiem, P. X. 1996. "Taggers Spray Over Vandal Image." *Chicago Tribune,* September 12, 1996. Metro Section, 1–2.

Chin, Diane. 2007. "Inadvertent Alienation: A Rhetorical Analysis of Pro-Service-Learning Arguments that Backfire." PhD diss., University of Illinois at Chicago, 2007.

Colby, Anne, T. Ehrlich, E. Beaumont, J. Stephens. 2003. *Educating Citizens: Preparing America's Undergraduates for Lives of Moral and Civic Responsibility.* San Francisco, CA: Jossey-Bass and Carnegie Foundation for the Advancement of Teaching.

Coles, William E. and James Vopat. 1985. *What Makes Writing Good: A Multiperspective.* New York: DC Heath.

Comas, Jordi T., B. Hiller, and J. Miller. 2005. "The Evolution of a Community of Practice: Stakeholders and Service in Management 101." In *Service-Learning in Higher Education: Critical Issues and Directions.* Edited by Dan Butin, 107–126. New York: Palgrave Macmillan.

Cone, Dick and S. Harris. 1996. "Service-Learning Practice: Developing a Theoretical Framework." *Michigan Journal of Community Service Learning* 3: 31–43.

Connors, Robert. 1995. "The New Abolitionism: Toward a Historical Background." In *Reconceiving Writing, Rethinking Writing Instruction.* Edited by Joseph Petraglia, 3–26. Mahwah, New Jersey: Lawrence Erlbaum Associates.

Coogan, David. 2006. "Service Learning and Social Change: The Case for Materialist Rhetoric." *College English* 57, 4: 667–693.

Cooks, L. and E. Scharrer. 2006. "Assessing Learning in Community Service Learning: A Social Approach." *Michigan Journal of Community Service Learning* 13, 1: 44–55.

Corrigan, Maureen. 2003. "You, as a Reader, are a Dope." (August 19, 2003). http://www.salon.com/books/letters/2003/08/19/corrigan/.

Crosswhite, James. 1996. *The Rhetoric of Reason: Writing and the Attractions of Argument.* Madison: University of Wisconsin Press.

Crowley, Sharon. 1991. "A Personal Essay on Freshman English." *Pre/Text* 12: 156–176.

————. 1998. *Composition in the University: Historical and Polemical Essays.* Pittsburgh, PA: University of Pittsburgh Press.

Cushman, Ellen. 1996. "The Rhetorician as an Agent of Social Change." *College Composition and Communication* 47: 7–28.

————. 2002. "Sustainable Service Learning Programs." *College Composition and Communication* 54: 40–65.

De Certeau, Michel. 1984. *The Practice of Everyday Life.* Berkeley: University of California Press.

Deans, Thomas. 2000. *Writing Partnerships: Service Learning in Composition.* Urbana, IL: National Council of Teachers of English.

————. 2006. "Genre Analysis and the Community Writing Course." *Reflections* 5, 1 and 2: 7–25.

Dector, Joshua. 2001. "Synergy-Museum." In *The Discursive Museum.* Edited by Peter Noever, 83-97. Vienna: MAK and Ostifldern-Ruit, Germany: Hatje Cantz Verlag. In New York: D.A.P. Distributed Art Publishers, Inc.

Derrida, Jacques. 1976. *Of Grammatology.* Translated by Gayatri Spivak. Baltimore, MD: Johns Hopkins University Press.

Downing, David, C. M. Hurlbert and P. A. Mathieu, eds. 2002. *Beyond English, Inc.: Curricular Reform in a Global Economy.* Portsmouth, NH: Boynton/Cook.

Eastwood, Carolyn. 2002. *Near West Side Stories: Struggles for Community in Chicago's Maxwell Street Neighborhood.* Chicago: Lake Claremont Press.

Engeström, Yrjö. 1990. *Learning, Working, and Imagining: An Activity Theoretical Approach to Developmental Research.* Helsinki: Orienta-Konsultit Oy.

Eyler, Janet and D. E. Giles Jr. 1999. *Where's the Learning in Service-Learning?* San Francisco, CA: Jossey-Bass Publishers.

Faigley, Lester. 1989. "Judging Writing, Judging Selves." *College Composition and Communication* 40, 4: 395–412.

Feldman, Ann Merle. 1996. *Writing and Learning in the Disciplines.* New York: HarperCollins College Publishers.

———. 2003. "Teaching Writing in a Context of Partnership." In *City Comp: Identities, Spaces, Practices.* Edited by B. McComiskey and C. Ryan, 203–215. Albany: State University of New York Press.

Feldman, Ann M., T. Moss, D. Chin, M. Marie, C. Rai, R. Graham. 2006. "The Impact of Partnership-Centered, Community-Based Learning on First-Year Students' Academic Research Papers." *Michigan Journal of Community Service Learning* 13, 1: 16–29.

Feldman, Ann M., N. Downs, and E. McManus. 2005. *In Context: Reading and Writing in Cultural Conversations.* 2d ed. New York: Addison, Wesley, Longman.

Felski, Rita. 1989. *Beyond Feminist Aesthetics: Feminist Literature and Social Change.* Cambridge, MA: Harvard University Press.

Fineman, Mia. 2004. "The Biennial that's Not at the Biennial." *The New York Times, Arts, Art and Design.* May 2, 2004.

Fish, Stanley. 1995. *Professional Correctness: Literary Studies and Political Change.* Oxford: Clarendon. Reprint. Cambridge, MA: Harvard University Press, 1999.

Fish, S. 2002a. "Is Everything Political?" *Chronicle of Higher Education,* Career Network. (March 29, 2002).

———. 2002b. "Say It Ain't So." *Chronicle of Higher Education,* Career Network. (June 21, 2002).

———. 2003. "Aim Low: Confusing Democratic Values with Academic Ones can Easily Damage the Quality of Education." *Chronicle of Higher Education,* Career Network. (May, 16, 2003).

Fleming, David. 2003. "Subjects of the Inner City: Writing the People of Cabrini Green." In *Towards a Rhetoric of Everyday Life: New Directions in*

Research on Writing, Text, and Discourse. Edited by Martin Nystrand and John Duffy, 207–244. Madison: University of Wisconsin Press.

Flower, Linda. 1997. "Partners in Inquiry: A Logic for Community Outreach." In *Writing the Community: Concepts and Models for Service-Learning in Composition.* Edited by L. Adler-Kassner, R. Crooks, and A. Watters, 95–117. Urbana, IL: NCTE.

Flower, Linda, E. Long, and L. Higgins. 2000. *Learning to Rival: A Literate Practice for Intercultural Inquiry.* Mahwah, NJ: Lawrence Erlbaum.

Foucault, Michel. 1993. "*What is an Author?*" In *Language, Counter-Memory, Practice,* Edited and translated by Donald F. Bouchard and Sherry Simon, 113–138. Ithaca, NY: Cornell University Press.

Fulwiler, Toby. 1984. "How Well Does Writing Across the Curriculum Work?" *College English* 46, 1: 113–125.

Gelmon, S. B., B. Holland, A. Driscoll, A. Spring, and S. Kerrigan. 2001. *Assessing Service-Learning and Civic Engagement: Principles and Techniques.* Providence, RI: Campus Compact, Brown University.

Gibbons, Michael, C. Limoges, H. Nowotny, S. Schwartzman, P. Scott, and M. Trow. 1994. *The New Production of Knowledge: The Dynamics of Science and Research in Contemporary Societies.* London: Sage.

Glassick, Charles. 1999. "Ernest L. Boyer: Colleges and Universities as Citizens." In *Colleges and Universities as Citizens.* Edited by R. G. Bringle, R. Games, and E. A. Malloy, 17–30. Boston, MA: Allyn and Bacon.

Goggin, Maureen Daly, ed. 2000. *Inventing a Discipline: Rhetoric Scholarship in Honor of Richard E. Young.* Urbana, IL: NCTE.

Goggin, M. D. and S. Beatty. 2000. "Accounting for 'Well-Worn Grooves': Composition as a Self-Reinforcing Mechanism." In *Inventing a Discipline: Rhetoric Scholarship in Honor of Richard E. Young.* Edited by M. D. Goggin, 29–66. Urbana, IL: NCTE.

Goodman, Robert and W. Fisher. 1995. *Rethinking Knowledge: Reflections Across the Disciplines.* Albany: State University of New York Press.

Gornick, Vivian. 1987. *Fierce Attachments.* New York: Simon & Schuster, Inc.

———. 2001. *The Situation and The Story: The Art of Personal Narrative.* New York: Farrar, Strauss and Giroux.

———. 2003. "A Memoirist Defends Her Words." *Salon Magazine.* (August 12, 2003). http://www.salon.com/books/feature/2003/08/12/memoir_writing/index_np.html.

Graff, Gerald. 2003. *Clueless in Academe: How Schooling Obscures the Life of the Mind.* New Haven, CT: Yale University Press.

Graff, Gerald and Cathy Birkenstein. 2006. *They Say/I Say: The Moves that Matter in Academic Writing.* New York: W.W. Norton & Company.

Gude, Olivia. 2000. "Placemaking in Chicago." *Chicago Public Art Group News-Magazine* 7, 1 (Summer 2000):1–16.

Haar, Sharon. 2002. "Location, Location, Location: Gender and the Archeology of Urban Settlement." *Journal of Architectural Education* (February 2002): 150–160.

Hall, David D. 1987. "On Common Ground: The Coherence of American Puritan Studies." *William and Mary Quarterly* 44, 2. (3rd Ser): 36–67.

Harkavy, Ira, J. Puckett, and D. Romer. 2000. "Action Research: Bridging Service and Research." *Michigan Journal of Community Service Learning* (Fall 2000): 113–118.

Harkin, Patricia. 1991. "The Post-Disciplinary Politics of Lore." In *Contending with Words.* Edited by P. Harkin and J. Schilb. New York: MLA.

Harris, Joseph. 1997. *A Teaching Subject: Composition Since 1966.* Upper Saddle River, NJ: Prentice-Hall.

———. 2003. "Opinion: Revision as a Critical Practice." *College English* 65, 6: 576–592.

Herzberg, Bruce. 1994. Community Service and Critical Teaching. *College Composition and Communication* 45, 3: 307–41.

hooks, bell. 1997. *Bone Black: Memories of Girlhood.* New York: Henry Holt & Company.

Hoskin, Keith W. 1993. "Education and the Genesis of Disciplinarity: The Unexpected Reversal." In *Knowledges: Historical and Critical Studies in Disciplinarity.* Edited by Ellen Messer-Davidow, D. R. Shumway, and D. J. Sylvan, 271–304. Charlottesville, VA: University of Virginia Press.

Hoskin, Keith W. and R. H. Macve. 1993. "Accounting as Discipline: The Overlooked Supplement." In *Knowledges: Historical and Critical Studies in Disciplinarity.* Edited by Ellen Messer-Davidow, D. R. Shumway, and D. J. Sylvan, 25–53. Charlottesville, VA: University of Virginia Press.

Hynes, James. 2001. *The Lecturer's Tale.* New York: Picador.

Keith, Novella Z. 2005. "Community Service Learning in the Face of Globalization: Rethinking Theory and Practice." *Michigan Journal of Community Service Learning* 11, 2: 5–24.

Kellogg Commission. 1999. *Returning to our Roots: The Engaged Institution.* National Association of Public Universities and Land-Grant Colleges. http://www.nasulgc.org/Kellogg/kellogg.htm.

Kirschner, David. 2004. "Enculturation: The Neglected Learning Metaphor in Mathematics Education." In *Proceedings of the Twenty-Sixth Annual Meeting of the International Group for the Psychology of Mathematics Education, North American Chapter*. Edited by D. McDougall and J. A. Ross. Vol. 2.7, 65–772. Toronto: OISE/UT.

Kitaj, Ronald B. 1989. *First Diasporist Manifesto*. New York: Thames and Hudson.

———. 2000. "The Billionaire in Vincent's Chair." In *Encounters: New Art From Old. R. Morphet*, 204. 152.4*61cm. Marlborough Fine Art, London: National Gallery Company Limited.

Knapp, Steven. 1993. *Literary Interest: The Limits of Anti-Formalism*. Cambridge, MA: Harvard University Press.

Kolb, David A. 1984. *Experiential Learning: Experience as the Source of Learning and Development*. Englewood Cliffs, NJ: Prentice-Hall.

Lanham, R. 1976. *The Motives of Eloquence: Literary Rhetoric in the Renaissance*. New Haven, CT: Yale University Press.

Lave, Jean and Etienne Wenger. 1991. *Situated Learning: Legitimate Peripheral Participation*. Cambridge: Cambridge University Press.

Lave, Jean. 1993. "The Practice of Learning." In *Understanding Practice: Perspectives on Activity and Context*. Edited by Seth Chaiklin and Jean Lave, 3–32. Cambridge: Cambridge University Press.

Lefebvre, Henri. 1991. *The Production of Space*. Malden, ME: Blackwell Publishing.

Limerick, Patricia N. 2000. *Something in the Soil: Field-Testing the New Western History*. New York: Norton and Company.

Luiton, Linda. 1998. "Will Development Bury the Barrio?" *The Chicago Reader* 27, 29 (Friday, April 24, 1998). 17, 18, 22, 24, 26–30.

MacGregor, Neil. 2000. "Director's Forward." In R. Morphet, *Encounters: New Art From Old*, 7. London: National Gallery Company, Limited.

Mailloux, Stephen. 1995. "Introduction: Sophistry and Rhetorical Pragmatism." In *Rhetoric, Sophistry, Pragmatism*. Edited by S. Mailloux, 1–31. Cambridge Literature, Culture, Theory Series. Cambridge: Cambridge University Press.

Mansfield, N. 2000. *Subjectivity: Theories of the Self from Freud to Haraway*. New York: New York University Press.

Mathieu, Paula. 2005. *Tactics of Hope: The Public Turn in English Composition*. Portsmouth, NH: Boynton/Cook.

Matsuhashi, Ann (née Ann Merle Feldman). 1981. "Pausing and Planning: The Tempo of Written Discourse Production." *Research in the Teaching of English* 15, 2: 113–134.

Maurrasse, David. 2001. *Beyond the Campus: How Colleges and Universities Form Partnerships with Their Communities.* New York: Routledge and Kegan Paul.

McCloskey, Deirdre. 1997. "Big Rhetoric, Little Rhetoric: Gaonkar on the Rhetoric of Science." In *Rhetorical Hermeneutics: Invention and Interpretation in the Age of Science.* Edited by A. G. Gross and W. M. Keith. Albany: State University of New York Press.

McManus, Ellen M. 2002. "Cultural Studies Into Case Studies: Making Writing Visible in the Composition Classroom." PhD diss., University of Illinois at Chicago.

McQuade, Donald. 1992. "Composition and Literary Studies." In *Redrawing the Boundaries: The Transformation of English and American Literary Studies.* Edited by S. Greenblatt and G. Gunn, 482–517. New York: MLA.

McQueen, A. 2001. "Gendered Encounters." Review of *Encounters: New Art From Old* by R. Morphet. *Art Journal* 60, 2 (Summer): 103-105.

Messer-Davidow, Ellen, D. Shumway, and D. Sylvan, eds.1993. *Knowledges: Historical and Critical Studies in Disciplinarity.* Charlottesville: University of Virginia Press.

Miller, Carolyn. 1984. "Genre as Social Action." *Quarterly Journal of Speech* 70: 151–167.

———. 1994. "Rhetorical Community: The Cultural Basis of Genre." In *Genre and the New Rhetoric.* Edited by Aviva Freedman and Peter Medway, 67–78. London: Taylor and Francis.

Miller, Susan. 1998. *Assuming the Positions: Cultural Pedagogy and the Politics of Commonplace Writing.* Pittsburgh, PA: University of Pittsburgh Press.

Morphet, R. 2000. *Encounters: New Art From Old.* London: National Gallery Company Limited.

Muthesius, Stefan. 2000. *The Postwar University: Utopianist Campus and College.* New Haven, CT: Published for the Paul Mellon Centre for Studies in British Art by Yale University Press.

Nelson, J. S., A. Megill, and D. McCloskey, eds. 1987. *The Rhetoric of the Human Sciences: Language and Argument in Scholarship and Public Affairs.* Madison: The University of Wisconsin Press.

Newman, Oscar. 1966. "The New Campus." *Architectural Forum* 5: 30–56. St. Louis, MO: Forest Park Community Center by Harry Weese & Associates.

Nietzsche, F. W. 2003. *Beyond Good and Evil.* Translated by R. J. Hollingdale. New York: Penguin Classics.

Noever, Peter, ed. 2001. *The Discursive Museum.* Vienna: MAK and Ostfildern-Ruit, Germany: Hatje Cantz Verlag. New York: D.A.P. Distributed Art Publishers, Inc.

North, Stephen. 1996. "The Death of Paradigm Hope, the End of Paradigm Guilt, and the Future of Research in Composition." In *Composition in the Twenty-First Century: Crisis and Change.* Edited by Bloom, Lynn Z., D. A. Daiker, and E. M. White, 194-207. Carbondale: Southern Illinois University Press.

Olson, Gary. 2002. *Justifying Belief: Stanley Fish and the Work of Rhetoric.* Albany: State University of New York Press.

Olson, Gary and Lynn Worsham, eds. 2004. *Postmodern Sophistry: Stanley Fish and the Critical Enterprise.* Albany: State University of New York Press.

Perry, David and Wim Wiewel. 2005. "From Campus to City: The University as Developer." In *The University as Urban Developer: Case Studies and Analysis.* Edited by David Perry and W. Wievel, 3–21. Armonk, NY: M. E. Sharpe.

Perry, David. 1995. "Making Space: Planning as a Mode of Thought." In *Spatial Practices: Critical Explorations in Social/Spatial Theory.* Edited by Helen Liggett and David Perry, 209–242. Thousand Oaks, CA: Sage Publications.

———. 2004. "The Great Cities Commitment: Leadership, Resources, Rewards and the Identity of the Urban Research University." (Paper, University of California, San Diego, for the Seminar on the Research University as Local Citizen, forthcoming in the Great Cities Working Papers Series).

Perry, David and Wim Wiewel, eds. 2005. *The University as Urban Developer: Case Studies and Analysis.* Armonk, NY: M. E. Sharpe.

Peterman, William. 1999. *Neighborhood Planning and Community-based Development.* Thousand Oaks, CA: Sage Publications.

Petraglia, Joseph, ed. 1995. *Reconceiving Writing, Rethinking Writing Instruction.* Mahwah, NJ: Lawrence Erlbaum Associates.

———. 1995. "Writing as an Unnatural Act." In *Reconceiving Writing, Rethinking Writing Instruction.* Edited by Joseph Petraglia, 79–100. Mahwah, NJ: Lawrence Erlbaum Associates.

———. 2000. "Shaping Sophisticates: Implications of the Rhetorical Turn for Rhetorical Education." In *Inventing a Discipline: Rhetoric Scholarship in Honor of Richard E. Young.* Edited by Maureen Goggin, 80–103. Urbana, IL: NCTE.

———. 2003. "Identity Crisis: Rhetoric as a Pedagogic and an Epistemic Discipline." In *The Realms of Rhetoric: The Prospects for Rhetorical Education,* Edited by Joseph Petraglia and D. Bahri, 151–169. Albany: State University of New York Press.

Philadelphia Inquirer. 1999. "Speech and Challenges: Universities Must be Free to Inspire Both." Editorial Section, September 26, 1999. E6.

Plato. 2003. *The Republic.* Translated by Desmond Lee. New York: Penguin Classics.

Posner, Richard. 2003. *Public Intellectuals: A Study of Decline.* (Paperback edition with preface and epilogue.) Cambridge, MA: Harvard University Press.

Pratt, Mary Louise. 1992. *Imperial Eyes: Travel Writing and Transculturation.* New York: Routledge and Kegan Paul.

Ransby, Barbara. 2003. *Ella Baker and the Black Freedom Movement: A Radical Democratic Vision.* Chapel Hill: University of North Carolina Press.

Readings, Bill. 1997. *The University in Ruins.* Cambridge, MA: Harvard University Press.

Rockquemore, Kerry A. and R. H. Schaffer. 2000. "Toward a Theory of Engagement: A Cognitive Mapping of Service-Learning Experiences." *Michigan Journal of Community Service Learning* 7: 14–24.

Rodin, Judith. 2003. "The University as Discourse Community." In *Public Discourse in America: Conversation and Community in the Twenty-first Century.* Edited by J. Rodin and S. P. Steinberg, 232–236. Philadelphia: University of Pennsylvania Press.

Rodin, Judith and S. P. Steinberg, eds. 2003. *Public Discourse in America: Conversation and Community in the Twenty-first Century.* Philadelphia: University of Pennsylvania Press.

Rose, Mike. 1989. *Lives on the Boundary.* New York: Free Press.

Rosen, George. 1980. *Decision-Making Chicago Style: The Genesis of a University of Illinois Campus.* Urbana: University of Illinois Press.

Russell, David. 1995. "Activity Theory and its Implications for Writing Instruction." In *Reconceiving Writing, Rethinking Writing Instruction.* Edited by J. Petraglia, 51–77. Mahwah, NJ: Lawrence Erlbaum Associates.

Russell, D. 1997. "Writing to Learn to Do: WAC, WAW, WAW—WOW!" *Language and Learning in the Disciplines* 2: 3–8.

Sands, Peter. 2007. "Towers of Ivory, Corridors of Linoleum: Utopia in Academic Novels." *Academic Novels As Satire: Critical Studies of an Emerging Genre,* Edited by Kimberly Rae Connor and Mark Bosco, 38–49. New York: The Edwin Mellen Press.

Sandy, Marie and Barbara A. Holland. 2006. "Different Worlds and Common Ground: Community Partner Perspectives and Campus-Community Partnerships." *Michigan Journal of Community Service Learning* 13, 1: 30–43.

Schroeder, Christopher, H. Fox, and P. Bizzell, eds. 2002. *Alt Dis: Alternative Discourses and the Academy.* Portsmouth, NH: Boynton/Cook Heinemann.

Scott, Joan W. 1991. "The Evidence of Experience." *Critical Inquiry* 17,4 (Summer, 1991): 773–797.

Shepard, Thomas. 1981. "Confessions." In *Collections of the Colonial Society of Massachusett* Vol. 58. Edited by George Selement and Bruce C. Wooley. Boston, MA: The Society.

Shor, Ira. 1996. *When Students Have Power: Negotiating Authority in a Critical Pedagogy.* Chicago: University of Chicago Press.

Simons, H. W. 1990. "The Rhetoric of Inquiry as an Intellectual Movement." In *The Rhetorical Turn: Invention and Persuasion in the Conduct of Inquiry.* Edited by H.W. Simons, 1–31. Chicago: University of Chicago Press.

Skinner, B.F. 1948. *Walden Two.* New York: Macmillan.

Smit, David W. 2004. *The End of Composition Studies.* Carbondale: Southern Illinois University Press.

Soja, Edward W. 1996. *Thirdspace: Journeys to Los Angeles and other Real-and-Imagined Places.* Malden, MA: Blackwell Publishing.

Soliday, Mary. 1994. "Literacy Narratives." *College English* 56, 5: 511–523.

Sterling, Terry Greene. 2003. "Confessions of a Memoirist." *Salon Magazine,* August 1, 2003. http://www.salon.com/books/feature/archives/2003/08/01/gornick/index_np.html.

Stygall, Gail. 1994. "Resisting Privilege: Basic Writing and Foucault's Author Function." *College Composition and Communication* 45: 320–341.

Syverson, Margaret. 1999. *The Wealth of Reality: An Ecology of Composition.* Carbondale: Southern Illinois University Press.

Taylor, Charles. 1989. *Sources of the Self: The Making of the Modern Identity.* Cambridge, MA: Harvard University Press.

Tompkins, Jane. 1996. *A Life in School.* Reading, MA: Addison-Wesley.

Trimbur, John. 2000. "Composition and the Circulation of Writing." *College Composition and Communication* 52, 2: 188–219.

———, ed. 2001. *Popular Literacy: Studies in Cultural Practices and Poetics.* Pittsburgh, PA: University of Pittsburgh Press.

Van der Wusten, H., ed. 1998. *The Urban University and Its Identity: Roots, Locations, Roles.* Boston, MA: Kluwer Academic Publishers.

Van Gogh, Vincent. 1998. *Portrait de l'artiste.* Oil on Canvas 1887 (original panel), 44x35cm. In Orsay, Post-Impressionism, Edited by C. Fréches-Thory, 95. Paris: Éditions Scala, 1986.

———— . 2000. *Worn Out: At Eternity's Gate,* Oil on Canvas 1890 (original panel), 62X44cm. In *Encounters: New Art from Old.* By R. Morphet, 211. London: National Gallery Company Limited, 2000; Otterlo: Kröller-Müller Museum. Photo by Indien Von Toepassing, Amsterdam.

————. 2000. *Van Gogh's Chair.* Oil on Canvas 1888 (original panel), 91.8x 73cm. National Gallery 3862. In *Encounters: New Art From Old.* By R. Morphet, 202. National Gallery Company Limited.

Venkatesh, Sudhir A. 2000. *American Project: The Rise and Fall of a Modern Ghetto.* London: Cambridge University Press.

Villanueva, Victor. 1993. *Bootstraps: From an American Academic of Color.* Urbana, IL: NCTE.

Voices of Cabrini. Chicago: Facets Multimedia. August 22, 2000. Documentary Film. Directed by Ronit Bezalel and Antonio Ferrera; Producer, Judy Hoffman Studio.

Walshok, Mary L. 1995. *Knowledge Without Boundaries: What America's Research Universities Can Do for the Economy, the Workplace, and the Community.* San Francisco, CA: Jossey-Bass Publishers.

————.1999. "Strategies for Building the Infrastructure that Supports the Engaged Campus." In *Colleges and Universities as Citizens.* Edited by Robert G. Bringle, R. Games, and E. A. Malloy, 74–95. Boston, MA: Allyn and Bacon.

Walvoord, Barbara. 1996. "The Future of WAC." *College English* 58, 1: 58–79.

Watkins, Evon. 2004. "Professional Distinction." In *Postmodern Sophistry: Stanley Fish and the Critical Enterprise.* Edited by Gary Olson and Lynn Worsham, 231–241. Albany: State University of New York Press.

Weber, Rachel, N. Theodore, and N. Hoch. 2005. "Private Choices and Public Obligations: The Ethics of University Real Estate Development." In *The University as Urban Developer: Case Studies and Analysis.* Edited by David Perry and Wim Wiewel, 285–299. Armonk, NY: M. E. Sharpe.

Wenger, Etienne. 1998. *Communities of Practice: Learning, Meaning, and Identity.* Cambridge: Cambridge University Press.

Wertsch, James, ed. 1981. *The Concept of Activity in Soviet Psychology.* Armonk, NY: M. E. Sharpe.

Wiewel, Wim and David Broski. 1999. "The Great Cities Institute: Dilemmas of Implementing the Urban Land Grant Mission." *Metropolitan Universities* 10: 29–38.

Willard-Traub, Margaret. 2006. Review: "Reflection in Academe: Scholarly Writing and the Shifting Subject." *College English* 68, 4: 422–432.

Williams, Raymond. 1978; 1977. *Marxism and Literature.* Oxford: Oxford University Press.

Wollstonecraft, Mary. 1993. *A Vindication of the Rights of Women* with Miriam Brody. New York: Penguin Classic.

Wright, Richard. 1998. *Native Son.* New York: Harper's Perennial Classics.

Yood, Jessica. 2003. "Writing the Discipline: A Generic History of English Studies." *College English* 65, 5: 526–540.

Index